THE VICTIM ADDICTION:
Release the drama of self-defeating emotional patterns

Victoria Lee Carlyle

The Victim Addiction:
Release the drama of self-defeating emotional patterns
By Victoria Lee Carlyle

All rights reserved. No part of this book may be reproduced in any form or by any means without permission in writing from the author, Victoria Carlyle.

Copyright © 2015, Victoria Carlyle

ISBN-10: 1943253005

ISBN-13: 978-1-943253-00-5

Printed in the United States.

Editing: Sherrie Nattrass, Cecily Markland and Jana Cox
Publishing: Transformational Life Publishing
Cover art: Brittney Hansen
Cover design and illustrations: Bonilla Design
Book layout and design: Jana Lee Cox, Legend eXpress Publishing, www.legendexpress.biz

Acknowledgements

The content of this book has been gathered over my lifetime, and I would like to thank those who have made a significant contribution through the years.

I am grateful for my children—Chase and Jessica, Adam and Kaci, Josh, Chelsie and Blake, Richelle, Kory, Ari, Shayah, Aiden and my special son David Johnson whose warm hugs and big smile always makes me feel loved—and to all my darling grandchildren for their love and support.

I appreciate my loving friends—LaCinda Lewis, Sherrie Nattrass, Colleen Hicks, Heather Scott and Jann Wyler—for their support and years of love, laughter, and joy. And, to my secretary, Dr. Irene Lebedies of Confidence Point Coaching, who has been a confidant and friend. I am also grateful for a few influential mentors—David Gilcrease of Resource Realizations and Lou Dozier and Barbara Fagan of Source Point Trainings and Duane Smotherman of Smotherman and Partners Consulting Group; Joyce Christie of NLP Global Initiative and Nadine Cooper of Changepoint behavioral counseling.

I appreciate Judge Mark Anderson who believed in me and gave me a chance to share my training, "The Power to Change."

A heartfelt thanks goes to Gabe Bonilla of Bonilla design and Brittney Hanson for the artistic way they have visually brought this book to life. I express my gratitude for Sherrie Nattrass of Attraction Cosmetics, Cecily Markland of Inglestone Publishing and Jana Cox of Legend eXpress Publishing for their loving support and editing skills; Transformational Life Publishing for providing the opportunity to release my book in an professional way.

Finally, this book would not be complete without expressing my immense gratitude for the inspiration and strength that has guided this work and my life. This book would not have been possible without this gentle but powerful direction.

Contents

Acknowledgements iii
Table of Contents v
The Victim Addiction Forward ix
Chapter 1: The Journey Begins 1
    Introduction...Navy Seals
Personal Power Pyramid. 4
    Explanation of the 5 Tiers

Tier I: The Power of Self-Awareness **11**

Chapter 2: Self-Awareness Defined 13
    Self-Awareness...Self-Talk...Thoughts...Comfort Zone
Chapter 3: The Comfort Zone 19
    Ben Carson...Caught in the box...Introducing our fear based Emotional Safety Zone...The difference between being an emotional victim and being victimized...Time to heal...Emotional Victim...Blame...Justifications...Resentment...Defense Mechanisms
Chapter 4: Structuring our thoughts, feelings, attitudes and beliefs . . 41
    We exchange ourselves for the approval of others...Buddha story
Chapter 5: Emotions. 47
    Heaven and Hell...Emotional Structuring...Anger...Guilt...Sadness...Depression...Giving Up On Life...Physical, Emotional, Sexual Abuse...Emotions are Powerful Motivators
Chapter 6: Beliefs 63
    The Establishment Of Our Primary Belief Systems
    Belief "I am a Burden"
Chapter 7: Perceptions 71
    Be Yourself...Emotional Filters...Behavior...The Unconscious way we give our power away...Emotional Victim Patterns...Victim Language...The Victim Addiction Defined

Tier II: The Power To Change **85**

Chapter 8: Change 87
    Perpetuating Fears
Chapter 9: The Convincing Influence of the
    Rational and Emotional Mind 93
    The War of the Worlds...Phantom Pains...Our Survival System...Facts What's Real / Feelings Feels Real...Intuition

Chapter 10: The Rational and Emotional Mind 103
   Rational, Logical Mind, or Cortex...Emotional Mind or Amygdala...
   Emotional Anchors...Emotional Triggers...Triggers Can Uplift...
   Consciously Processing
Chapter 11: Amygdala Hijacking. 117
   Amygdala Hijacking...Emotional Timing
Chapter 12: Taking Things Personally. 129
   Taking Things Personally...Emotional Validation
Chapter 13: Victim Behavior 137
   Helpless Victim Patterns...Faultless Victim Patterns

Tier III: The Power of Living an Accountable Life 143
Chapter 14: Accountability. 145
   The Other Side of Victim – Accountable...Living an Accountable Life...
   Unconscious Victim Language...Conscious Accountable Language...
   Accountable Patterns
Chapter 15: Conscious Choice 151
   What is Conscious Choice...The Wolves Within...Choices Defined
Chapter 16: Evidence 157
   Evidence for Change...Instant Change...Repetitious Evidence For Change
Chapter 17: Restructuring 169
   Semmelweis...Restructuring...Mother Teresa...Positive Solutions
Chapter 18: Mastering Our Emotions 179
   Drunk Laborer...Emotional Change...Face The Pain To Stop The
   Pain...Change Your Thoughts...Shutting Off Uncomfortable Emotions
Chapter 19: Establishing New Neural Pathways 191
   Jacob Barnett...Neurons...Neural Pathways The Super Highway of
   Our Mind...Habits...Restructuring Neural Pathways...The Power of
   the Human Mind

Tier IV: The Power of Transcending Perceptions 203
Chapter 20: Letting go of Painful Memories 205
   Mastering Our Emotions ... Grief, Loss and Regrets...The Gift of an
   Amygdala Hijacking...Secrets and Lies
Chapter 21: Learning to Forgive 221
   Forgiveness...Reconciliation...Taking Back What Once Was Lost...
   From Bad to Worse...Freedom in Forgiveness
Chapter 22: Empowering Beliefs 231
   Governor of Tennessee...Creating Powerful Beliefs...Our Beliefs
   Define How We Feel...When Detrimental Beliefs go Unnoticed...
   Beneficial Conscious Beliefs...Detrimental Unconscious Beliefs...
   Restructuring Beliefs

Chapter 23: Trusting Yourself 247
    Trust...Self-Trust...Internal Instincts
Chapter 24: Attitude 253
    The Kind of Guy You Love to Hate...Choosing our Attitude

Tier VI: The Power of Emotional Transformation L.O.V.E. 261
    Nicholas James Vujicic
Chapter 25: Learn 265
    Primitive Structuring...Brain Chemicals – Source of Emotional Transformation...Tribal Rituals for Depression...Keeping a Mood Journal...Notice Identify and Express Emotions...Identifying Destructive Emotional Patterns...Clarifying Intensity of Emotional Patterns...Avoiding Emotional Patterns...Expressing Feelings... Recognizing Painful Feelings...Beneficial Feelings...Supporting Others
Chapter 26: Overcoming Obstacles 285
    Overcoming Triggers...Overcoming Loss...Overcoming Grief... Unexpected Change...Charlie Boswell...Restructuring Failure and Overcoming Fear...Overcoming Emotional Blindness...Strategies for Overcoming Obstacles
Chapter 27: Values 305
    Clarifying Values...Defining Values...Living Our Values...Establishing Personal Boundaries...When Boundaries are Violated...Establishing Trust
Chapter 28: Engage 317
    Celebrating Transformation...Rational and Emotional Brains Analogy... Designing the Life You Love...Playing...Laugh...True Wisdom... Gratitude...Living in Full Potential...Inside the Emotional Safety Zone...Transforming The Victim Addiction...Elevating Mechanisms... Aligning Our Values
Chapter 29: Accessing Your Inner Motivation to Succeed 335
    Creating a Happy Life...Positive Affirmations...Mind Mapping... Vision Board...Restructuring Ineffective Habits...Don't Hope ... Decide

The Victim Addiction

"The Victim Addiction speaks to the familiar conflict that occurs as self-defeating emotional patterns separate us from our personal power."

~ Victoria Lee Carlyle

I have always loved the idea of going to a masquerade ball. I think wearing an amazing gown and hiding behind a lovely sequined mask while being escorted by an interesting man, wearing a perfectly designed mask of his own, seems like something right out of a fairytale.

Can you imagine how fun it would be to create the perfect mask? One that not only looked stunning on the outside, but a mask that would also create stunning results in every aspect of life.

Yet, without even realizing it, each of us has already done so. The unfortunate part for most is that the mask we have created doesn't necessarily reflect the true beauty we wish to portray.

> Can you imagine how fun it would be to create the perfect mask? One that not only looked stunning on the outside, but a mask that would also create stunning results in every aspect of life.

When I first set out to create a cover for this book, I thought it would be fun to use an image of a crazy rollercoaster to depict life's ups and downs; but a line from a poem I had read long ago kept running through my mind. The poem is about the masks we wear, and the line reads, "Please hear what I am not saying." This line brought back memories of all the times in my life I felt like I was not good enough or wasn't appreciated. It even reminded me of times when I desperately wanted love, but because I had suffered so much abuse in my life I couldn't recognize love and would inadvertently set myself up for more pain.

That simple phrase released a flood of memories from the many years I had been caught in what I now call The Victim Addiction. However, it also reminded me of the strength I gained as I shed the mask of pretense and put on an entirely different mask; the mask called the "real me."

I wanted to create an image that would portray the ability we have when we connect to a powerful source of truth that has the ultimate strength to create a rich and satisfying life. I had an idea, and turned to the beautiful artist Brittney Hansen who was able to help me create the perfect look.

The objective was to use the masks to illustrate two options that we, as humans, will always face. The first option is to maintain familiar emotional patterns where we unconsciously give our power to our past hurts and resulting circumstances. The second option is to take back our personal power by getting beyond our fears and painful emotions. This conscious action will inspire a powerful inner motivation to succeed.

The Mask of Silent Misery

Sadly, many of us are among those who wear the mask of silent misery. We feel mistreated, misplaced and misunderstood as we struggle to cope with the confusion of unresolved pain and sorrow. When our buttons get pushed and these repressed feelings come out, we react by getting angry, frustrated, confused or hurt, and often blame others for the way that we feel. Then, because we don't know how to recognize, manage, control or change these uncomfortable emotional patterns, we simply dismiss them, believing that this will help us remain mentally and emotionally stable.

The problem is, those who hide behind the mask of misery never seem fully present, engaged or connected to the people around them. Their lives may appear satisfactory on the outside, but there is a connection missing and they never experience the deep, fulfilling relationships that they truly desire.

The mask on the right side of the cover portrays what can occur as we stop giving our power away to our circumstances. It depicts what can result when we stop being hurt, offended, frustrated or angry and, instead, build the trust, love and forgiveness needed to create a happy life.

Nobody wants to feel powerless over their life; yet, living in a society where The Victim Addiction is a prevalent part of societal norm can make it a bit challenging to notice the subtle ways we create our own unhappiness. For some, the thought of living the life they have always wanted really does seem like an unrealistic fairytale.

Rest assured, there is a way to make your dreams come true and create stunning results in every aspect of your life. This book was written to help you rise to your full potential. These philosophies will introduce you to solid, proven principles that will free you from unconscious emotional patterns that would otherwise hold you back. The concepts are offered in a nonjudgmental, down-to-earth and easy-to-comprehend way. To help you personalize and incorporate these concepts, interactive processes have been included throughout the book.

Also included are some of my real-life experiences of heartache, struggle, pain—and ultimately, success. I share these ideas with you, hoping you will put them to use so you, like me, will enjoy the life-changing benefits they have to offer.

Consider Your Destination

So as you set forth on this journey of discovery, take a moment to figure out what a rich and fulfilling life really is.

You can begin by asking yourself a few simple questions.

- Does my life look and feel the way I want it to look and feel? If not, what would I like to change?
- Do I worry more about how my life looks or how my life feels?
- Does my happiness depend on others or am I happy with myself?
- Do I seek advice from others or do I trust the decisions that I make?
- What would I have to change to create the life I always thought I would live?

These are a few simple questions to ponder. It's important that you don't overthink or complicate this task. Throughout this adventure you will notice subtle changes begin to occur as your awareness regarding your ineffective thoughts, feelings, attitudes and beliefs start to increase.

Mother Teresa has been a great inspiration in the way she not only changed her own life, but in how her life changed a nation and the world. She once said of herself, "I am just an ordinary person with an extraordinary story."

I, too, am just an ordinary person and this is my extraordinary story—a story of Courage, Choice and Conscious Change.

Embark with me now on this extraordinary quest as you begin to design your life the way you have always dreamed it would be.

Enjoy the journey!

Chapter 1

The Journey Begins

"The purpose of this book is to help you become conscious of your past experiences, not controlled by them."

~ Victoria Lee Carlyle

This book has been written to assist those who struggle with ineffective emotional patterns. It will also be beneficial for those who are trying to help someone they love who suffers from or is blinded by the effects of detrimental emotional patterns.

These patterns are unconscious, but they have the power to disrupt relationships, sabotage happiness and hold people back from their ability to succeed. Consciously creating success includes enjoying life to the fullest, sustaining loving relationships, establishing financial security, and having a career that you enjoy while creating memories that will last a lifetime. Essentially, it is living the life that you have always wanted.

The concept of success includes enjoying life to the fullest, sustaining loving relationships, establishing financial security, having a career that you enjoy while creating memories that will last a lifetime.

Speaking of memories that last a lifetime, I recently relived the sweetness of one such memory. I was traveling in my car and listening to the radio, when I heard "God Bless the USA," by Lee Greenwood. I was surprised at the instant rush of emotion that came to my mind as I pictured my son, scared as can be, singing this song in public for the first time. A smile crossed my face as I remembered how, after his performance, he burst into tears and was too embarrassed to go back out on stage to receive a standing ovation.

With my heart tender, I continued to listen to the words of the song and was overwhelmed with gratitude as I thought of all the men who have died for our freedom. This feeling reminded me of an article I had read about the Navy SEALs. I had been impressed with their unwavering dedication and love for their country. These men not only stand for what is right, they have the honor and moral courage to get beyond their fears and put their lives on the line for every mission they undertake.

I had read how, in one particular SEALs operation, one of their helicopters crashed at a crucial stage. The team recovered quickly, immediately readjusted their plan and forged ahead to accomplish their goal.

The article described the courage of one team member, who, without hesitation, grabbed two people thought to be wearing explosive vests and used his own body to shield the rest of the team from the blast.

I began to wonder how those in these Special Forces are able to override their emotional attachments and natural fear responses to remain clearly focused on their objective.

I truly admire how these men put their lives on the line, control their emotions and still have the ability to think clearly enough to remain kind and gentle to those innocently caught up in the operation.

The SEALs Training Secrets

I began to study the innovative training methods that create the physical, mental, and emotional strength it takes to become some of the most courageous men on earth. Don't get me wrong. It's not that these brave, dedicated men don't feel the fear; it is that they have the ability to get beyond their fear, clearly focusing on one stage at a time until their mission is complete.

The SEALs training is considered to be the toughest in the world. To accomplish their assignments, they must have the clear, conscious ability to override their automatic fear response so they can pay attention to little details that, if ignored, could get them killed.

Because panic is not an option, cadets are trained by being placed in high-stress situations of panic, fear and doubt, and are required to face such situations over and over again until they become comfortable in uncomfortable situations.

One of the most challenging exercises they face is in the BUDS training where the final test is to override the body's natural survival instinct and face the fear of drowning. In this test, the cadets enter the water with a trainer who constantly attacks their air supply. Even though they have practiced untangling their oxygen equipment thousands of times, there is almost nothing more frightening for the human mind than to face the fear of drowning.

There is an important aspect of the training that is truly amazing. The Navy noticed that the minute the cadets learned to override the natural survival instincts of panic, fear and doubt, their confidence went up because they no longer had the same fear response controlling them.

Every one of us can benefit from the innovative tactics the Navy has used to assist cadets in advancing through the SEALs training.

Just as the SEALs train to become the best in their field, The Victim Addiction is dedicated to providing you with the understanding and support you need to overcome your own automatic fear responses.

As we consciously face our emotional fears, we begin to feel comfortable in uncomfortable situations. The byproduct of feeling comfortable and gaining control over our emotional reactions is that our confidence will go up. We feel more secure with ourselves because we no longer have the same automatic responses controlling us.

As we come to understand The Victim Addiction and the unconscious power it has had over us, we increase our ability to become free from the emotional patterns that bind us and, instead, access tools to successfully triumph in every area of our lives.

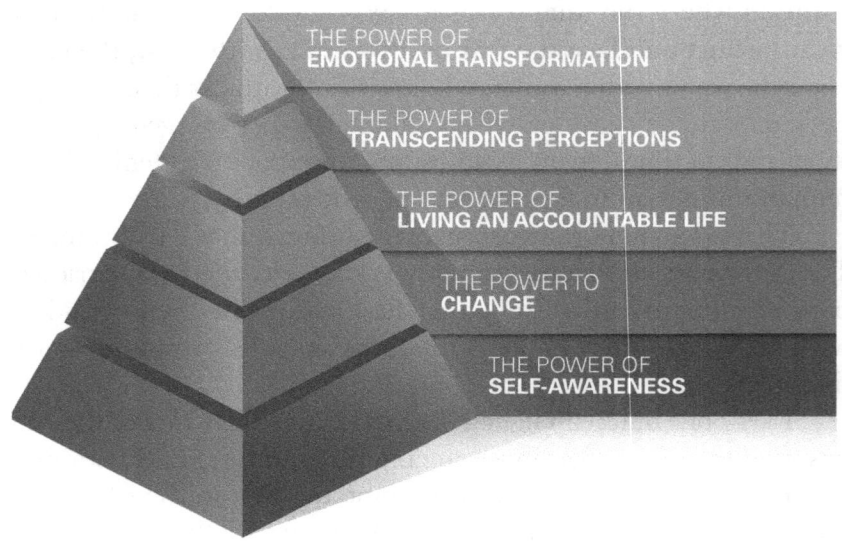

The Personal Power Pyramid

"Without change, something sleeps inside us, and seldom awakens."

~ Frank Herbert

The antidote to The Victim Addiction is the Personal Power Pyramid.

The pyramid is a visual guide that will heighten your level of consciousness. It builds as each concept is introduced, ultimately opening the insights necessary to obtain lasting change.

Each aspect of the pyramid will enhance your ability to make clear, decisive choices that will allow you to overcome the unconscious patterns of The Victim Addiction.

Tiers of the Personal Power Pyramid

The beginning tier, Tier I, is the Power of Self-Awareness. The objective here is to learn to become more inquisitive and to raise your self-awareness. The more inquisitive and conscious you become, the more you will recognize how you unconsciously give your power away to The Victim Addiction. In Tier I, it is important to be curious and not critical as you notice the emotional and behavioral patterns that get in the way of your happiness and growth.

Tier II is the Power to Change. In this tier, you discover the distinct differences of the rational and emotional mind. You will also gain valuable information that will give you the ability to access the power to change anything in your life.

In Tier III, the Power of Living an Accountable Life, you learn the difference between living in The Victim Addiction and living an Accountable Life. In this tier, you examine the energy and strength that comes as you release the emotional hold painful experiences have had over your life. At the same time, you will explore the incredible freedom that comes with the power of conscious choice.

In Tier IV, the Power of Transcending Perceptions, you explore the unconscious belief systems that shape the thoughts, feelings, and attitudes that direct your behaviors. In this tier, you discover ways to consciously override your fear-based beliefs with empowering beliefs, which will create new attitudes that will change your life for the better.

In Tier V, you reach the pinnacle of the Personal Power Pyramid and enjoy the Power of Emotional Transformation. This tier is the foundation of personal freedom, as everything you have worked for comes together. Here you learn to implement effective tools you have gained throughout this book. The lasting change you have experienced will not only help your life, but will also have a powerful impact on the lives of those around you. In this tier, you gain tools to overcome obstacles and establish foundational values. These values will give you the ability to set personal boundaries. Once you overcome your obstacles and establish the core values you want to live by, you gain the ability to set personal boundaries, build loving relationships, establish financial security, enjoy your career and create remarkable memories that will last a lifetime.

As you put into practice the processes, thoughts and ideas introduced in this book, you will gain the self-trust needed to truly own your personal power. Moving into your personal power will take conscious rigor and, at times, may seem uncomfortable and overwhelming, but don't give up, the rise to attain the greatness you possess is worth any time you may invest. Plus, your investment will come back in abundance, because it's a lasting change that only you can control and create.

Loveland, Colorado, artist Bobbie Carlyle's sculpture of "Self Made Man" depicts a man chiseling himself out of stone. This is a powerful example of the pain we must face to mold ourselves into the person we choose to become. The time is now, to realize that you have everything you need to impact your life and consciously connect to your inner motivation to succeed. You alone have the power to rise to your greatness and create the rich, satisfying, happy life you have always wanted to live.

"Self Made Man" is a sculpture by
Loveland, Colorado, artist Bobbie Carlyle[2]

The Rise to Greatness

In order to rise to our greatness, we must be willing to address times in our life when we have felt unappreciated, overlooked, unrecognized or when we weren't acknowledged in the way we wanted to be.

---
[2] Photograph of "Self Made Man" used with permission from artist, Bobbie Carlyle. See more about Bobbie Carlyle Sculpture at www.BobbieCarlyleSculpture.com.

The Journey Begins

Did you know that any time we are hurt, offended, blaming, frustrated, angry, or even when we feel attacked, criticized, stupid or abandoned, we are experiencing symptoms of The Victim Addiction?

So how can we get out of The Victim Addiction and experience life to our full potential?

The solution is simple. It begins by believing we have the power to make things better.

Yet sometimes, even when we have made strides forward, we may not feel like things are better.

In fact, I can have all the skills to create an amazing life, but if I don't feel I am successful, I can sabotage everything I've accomplished. This occurs because what I know and how I feel are two completely different things. Some people experience tremendous success, yet still feel like a failure. Others have a wonderful job and a good family life but carry unconscious burdens and have a hard time enjoying the benefits of their hard work.

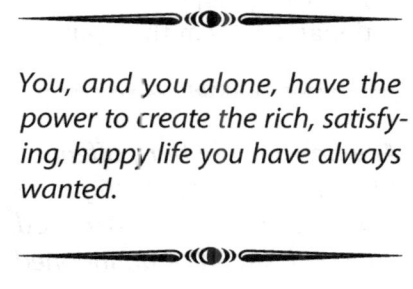

You, and you alone, have the power to create the rich, satisfying, happy life you have always wanted.

Have you ever thought about the difference between what you know to be true and what you feel to be true?

What we *know* comes from the rational mind. The rational mind is the processing center of the brain and will assist us as we logically plan, strategize and prepare to create productive results. The rational mind brings great value to our ability to succeed, but the true drive and determinant of success will come from the power of our emotional mind.

The Power of the Emotional Mind

How we *feel* comes from the emotional mind. The emotional mind does not think or comprehend our current reality. It is protective and always on guard for danger but cannot differentiate between real danger and perceived danger.

The emotional mind is extremely powerful because it has more neural connections than any other portion of the brain. Neural connections are like roads on a one-way highway, which means that information going from the emotional mind to other portions of the mind only travels in one direction. Because the emotional mind has massive amounts of active neural pathways, the influence it has over our thoughts, feelings, attitudes and beliefs are substantially stronger. This understanding is extremely important when you consider that the emotional mind does not know the difference between what it sees and what it remembers and cannot comprehend our current reality. Because it can only recognize sensory details of incidents we have already experienced, this part of our mind influences our perceptions by tapping into sensory memories of past events.

Every experience we have will establish both rational and emotional details in the brain. The rational factors include all the logical details, such as the who, what, when, why and how. The emotional components include all the sensory memories with all the sights, sounds, smells, emotions and physiological sensations that occurred during the original event.

Any time we are hurt, offended, blaming, frustrated, angry, or even when we feel attacked, criticized, stupid or abandoned, we are experiencing symptoms of The Victim Addiction.

These logical and emotional factors will anchor the details of each experience in different portions of the brain. Once an incident has been anchored, it can be triggered by any of the sights, sounds, smells, emotions or physiological sensations that are perceived as similar to the original event. When we are triggered, we can feel just as frightened, angry or insecure as we did when the original event occurred.

Learning how our mind has anchored certain events and understanding the impact these events have on our thoughts, feelings, attitudes and beliefs will help us connect to the drive and determination needed to overcome emotional obstacles and gain the freedom to direct every area of our lives.

The more curious we become about our emotional reactions, the more we will recognize how we give our power away to The Victim Addiction. This awareness will give us the ability to notice the unconscious emotional patterns that bind us, while increasing our conscious ability to change.

Another element of learning will come from experiential processes placed throughout this book. The purpose of these processes is to help you learn how to get curious, not critical, when it comes to your unconscious emotional patterns and reactions. Curiosity will give you a better understanding as to why you think, feel and act the way you do.

Not all of the questions in each of the processes will apply to every individual. However, even if one does not apply to you directly, it may pertain to someone with whom you have influence. Because of this, I suggest that you take time to familiarize yourself with each of the processes.

Tier I
The Power of Self-Awareness

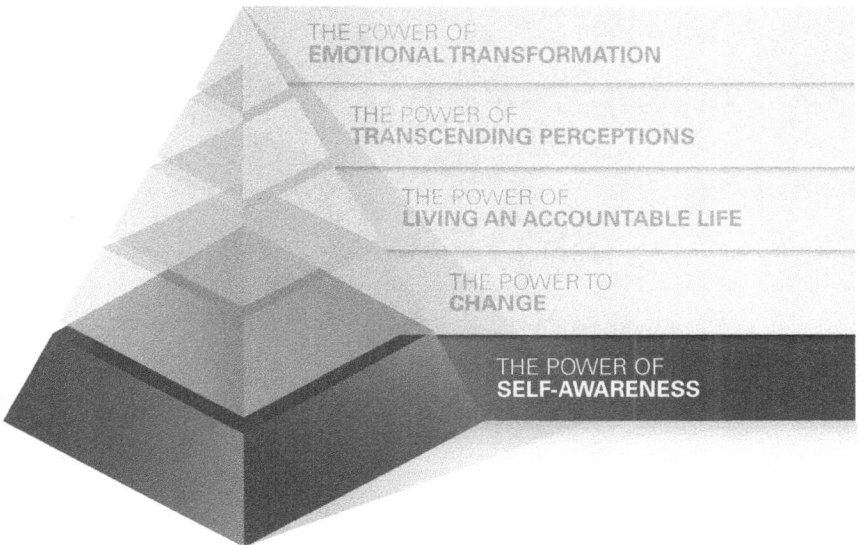

"Your visions will become clear only when you can look into your own heart. He who looks outside himself, dreams; he who looks inside, awakens."

~ C.G. Jung

Self-awareness is the first tier and the starting point for obtaining personal power. This tier can be the most difficult part of the pyramid because we are identifying our triggers and noticing the ineffective patterns that engage our defense mechanisms. Because it is uncomfortable to look at our unproductive patterns it can make it challenging to be objective. Our defensive habits have the power to block our ability to notice the unconscious ways we generate our own misery by blaming, denying, justifying or lying to ourselves.

Have you ever noticed the different ways that you sabotage your happiness by avoiding conflict or trying to control others? Are there areas in your life where it is more important to be right than to encourage happiness and peace? Let's explore the self awareness needed to understand why this occurs.

Chapter 2

Self-Awareness Defined

If your emotional abilities aren't in hand, if you don't have self-awareness, if you are not able to manage your distressing emotions, if you can't have empathy and have effective relationships, then no matter how smart you are, you are not going to get very far.

~ Daniel Goleman

Each of us has the ability to consciously choose the outcomes in our lives. Becoming self-aware enhances our ability to unlock the unlimited potential of our mind by revealing the unconscious emotional patterns that limit our happiness and growth.

What is Self-Awareness?

Self-awareness is the conscious ability to notice the automatic mindless ways our emotional thoughts, feelings, attitudes and beliefs influence our perceptions, and control our behaviors.

Learning to consciously identify and direct the emotional patterns that interfere with our happiness and growth will give us the freedom to live more fully within our personal power.

Without self-awareness, we continue in blindness. We blame, justify and deny our current circumstances, believing those circumstances are something outside of our power to manage, control or change.

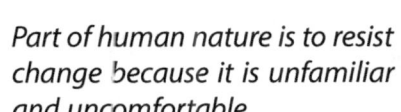

Part of human nature is to resist change because it is unfamiliar and uncomfortable.

Change can be hard. Part of human nature is to resist change because it is unfamiliar and uncomfortable and it challenges what we emotionally believe to be true. So again, the only way to create lasting change is by consciously observing our emotional perceptions and noticing the gap between where we are and where we want to be.

Becoming self-aware will bring our ineffective emotional patterns to the surface, which will increase our ability to differentiate facts over feelings or consciously decipher between what is real versus what we feel to be real. Most of the time *"what is real"* and the emotional perception of *"what we feel to be real"* are very different. How we feel about an emotional situation can change our perceptions, leading to illogical conclusions that produce irrational thoughts and unpredictable behaviors.

By working through the processes in this book, you will begin to decipher your perceptions and discover your emotional patterns. Once your emotional patterns come to light, you will be able to determine whether the way you think, feel and act enhances your happiness or unconsciously sabotages your power to succeed.

How we feel about an emotional situation can change our perceptions, leading to illogical conclusions that produce irrational thoughts and unpredictable behaviors.

The processes will also help you understand how you have organized the habits of your mind. Each process is designed to gradually increase your awareness and give you the conscious ability to let go the ineffective emotional patterns that get in the way of your happiness and growth. The more consciously you engage in the processes, the more confidence you will have to design your life the way you want.

The Process of Self-Awareness

Self-awareness is the first process. The purpose of this process is to introduce you to the power that comes from conscious awareness. You will begin by noticing your physical state throughout the day. Try to notice the different elements that alter your physical or emotional well-being.

1. Several times a day, perhaps on the hour every hour, note the way you feel – your body's reaction to external stimuli. For example, notice how your body feels. Are your shoulders tight? Are your eyes heavy? Notice your breathing, heart rate, posture, etc.

2. Note what is happening when you meet with your boss, are at lunch with friends or arguing with your child, etc.

3. Notice how the circumstances in your life affect your mood. Are you happy? Sad? Angry? Tense?

4. Where are your thoughts focused? Do your thoughts enhance your energy or bring you down?

5. Write your responses in a journal and draw logical conclusions, such as: "When I argue with my sister, my jaw aches from clenching my teeth, my hands sweat, and I usually get a headache. After talking with my boss my mood changed drastically. When I first sat down with my friends I was happy, but immediately became exasperated and angry. After talking to my son I was irritated and I thought to myself, why can't he just do what I ask? or, When I feel discouraged I remember all the other times people have hurt, disrespected or disregarded me."

Here is a little experiment that will also enhance your awareness, as you are reading the newspaper or watching the news on TV, notice any emotional fluxes or variations—notice which news stories impact your thoughts, feelings or tap into your beliefs. Also notice when your mind throws out something that seems illogical or is completely irrational for a particular situation, then note any reaction that should occur.

Journal any thoughts or ideas that will encourage growth and promote change

Self-Talk—Interpreting Our Thoughts

Another part of becoming self-aware is to notice your thoughts. There is an old Chinese proverb that says, "A bird that sings does not sing because it has an answer, it sings because it has a song."

Are you fully aware of the song that plays in the background of your mind?

Noticing where our thoughts go and how we talk to ourselves is a key to greater self-awareness.

Have you ever walked up to someone and said, "I'm good enough, I'm smart enough, and, doggone it, people like me!" (Stuart Smalley)

Yeah ... me neither! But have you ever wondered why sometimes your thoughts seem to draw you toward things that are discouraging and not toward how absolutely amazing you are or can be?

Have you ever stopped to notice your thoughts? Or better yet, have you ever tried to quiet the constant chatter that goes on in your mind? Try it now. Set a timer for one minute, close your eyes, clear your mind, and think of absolutely nothing for the next 60 seconds.

How did it go? Were you able to quiet your mind?

Did you know that you think more than 60,000 thoughts a day, making it nearly impossible to quiet the mind chatter?

At some level, we are always having an internal dialogue with ourselves.

The Impact of Our Thoughts

There are times when your thoughts can actually limit your ability to succeed. For example, how many times do you avoid taking action on things you know will improve your life? Typically, in those instances, it is not that you lack the time, talent, knowledge or ability to change, it's simply that your thoughts or perceived inadequacies sabotage you.

Self-Awareness Defined

Self-awareness is the bridge to the personal power it takes to overcome the circumstances that get in the way of a rich and fulfilling life.

Have you ever pondered the thoughts that contribute to the way you view the world? Or, have you considered how your thoughts convince you to avoid change?

Noticing what your natural tendency is when you face a challenge or can't do something easily is essential for your continued progression.

When you get frustrated, do you get angry or over-complicate things? Or, do you give up and say, "I can't do this!" so you don't even try?

Think Outside the Box

As long as ineffective thoughts and emotions are free to run in the unconscious mind, they will continue to distort your experiences. Say you were trying to solve a problem, but your thoughts tell you, "I can't do this," and you begin to feel stupid; what is the likelihood that you will be able to solve the problem? In fact, how can you accomplish anything if "I am stupid" is always running in the background of your mind? What makes interrupting these types of patterns hard is that some thoughts are so familiar and habitual that you don't even notice when they're running.

"Think outside the box" has become a commonly used phrase. It suggests that the way to innovation, creativity and problem solving is to look at things in a way that is new. In the next few chapters, we will be discussing a great deal about the mental box in which we trap ourselves. Becoming aware of your own thoughts and feelings is the first step in being able to ultimately "think outside" that box and move beyond where you currently are to where you want be, and a great place to begin is with your thoughts. Because our thoughts are conscious it can be very helpful to pay attention to the different thoughts we have throughout the day. Some of our thoughts lift our energy, and some thoughts bring our emotional energy down.

THE PROCESS OF NOTICING YOUR SELF-TALK/THOUGHTS

The purpose of this process is to help you notice how your thoughts influence the way you feel and how those feelings impact your perceptions and behaviors.

This week, notice where you place your energy by looking at your "self-talk."

At least three times a day, consciously notice the subjects you are thinking about. Are you associating your emotional energy on things that build you up or on things that tear you down. Create a list of your thoughts. Let's call the uplifting thoughts our Fantabulous List, and the list of those thoughts that bring you down or discourage you, call it the Craptacular List.

In order to become truly self-aware, it is important that you do not make yourself wrong about the way you think or feel. Instead, understand that these types of feelings are helpful indicators that the way you have structured your perceptions may need some adjustment.

When you avoid self-judgment you allow yourself the opportunity to identify some of the ineffective ways you sabotage your happiness and growth. With this in mind the "Craptacular" thoughts you have should never be ignored or overlooked. These thoughts will give you the valuable information you need to use as a benchmark, as you notice the gap between where you are and where you want to be. These thoughts can also help you understand the detrimental ways you hold yourself back. Once you notice the ways you hold yourself back, you gain the conscious ability to make necessary changes that will enhance your confidence to direct your life the way that you want.

As you write these lists, it is important to understand that the unconscious mind is in charge of our survival system and will use illogical feelings of fear as a shield to prevent you from making any uncomfortable change that involve risks. That fear factor could block you from noticing familiar emotional patterns that get in the way of your conscious ability to succeed.

Journal any thoughts or ideas that will encourage growth and promote change.

Chapter 3

The Comfort Zone

"Coming out of your comfort zone is tough in the beginning, chaotic in the middle, and awesome in the end ... because in the end, it shows you a whole new world! Make an attempt."

~ Manoj Arora, from *The Rat Race to Emotional Freedom*

One of the most important steps in self-awareness is to become aware of your comfort zone.

I am going to use the box shown here as a representation of our Comfort Zone.

Our Comfort Zone

There are a lot of wonderful things in our comfort zone. Most people say their comfort zone is a place where they feel safe and familiar. Our comfort zone is the automatic rut of everyday life where we get in our car, go to work, come home, watch TV, go to bed, get up, and do it all over again! On a logical level, the comfort zone feels familiar and safe.

BUT! There is an unconscious place in our comfort zone where The Victim Addiction rules. We go to this place when we are frustrated, discouraged or feel lost. In this place, our thoughts and feelings box us into a mentality that seems to defeat us and makes our circumstances seem permanent. It's a place where logic fades and fear takes over.

I am going to refer to the place where fear takes over as our Emotional Safety Zone.

The image below is a representation of the fear-based place in our comfort zone called the Emotional Safety Zone.

When we are in our Emotional Safety Zone, we don't view the world as the world is; we view the world based on our perceived fears. At times, this perception can seem uncomfortable, and so we mindlessly blame and accuse others for the way we feel, while we remain totally oblivious to our own thoughts and actions.

Although our safety zone is set up to protect us from our perceived fears and to keep us emotionally safe, it also prevents us from seeing our own misperceptions. In the Emotional Safety Zone, our feelings

The Comfort Zone

become our reality, which can distort our perceptions and affect our behaviors. That's how it was for a young African American boy born in the poverty-ridden climate of Detroit.

Ben Carson

Ben Carson was born in the '50s in the hardened, inner-city area of Detroit. At an early age, he convinced himself that he was stupid and incapable of learning or excelling. As a student in a predominantly all-white school, he was at the bottom of his class and was often ridiculed by other classmates. To protect himself from the disapproval of others, Ben developed a violent temper.

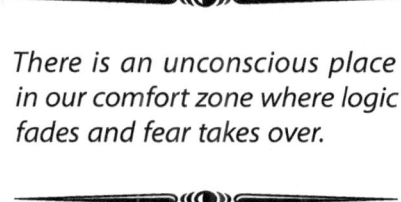

There is an unconscious place in our comfort zone where logic fades and fear takes over.

Ben's mother was a hardworking, very organized woman, who taught her children that anything was possible. Because she was undereducated, she insisted that her sons work hard in their education. To help her sons with their academics, she had her boys read and report on two library books per week. Even though she couldn't read very well she carefully went over their reports and gave a mark to indicate the report was complete.

At first, Ben was angry about giving up his free time and having to spend it reading. After a few short weeks, though, Ben began to realize all the wonderful things he could learn within the pages of a good book. He began studying and learning about a wide variety of subjects.

Ben's love of reading helped him excel and moved him to the top of his class. But, even though he was doing exceptionally well in school, Ben's temper was still out of control and he attacked others over the slightest provocation.

He recalls trying to hit his mother with a hammer because she suggested that he change his clothes. He also caused a head injury to a classmate over a disagreement regarding a locker.

One day, when he stabbed a friend because of a disagreement over a radio station, Ben realized that his anger was completely out of control and he needed to change.

Hiding in the bathroom with a Bible in his hand, he asked God to give him the courage to change. He found inspiration in the book of Proverbs in a passage that said, "Better a patient man than a warrior."

Ben began to ponder about his anger problem, trying to understand how his perceptions and behaviors may have been contributing to the problem. What he realized was that much of his anger occurred even when things did not involve him. He would feel personally attacked as if those things were intentionally directed at him.

He honestly thought everyone was attacking him because he was a poor, black kid, even when that wasn't happening at all. He was completely blind to the fact that he was making destructive choices based on his feelings, not facts; and those feelings were creating his results.

It wasn't until he had the traumatic experience of stabbing his friend and then recognizing it was over something completely insignificant, that he knew he must change. As he questioned his emotional patterns, he began to comprehend how slanted his view of others had become.

When he stopped taking things personally, he was able to overcome his challenges and view situations from another perspective. It was then that he realized he had the full power to change his emotional reactions. The moment he consciously took control of his emotional reactions his life began to change.

After he graduated from high school with honors, Ben worked hard to support himself through college so he could move on and pursue a medical career. He received his bachelor's degree from Yale University, and earned a medical degree from the University of Michigan School of Medicine.

At age 33, he became the Director of Pediatric Neurosurgery at John Hopkins Hospital, the youngest major division director in the hospital's history. Ben went on to perfect his skills as a neurosurgeon and eventually became famous for his groundbreaking work in separating conjoined twins.

Ben Carson's talents are an incredible blessing to the world, and he has been honored for his many unprecedented breakthroughs and contributions in his field.[1]

---

[1] *Gifted Hands: The Ben Carson Story* (2009) (TV Movie). A Johnson & Johnson Spotlight Presentation. Premiered Saturday, February 7, 2009 (TNT).

It was only when Dr. Carson began to question his emotional patterns of anger that he was able to access the power to change his situation.

Where Logic Fades and Fear Takes Over

What we must remember is that when we are in our Emotional Safety Zone, our logic fades and fear is what directs our thoughts, feelings, attitudes, beliefs and our behaviors. However, when we identify the emotional patterns that drive that fear, we gain the power to direct those thoughts, feelings, attitudes and beliefs in successful ways.

Some of the fears that drive our Emotional Safety Zone include:

- Fear of failure
- Fear of rejection
- Fear of loss
- Fear of changes
- Fear of judgment
- Fear of humiliation
- Fear of being alone
- Fear of being hurt

When we are in a place of fear, our defense mechanisms go up and our emotional mind goes into an over-protective mode to create a sense of safety. In this over-protective Emotional Safety Zone, our mind quickly links our current interaction to other times when we have felt similar failure, rejection, loss, panic, or pain and attaches those past feelings to our current situation.

This "triggers" a fear-based reaction and our behaviors and actions are instantly controlled by the emotions of past events. When triggered, the emotional mind will "sabotage" our reasonable thinking and override the reality of our current situation.

Caught in the Box

Again, the place that unconsciously takes over when we feel criticized, angry, frustrated, disrespected or hurt is called the Emotional Safety Zone.

While it may feel safe and familiar, it is in this Zone that the unconscious mind takes control of our thoughts, emotions and beliefs, and we automatically repeat the same patterns over and over.

That is why we have times in our lives when we experience a momentary lapse of reason and are left to wonder, "What was I thinking?" The reality is, you weren't!

THE PROCESS OF RECOGNIZING UNCONSCIOUS FEARS

The purpose of the fear process is to notice the unconscious fears that block your progression and limit your emotional well being.

Look at the fear list:

- Fear of failure
- Fear of rejection
- Fear of loss
- Fear of changes
- Fear of judgment
- Fear of humiliation
- Fear of being alone
- Fear of being hurt

Specifically identify times in your life when unconscious fears have placed limits on your ability to make decisions.

For example, do you hesitate sharing your opinion for fear of ridicule, judgment, or rejection?

As you identify your self-imposed boundaries notice any fear based judgments or beliefs that keep you in your limits.

Notice any justifications you have created to substantiate your reactions.

Journal any thoughts or ideas that will encourage growth and promote change.

When the emotional mind takes control, it is important get curious, not critical about the emotional patterns that bind you. When you are critical, you generate more fear and feel less empowered. Curiosity will give you the conscious ability to override your fears and move forward in a more productive direction.

Because the emotional mind lacks logic and is unconscious, we are unaware of the influence our fears have over the choices we make. While these choices may make us "*feel*" safe, the familiarity is what keeps us stuck in emotional patterns that ultimately get in the way of our happiness and our growth.

I know it may seem illogical, but remember the emotional mind triggers uncomfortable feelings to protect us. The emotional mind's motto is similar to that of the Navy SEALs' and that is, "The only easy or emotionally familiar day was yesterday." That is why we stay in our comfort zone—because it is familiar, so it "*feels*" comfortable and safe even when, in reality, we are neither comfortable nor productive and at times we are not even safe.

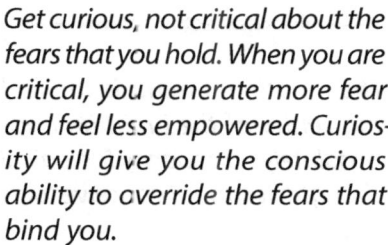

Get curious, not critical about the fears that you hold. When you are critical, you generate more fear and feel less empowered. Curiosity will give you the conscious ability to override the fears that bind you.

Let's take a minute and discuss why this irrational safety occurs.

Essentially, we have two portions of the mind that influence our reality. The left brain is rational and and uses feelings to process our reality.

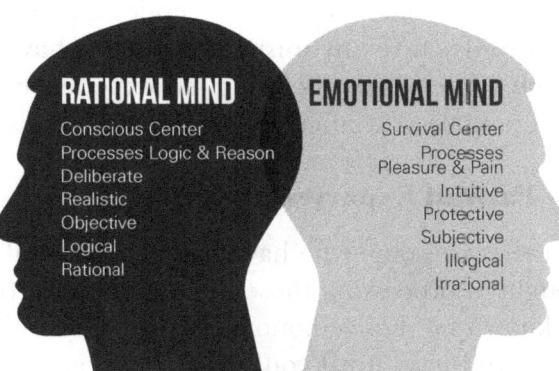

Because the emotional mind is part of the survival system, it is fully developed at birth and has more neural connections than any other portion of the mind. The emotional mind is the feeling center of the brain and has absolutely no capacity for logical thought. It cannot conceive facts or reality. Since the emotional mind is part of the survival system, it will use defense mechanisms as a coping device to keep us safe from things that may cause us emotional harm.

The only way the emotional mind can communicate potential danger is through feelings. It is up to us to decipher what is real and what the mind has perceived to be real.

> *The emotional mind is the feeling center of the brain and has absolutely no capacity for logical thought. It cannot conceive facts or reality.*

The only way to bridge the gap between our emotional mind and our rational mind is through our feelings. That is why it is so important to notice the intensity of our feelings and consciously decipher if the intensity is logical for the current situation.

The rational mind is very important to our emotional growth, but the rational mind can take up to 30 years to fully develop. Unlike the emotional mind which communicates to us through feelings, the rational mind communicates through logical thought and reasoning. It also is the place where we analyze our feelings and where we can process past events. We process past events by becoming consciously aware of the thoughts, feelings, attitudes and beliefs that influence our perceptions. Once we become aware of what drives our perceptions, we have the ability to consciously restructure any misperceptions we have acquired. It is only through consciously processing our experiences that we can truly manage, control or change the choices that we make.

Looking at Painful Experiences

I know there are some who have had very painful experiences and the thought of processing those memories seems frightening. I want you to know that those emotional events will continue to cause you heartache and pain until you bring the thoughts, feelings, attitudes and beliefs to a conscious level where they can be analyzed and released. Your feelings may make you feel tremendously unsafe, so it might be best to start slowly.

1. You can start by writing down your feelings and experiences. Remember, it may seem illogical, but that's okay.
2. Ponder the impact painful events have had on your life. Give yourself time to acknowledge and grieve all the things you have lost.
3. Continue processing by talking to someone you trust. Talking about your struggles will give you a better view of your pain, relieve the pressure you have felt and help you understand that you are not alone.
4. Forgive yourself for any guilt or shame you have carried and then forgive others so you can truly put your pain behind you. Forgiving others is important, as it will release any power those who have hurt you may have had.

Introducing the *Fear-Based Emotional Safety Zone*

"Everything you've ever wanted is on the other side of fear."
~ George Addair

The Emotional Safety Zone sabotages our potential by keeping us in a place that is familiar, while blinding us to the ways we recreate detrimental emotional patterns in our lives.

I know how destructive these types of patterns can be because I lived in these self-generating patterns for more than 40 years of my life. Here is a simple example of how my Emotional Safety Zone would compromise my happiness:

I had several children still at home when I decided to go back to school to get my psychology degree. I worked extremely hard to get straight A's. If I got an A-, I was devastated. I remember one teacher who gave me an A- because I fell short by a 0.3 percentage point of an A. I was furious!

I worked hard in that class. This arrogant teacher had no idea the things I had sacrificed to get an A! My friends laughed at me and said, "Remember, C's get degrees!" That didn't help. Couldn't they see I was doing the best I could?

It took me a long time before I realized all of the ways I had put my life on hold for my A's—all of the things I did not do with my children because I had to measure up.

But to whom was I measuring up? No one cared if I got A's. The only one I was proving anything to was myself. I was always trying to be good enough even when there was nothing or no one to compare myself to.

The problem was, I didn't understand the unconscious power that was influencing my behaviors; if people tried to convince me that I did not have to work so hard, I would get defensive and feel hurt or attacked.

This is how the Emotional Safety Zone drained my energy and sabotaged my intentions. When I was in school, I would spend twelve hours on a simple paper because it had to be good enough. Then, when I turned it in, I would experience the same old thoughts, which left me feeling that familiar self-destructive disappointment.

I would think:
- "It's not good enough."
- "I should have spent more time on it."
- "Even when I do my best, I feel like a failure."

- "I should have been more organized."

Of course, I was happy when I got an A because, despite my internal dialog, an A meant "I" was good enough—at least for the moment. However, it wouldn't take long before the *"I have to prove myself"* cycle would start all over again! The Emotional Safety Zone is a self-imposed mental boundary, which maintains safety in familiarity. This familiarity creates a false sense of security.

That familiarity, or what we have always known, puts us in an unconscious, powerless state in which we blindly give our power, trading it for blame, justifications and denial. It is in this place that our defense mechanisms take over to shield us from reality.

Then as a result, we feel powerless or out of control; we feel like we are being dominated or that we have to dominate others to regain control. It is in this powerless mental state that we become victims of our own emotions.

THE PROCESS OF FEELING POWERLESS

The purpose of this process is to become aware of the different areas in your life where you feel limited in your ability to manage, control or change your situations.

In what areas of your life do you…

- Feel powerless?
- Feel that you cannot manage, control or change?
- Feel that you are being dominated or feel a need to control things around you to be okay?

Journal any thoughts or ideas that will encourage growth and promote change.

Emotional Victim Versus Being Victimized

I would like to emphasize that being an *Emotional Victim* is different than *Being Victimized*.

Being victimized is when you have had an experience in which your power has been forcefully taken from you, such as during a rape, robbery, or other forms involving violence or severe abuse. If you have had an experience in which you have been victimized, even if you have suppressed the event, you may feel angry, sad, confused or scared. If you are ready to face the pain and move in a different direction, the things you learn in this book will be very useful in assisting you to consciously process your pain and take back your personal power.

However, until you comprehend the unconscious ways the emotional mind "protects" you and learn how to consciously process your pain, you will find that certain elements of your Emotional Safety Zone will continue to perpetuate your pain and sabotage your healing process.

Being victimized is when you have had an experience in which your power has been forcefully taken from you.

The emotional mind's job is to conceal detailed memories of extreme emotional events so they won't hurt you again. The problem is, every time something in your current environment seems even vaguely familiar to a past painful event, it will trigger feelings of fear, and instead of facing the pain an automatic fight or flight response will take over.

If you've had a traumatic event, you may be feeling like these events have taken control over your life and they have even defined, at least to some degree, how you feel about yourself. But any time your perspectives are based on the way you feel, you will have a hard time imagining that your life can ever be any different. When you base your perceptions on reality, you gain the ability to separate from the destructive emotions caused by others and move on to truly enjoy life again.

Time to Heal

It is important to regain personal safety by acknowledging the feelings that connect you to painful events.

You can start by noticing which environments or relationship patterns cause you to feel uncomfortable. Remember, if it feels real, unconsciously you believe the fears you are feeling are pertinent to your current situation and, in most cases, you will create a rational illusion to validate that the way you are feeling is relevant to your current situation.

In order to get past this emotional trauma, you must face your fears over and over again. Each time you face your fears, you release some of the intensity your emotions hold, which will make your next emotional encounter of this event easier to handle.

Looking at the painful things that have happened to us can be frightening, but having the courage to question our emotions will give us the strength we need to let go of the sorrow and create something new. It may be beneficial to journal your thoughts and feelings. Keep in mind that emotional experiences hidden in the unconscious mind will oftentimes come out illogically. Pay particular attention to your illogical thoughts, as they create the energy that fuels your fears.

Keep reading to find out how to take your power back and create the self-worth, inner peace and happiness you deserve!

Emotional Victim

Unlike someone who has been victimized and had their personal power forcefully taken away from them, an Emotional Victim blindly gives their personal power away, and then ends up feeling victimized.

When I am being an emotional victim, I am in a place where I *feel* like my power has been taken from me, and I *feel* like a victim—when in all actuality, I am unconsciously giving my power away. I am victimizing myself and at times will blindly victimize others as well.

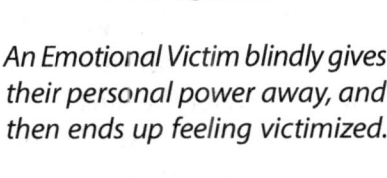

An Emotional Victim blindly gives their personal power away, and then ends up feeling victimized.

As an emotional victim, I justify my inadequacies, and I blame others or myself for my lack of happiness and success.

Remember, the emotional victim doesn't emerge when everything is great and life is rolling along. It is an unconscious function that lingers somewhat dormant and comes out in times of challenge. For most of us, the unconscious emotional victim is only prevalent when we are in a heightened emotional state, such as times of extreme loss, change, failure or rejection. We don't consciously choose to go there; most of the time, we don't even realize when we are there.

Let's face it, nobody wakes up in the morning and says, "Hmm ... I wonder how I can victimize myself today?" No one consciously chooses to allow their emotions to overtake their thoughts and behaviors. In fact, the emotional victim is completely in the dark as to what is truly driving them. So when our emotions take over, we may casually pass it off as, "This is just the way I am," or "I don't know what came over me."

The truth is, you will remain an emotional victim—and the bouts of irrational, emotional behavior may even become more frequent until you start acknowledging the detrimental thoughts, feelings, attitudes and beliefs that keep you in The Victim Addiction.

Understanding how we give our power away to the emotional victim will help us gain the self-awareness needed to access full power over our emotional lives.

Understanding how we give our power away to the emotional victim will help us gain the self-awareness needed to access full power over our emotional lives.

The dedication it takes to consciously change our detrimental emotional patterns will also assist us in healing any pain or sorrow caused by our unconscious habits.

For example, I worked with a man who suffered abuse as a child. One day, he was talking with his brother about the excuses their father had for the hurt he had caused. The longer the brothers spoke, the more they realized how much resentment they harbored. Both resented how their father avoided taking any responsibility for his violent, inappropriate or harmful actions. He justified his actions by saying, "I lost control"—as though he was not to be blamed for the injuries he had caused.

After the brothers learned ways the emotional victim automatically takes over, it was easier for them to understand how their father could feel he had no choice in the way he directed his emotions.

When we become aware of the ways we have unconsciously hurt others, we not only have the ability to forgive ourselves for our behaviors, we can also admit our inadequacies and ask for forgiveness when our actions hurt others. This understanding will allow us to forgive the unconscious ways we give our power away and open the door to fulfilling relationships.

THE PROCESS OF NOTICING THE EMOTIONAL VICTIM

The purpose of this process is to notice emotional victim patterns in yourself and in others.

- Identify any emotional patterns that limit your ability to succeed in any area of your life. (Note: Emotional patterns include any ineffective thoughts, feelings, attitudes or illogical beliefs, such as: "I could never do that.")
- What are the unrealistic or illogical thoughts or perceptions that limit your growth and lead you to feeling unable to change your circumstance?
- Realistically evaluate whether your perceptions are grounded in facts or driven by feelings. Use a two-column chart to compare perceptions based on facts and perceptions based on feelings.
- Create another two-column chart to identify the results you are producing. On one side, put: "I am producing the results I desire." On the other side, write: "I am not producing the results I desire." Example: "I enjoy my friends" and on the other side "I am really lonely."

Explore the thoughts, feelings, attitudes, and beliefs that support the results you currently have. Example: "What I want is to feel that people respect me. The actions that might prevent me from feeling that way are that I get angry at others when I feel disrespect."

In order to let go of The Victim Addiction you must realize that part of owning your personal power corresponds with the harmful actions that you tolerate from others. You can begin standing up for yourself by becoming aware of the things that you tolerate and then consciously choosing to do things differently.

This week, spend some time identifying relationships that cause you to feel bad about yourself or make your defenses go up. Look at various relationships such as work, dating, marriage, parent/children, sibling, etc. Analyze your reactive thoughts, feelings, attitudes, and beliefs that freeze you in an emotional state. The ultimate goal is to restructure the reactive patterns. Once you have determined why you feel the way you do, take conscious action to redirect your emotional energy so you can produce the results you want. It may be difficult to create something new with someone whom you share a painful history, so begin standing up for yourself in less threatening ways, like asking for a well-deserved raise or sending your food back at a restaurant.

Journal any thoughts or ideas that will encourage growth and promote change.

THE PROCESS OF NOTICING EMOTIONAL PATTERNS OF OTHERS

The purpose of this process is to take notice of common emotional patterns of those around you.

As you begin to observe others, you will notice common emotional patterns that show up in the way they interact with others so you don't have to get offended or take things personally.

- What judgments do you notice toward them?
- What tone do they use?
- How do they behave?
- Do you notice similar patterns in yourself? Are you taking the emotional behaviors of others personally?
- When others are upset, what are their consistent actions toward people around them?

Journal any thoughts or ideas that will encourage growth and promote change.

Separating ourselves from others' emotional patterns will give us some insights into our own emotional patterns that keep us in The Victim Addiction. We also realize, "We cannot change what we cannot see," and neither can others. When we begin to notice the emotional

The Comfort Zone

patterns of others, we can support their emotional growth by pointing out specific patterns that get in the way of their happiness and growth. But keep in mind that you cannot change someone if they are not ready to change, or feel emotionally unsafe, so it is important to stay out of judgment and be as specific as you can by pointing out several instances where familiar patterns have caused unhappiness and pain.

One element of the Emotional Safety Zone is that we prefer what is familiar—even when what is familiar causes our pain. Because we don't want to look at the pain, we often blame others for the way we feel.

Blame

Blame is a way to release our pain and frustrations by transferring our feelings to someone else. With blame, we believe that "someone or something outside ourself" is taking our power and causing our discomfort. Because this belief feels so convincing, it seems real, and in the moment we feel better. Blame allows us to transfer all our negative feelings to others and keeps us from having to assume any responsibility for the choices we have made or the pain we have caused.

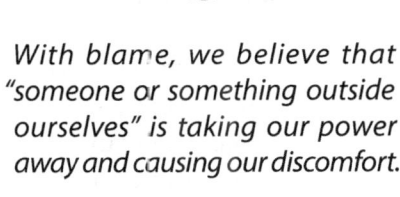

With blame, we believe that "someone or something outside ourselves" is taking our power away and causing our discomfort.

When we believe, "It's not my fault I feel this way; it's yours!" we can resent others for making us feel angry, frustrated, lonely or sad.

The Blame Game

The blame game is one of the ways we inadvertently enter into a powerless state and can be the most damaging of all defense mechanisms.

We use the blame game to avoid feeling the conflict of pain, guilt or shame. If I can't handle my emotions and I don't want to change or look inside to see how I could be the cause of my own pain and suffering, I will blame others and transfer the conflict I feel inside to them. Then, because I have shifted the blame and the conflict is not my fault, I don't have to feel guilty or change my actions.

There is an instant feeling of satisfaction when we make ourselves right in this way. Many people would rather blame others so they can be *right* about their misery, than look at their choices and make the changes necessary to be *happy*.

I was in a relationship for 28 years with a person entangled in the blame game. He would say, "You think I'm a monster." Now, I really never thought any such thing, but because he was living in a world of secrets and lies, he felt guilty. Unfortunately for him, the way he coped with his guilt was with blame and anger. He didn't want to change his behavior, even though the choices he was making created a tremendous amount of internal angst and suffering. It was easier for him to blame me for how he was feeling about himself, than to go inside and do the real work. Eventually, he had generated so much guilt and resentment that he chose to remove himself from our relationship.

It can be very uncomfortable to look at the choices we make that create our pain and suffering. It is easier to hold onto unrealistic expectations and transfer our shortcomings on to others by blaming them for the way we feel.

Do you notice areas in your life where you avoid taking ownership for your actions by blaming others?

Justifications

A few other ways we give away our power is through justifications and denial.

We may be conscious that we have a problem but are unaware or unwilling to admit to the effects the problem continues to have on our relationships or our lives. Our problem has become so familiar that we are blinded to the consequences, and we justify our behavior as, "This is just the way I am." Our justification changes our perspective and we no longer view the problem as our problem.

In fact, part of justification includes rationalizing the problem. This is where the emotional mind enrolls the rational mind to find evidence to support the idea that how we feel about the problem is not

The Comfort Zone

our fault or our problem. We truly believe things like: "This is just part of the unique way we are made up." Then, when we hurt someone we care about, we can separate from any uncomfortable feelings that may occur by denying our actions and remain completely unaware of the impact. *The truth is, our behavior is the cause of our pain and the problem.*

Because I don't want to hurt the ones I love, I must be loyal to the way I have rationalized the justifications. Some of my justifications may sound like: "You just don't understand me" or "I am old enough to act however I want."

Panic sets in when I begin to think about change because I don't want to change. I am very comfortable with the familiar way things are, and I begin to mentally justify my position. When I am confronted, I get angry and defend the problem. Then, I deny that the circumstance that hurt my loved one is "about me," or that, "I am the cause of others' pain and suffering."

Once I justify and blame my pain on someone else, the suffering begins to release, and I feel satisfied with the fact that I am right and it is not me who is causing the pain.

Denial blinds me from my blame and justifications. Once I justify and blame my pain on someone else, the suffering begins to release, and I feel satisfied with the fact that *I am right and it is not me who is causing the pain.*

When I feel better, I open the door for the blame, justification, and denial cycle to start all over again.

THE PROCESS OF BLAME AND JUSTIFICATION

The purpose for this process is to look at the ineffective ways you transfer your feelings onto others through blame and justification.

Identify areas in your life where blame takes your personal power and compromises your relationships.

- Where are you automatically blaming your actions on others?
- When do you make excuses for yourself to justify your behavior?
- Are there areas in your life where you feel powerless and quietly blame yourself?
- How does blame impact the relationships around you?

Journal any thoughts or ideas that will encourage growth and promote change.

Resentment

Blame, justification and denial not only shift responsibility, these practices will create additional resentment toward others for our suffering and pain. Once we start pointing the finger at someone else, we look for excuses that will validate our attitudes towards them. It's easy to feel like a martyr and find ways others take advantage of us so we can blame our suffering on things we believe are outside of our ability to control. Sometimes resentment starts out because someone has violated our trust or deeply hurt us; we feel vulnerable and our Emotional Safety Zone kicks in to protect us from further pain. We may feel that this protection helps us cope with our pain as we inadvertently begin to withdraw from close relationships. The loneliness and feelings of abandonment transfer into other areas of our lives. Unconsciously, we begin to resent everyone for everything and validate this resentment by creating evidence that "something or someone beyond our ability to control" is the real problem.

About two years after my divorce I was in a relationship with a man who suffered from obsessive-compulsive disorder. Tristan had many wonderful qualities—he was kind, loving, and very helpful. He would tell me all the time that he had "never loved anyone as much" as he loved me.

He also appreciated the love I gave him in return.

Tristan had enough evidence throughout his life to know that he had a hard time living around other people."

Tristan's *Denial* was, "I don't have obsessive compulsive disorder."

His *Emotional View* was, "I can only feel peace when things in my home are perfectly clean, symmetrical and well organized."

His *Struggle* was, "Change, no matter how small, is very hard."

His *Behavior* was, "Finding peace in daily rituals."

His *Belief that supported his Emotional View* became, "Everyone loves Tristan's environment, but no one loves Tristan."

His *Defense Mechanism* became resenting those who disturbed his perfect peace.

This resentment caused so much conflict within him that he turned his back on a relationship he claimed he had been looking for his entire life.

Most defense mechanisms blind us to our behaviors and compromise our happiness.

Defense Mechanisms

Our defense mechanisms are self-imposed guards that assist the emotional mind in protecting us from feeling uncomfortable or experiencing pain.

We all have *defense mechanisms* to help us avoid feeling uncomfortable. One of Tristan's defense mechanisms was resenting others for the anxiety he felt.

Have you ever thought about the defense mechanisms that you use?

A few common defense mechanisms include:

- Anger
- Hiding
- Overeating
- Excess sleep
- Drugs or alcohol

THE PROCESS OF DEFENSE MECHANISMS

The purpose of this process is to notice the automatic defense mechanisms that you use and how those defense mechanisms are preventing you from experiencing change.

Becoming more aware of the ways that you emotionally protect yourself will help you consciously create a starting point for lasting change.

- Specifically identify the types of defense mechanisms that are most common for you.
- Now pinpoint the various interactions that bring up your defense mechanisms to the surface.

Journal any thoughts or ideas that will encourage growth and promote change.

Chapter 4

Structuring our Thoughts, Feelings, Attitudes and Beliefs

"Our greatness lies not so much in being able to remake the world, as being able to remake ourselves."

~ Gandhi

There are four sides that construct the mental walls of our fear-based Emotional Safety Zone.

The **first** wall of the *Emotional Safety Zone* is **Structuring**.

Structuring

As human beings, we enter the world without any preconceived notion of how the world works. As we develop, our experiences structure our thoughts, feelings, attitudes and beliefs, and we begin to make sense of the world around us.

Although the structures of our early childhood help us learn and grow, they eventually become irrelevant. However, these invalid perceptions will continue to affect our thoughts, feelings, attitudes and beliefs throughout our lives. It is not until we become consciously aware of our faulty perceptions and reactive behavior that we have the ability to change.

Our early structuring starts out in a survival stage so we can get our needs met. This structuring is self-focused, naïve and innocent. Have you ever noticed how open, honest and authentic little children are? They don't see a problem in letting you know how they feel.

I love this quote by Dr. Seuss:
"Be who you are, and say what you feel, because those who mind don't matter, and those who matter don't mind."

Wouldn't it be great if nothing held us back from being who we are? I'm not talking about screaming until we get our way. I'm talking about simply asking for what we want and not waiting around for others to read our minds in order to get our needs met.

Unfortunately, many of us learned long ago how to hide our emotions and to be careful in what we ask for. As children, we wanted to be loved and accepted so we noticed the body language and social cues of those closest to us and changed ourselves for their approval.

"Be who you are, and say what you feel, because those who mind don't matter, and those who matter don't mind."

Children are innocent and full of wonder; they don't realize that sometimes a loved one's reaction has more to do with the pressures of life than the love they have for the child.

I witnessed a scenario that illustrates how a traumatic event can occur from a simple interaction.

I had been standing in a bookstore near the women's restroom, when all of a sudden my thoughts were interrupted by the joyful sound of clapping and praise.

My curiosity was piqued, so I moved closer to the restroom door. I could hear joyful words of praise coming from a happy child, and the desperate shushing of a woman, as she tried to contain the child's

Structuring our Thoughts, Feelings, Attitudes and Beliefs

excitement. The harder the woman tried to quiet the child, the more enthusiastic the child became.

I am sure this child had just finished her own potty training experience, so she knew what grandma had done in the bathroom was to be acknowledged and celebrated! Trying to help her grandmother understand how proud she was of her, the child said, with all of the energy she could muster, "Wow! Grandma! That is SO BIG! I am SO PROUD OF YOU!" With a stern tone and some sharp words, the grandmother put an abrupt end to the child's celebration.

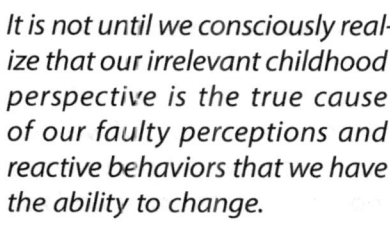

It is not until we consciously realize that our irrelevant childhood perspective is the true cause of our faulty perceptions and reactive behaviors that we have the ability to change.

I know it was not the grandmother's intention to hurt the child; she was probably just embarrassed and didn't want the child to tell the whole store what she was doing in the restroom.

I heard them washing their hands so I quickly walked away before they came out. Seconds later, I saw them hurrying toward the exit. The child was walking a step or two behind her grandmother and I noticed a little tear running down her cheek. To a child, this type of event can be confusing and very traumatic.

We Exchange Ourselves for Others' Approval

As children, we were authentic. We spoke our truth! If we were mad, we showed it, but when our honesty created an emotional reaction in others, we took it personally and felt sad. Because we were not old enough to evaluate the situation appropriately, we began to feel like we were bad or wrong for the way we that we expressed ourselves. We may have even structured the belief that, "It is not safe to express my feelings." As long as childlike beliefs like these stay active in our unconscious mind, they have the ability to create havoc in the way we perceive the world.

The previous story offers a prime example of how easily a child could decide: "Getting excited about things makes people mad and that makes me feel bad." It can be extremely painful for a child to feel it is not safe to get excited and that enthusiasm must be suppressed in order to gain approval. The little girl in this story probably loves her grandmother and, instead of risking disappointing her again, she chooses to hide her enthusiasm.

Let's say, years later this girl is engaged to be married, but those around her are concerned because she doesn't appear to be very excited about the upcoming wedding. Because she has unconsciously suppressed the ability to feel excitement, when questioned about it, she feels confused and begins doubting her decision to marry.

> *As children, we were authentic. We spoke our truth! If we were mad, we showed it, but when our honesty created an emotional reaction in others, we took it personally and felt sad.*

Then, after the wedding, as she experiences the normal adjustments of married life, any time she feels uncomfortable, her internal reservations may stir the feelings of hesitation she experienced before she was married. In her confusion, her feelings intensify and she withdraws a bit. Her husband wants her to be happy so he starts questioning her quiet behavior. Because the true source of her uncertainty is unconscious, she becomes defensive and silently blames her new husband for the way she is feeling. Her unconscious suppression continues to cause her to feel unsettled and eventually sabotages her ability to create the necessary bonding for her new relationship to grow.

It is interesting how perceptions from simple childhood events can impact us in our adult lives.

This is how the emotional cycle works:

A simple childhood event occurs, and we feel bad; then, we emotionally anchor an adverse belief that changes the way we view ourselves and distorts the way we view others.

The majority of our emotional structuring occurs when we are too young and inexperienced to comprehend what is really going on around us. During this age of vulnerability, many frustrating situations occur that we don't know how to overcome. We eventually figure it out, but the initial thoughts, feelings, attitudes and beliefs have already been established, and we have unconsciously compromised our true nature in order to adapt to our surroundings. A good analogy of how we suppress our feelings and conceal our true nature can be found in the following story.

In 1957, a monastery in Thailand was being relocated, and a small group of monks were put in charge of moving a sacred clay Buddha. In the midst of the move, one of the monks noticed a crack in the large statue. Concerned about further damage, the monks decided to wait for a day before continuing with their task. When night came, one of the monks went to check on the giant statue. He shined his flashlight over the entire Buddha. When he reached the crack, he saw something reflect back at him. The monk was curious, and he got a hammer and chisel and began chipping away at the clay that was covering the Buddha.

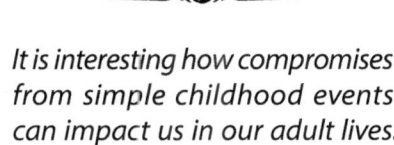

It is interesting how compromises from simple childhood events can impact us in our adult lives.

As he knocked off piece after piece of clay, the Buddha got brighter and brighter. After hours of work, the monk looked up in amazement to see standing before him a huge solid gold Buddha. Many historians believe that several hundred years earlier, when the Burmese army was preparing to attack Thailand, the Thai monks had covered the Buddha with clay to keep it safe from being stolen. When the Burmese army did attack, all the Thai monks were killed, so it wasn't until 1957, when the monks were moving the precious idol, that the great treasure was discovered.[1]

Like the Buddha, there is a great treasure in each of us, but the emotional mind adds protective layers around our inner beauty. To uncover our real self, we must find the courage to consciously chip away the layers of our emotional thoughts, feelings, attitudes and beliefs that keep our inner power hidden.

Anytime we unconsciously protect ourselves from feeling uncomfortable or experiencing pain, our Emotional Safety Zone takes over, and we place mental layers of protection around who we really are. We then

---

[1] Canfield, Jack and Mark Victor Hansen, *Chicken Soup for the Soul* version III.

justify our behaviors and blame others for the detrimental ways we feel about ourselves.

The Process of Identifying Childhood Structures

The purpose of this process is to assist you in identifying childhood structures that interfere with your current perspective.

It is very challenging to identify anything that remains on an unconscious level. That is why it is so important to distinguish the emotional impact certain things in your environment can cause. When looking at ineffective childhood structuring, one area to reflect upon are phrases you may have heard throughout your childhood and identify how they may be influencing your current perceptions. Consider phrases such as: "I am so ashamed of you," "Why are you such a baby" "Who do you think you are?" "Why do you have to be so obnoxious," or "I told you to behave!"

These types of repetitious phrases can sabotage our self-worth and limit our potential without us even realizing it.

- What are some of the repetitious phrases you heard as a child?
- How might the phrases you notice affect your thoughts?
- Is the way you feel about yourself limiting your ability to create create loving relationships?
- What other ways might the way you have structured your childhood events be slanting your perspective?

Journal any thoughts or ideas that will encourage growth and promote change.

Chapter 5

Emotions

"Do not let another day go by where your dedication to other peoples' opinions is greater than your dedication to your own emotions!"

~ Steve Maraboli

The **second** wall that keeps us in our Emotional Safety Zone is **Emotions**.

Heaven and Hell

An old Zen master sat in deep meditation with his eyes closed, legs crossed and his hands folded upon his lap.

Suddenly, his meditation was interrupted by the harsh and demanding voice of a Samurai warrior. "Old man! Teach me the difference between heaven and hell!"

The Samurai impatiently waited for the answer, growing more and more agitated with each passing second.

"You wish to know the secrets of heaven and hell?" replied the master at last. "You whose breath is foul and very appearance is revolting? A man who carts a rusty sword in a tattered sheath? Why should I waste my time with the likes of you?"

The Samurai, consumed with pride and filled with rage, uttered a vile curse. He drew his sword and raised it high above the master's head.

"**That** is *Hell!*" said the master gently.

In a fraction of a second, the Samurai was overcome with awe, as he looked at this gentle teacher who had the courage to put his life on the line in order to teach the Samurai the valuable lesson that he had come to learn.

With tear-filled eyes, the Samurai put his palms together and bowed in gratitude for the insights he had received.

The master looked up and quietly said, "And that, is *Heaven!*"[1]

When we mindlessly allow ourselves to operate outside of rational thought, we become victims to our emotions, and gradually lose touch with reality.

In days of old, a Samurai was held with the utmost respect. Samurais were well educated and lived noble lives full of integrity and honor. Who knows what happened in *this* particular warrior's life that took his virtue. His shift may have happened so subtly he may not have even noticed how he had gradually placed his honor aside, allowing rage to consume his dignity and rule his path.

This story illustrates how, when we operate outside of rational thought, we become victims to our emotions, and can gradually lose touch with reality. We blindly give our emotions the power to control our path and then turn our lives over to automatic reactions and illogical behaviors. When we veer from our personal power, we become vulnerable and create a wall of self-sufficiency by physically

---

[1] Secrets of Heaven and Hell, Adapted from story by John W. Groff Jr., *A Third Serving of Chicken Soup for the Soul*.

and emotionally distancing ourselves. Then, we blame others for our loneliness and confusion.

That was the case with the Samurai in the story above. Somehow he got so far off the beaten path that he had forgotten who he was. Yet, one simple act of courage from the master brought the Samurai back to his senses, giving him the conscious awareness needed to find the answers he had been searching for.

The answer to any question you may have concerning your future is already within your grasp. What you must learn is how to ask the questions that will bring illogical emotional patterns to a conscious level so you can resolve them. Getting curious about the emotional structures that direct your life is the key to unlocking your Emotional Safety Zone.

Emotional Structuring

Because we are, and always will be, emotional beings, it is essential that we learn how to manage, control and enjoy the passion, drive and determination that come with our emotional life.

The truth is most of us have been left on our own not only to decipher our own feelings but also to interpret the emotions of others.

The first stage of our emotional growth occurs in infancy. Have you ever smiled at a baby just to see their face light up as they smile back. Have you watched a two-year-old pat the back of someone who seemed sad?

Neuroscientists believe that much of the brain circuitry essential for perceiving emotions makes a dramatic shift between the ages of 5 and 7. In this stage of our conscious development, we begin to structure our feelings by creating attachments and emotional patterns.

The challenge with these unconscious structures is that many of us have never been taught what to do with the feelings we experience. As children, our main focus is directed towards an education in academics. There isn't a place to get curious or ask questions about our emotional experiences. The truth is most of us have been left on our own, not only to decipher our own feelings, but also to interpret the emotions of those around us. Because some adults in our lives handled frustrating situations inappropriately, we grew up feeling like some of our emotions were "bad or wrong." These feelings were also reinforced every time we were reprimanded for innocently acting upon our natural passionate qualities.

Were you ever forced to say, "I'm sorry," even when you didn't want to, because you weren't? Crying because your feelings were hurt was definitely not allowed, so you taught yourself not to cry when you were hurting. Are you still apologizing or in relationships where others expect an apology, even when you have no idea what you have done "wrong"?

Remember that much of our emotional circuitry was established before we had the conscious ability to grasp the world around us. This lack of knowledge could explain why some people have such a hard time dealing with emotional problems throughout their adult life.

Emotions are an essential part of our learning and growth. Each biologically wired emotion is an innate guide connected to an action designed to assist us in creating a well-balanced life.

Gratifying, productive emotions increase energy to meet new challenges and allows us opportunities to experience happiness and growth.

Emotional Survival System

Uncomfortable emotions, such as fear, sadness and anger, are an evolutionary part of our survival system. Without a proper understanding of how the survival system works, when panic, fear, or doubt is triggered, our emotional mind will seize our thought processes and take control of our perception and reactions.

These biological responses are extremely useful in protecting us when our lives are truly in danger. However, there are times when *perceived dangers* cause emotional reactions that are not necessary for our preservation or protection. In these situations, the mind will produce *psychological and physiological reactions that are just as strong and alarming as if we were in real danger.*

Perceived danger is experienced as real danger. As mentioned previously, our fears may include fear of change, fear of failure, fear of rejection, fear of getting hurt, and so on. When these types of fears are triggered, we can feel like we are in real danger, which can cause us to attack, hold back, withdraw, or even panic.

When we avoid our emotions by burying them, we lose the freedom to enjoy life to the fullest. When left in an unconscious state, our emotions will attach to other painful or uncomfortable situations, which will increase the intensity of our fears. The more emotions we attach to fearful events, the more confusing and illogical they become. Understanding the illogical structures will help us change every area of our lives.

There are times when perceived dangers cause emotional reactions that are not necessary for our preservation or protection. In these situations, the mind will produce psychological and physiological reactions that are just as strong and alarming as if we were in real danger.

I've heard it said, "Feelings buried alive never die." These feelings never die because we cannot process anything that remains in an unconscious state. We must separate the feelings of our emotional events on a conscious level, where we can realistically decipher our fears. Once we are consciously aware of our emotional structures and fears, we have the ability to logically process, analyze and change in ways that are relevant to our current reality.

It is helpful to realize that the unconscious mind feels, it does not think. When we consciously bring feelings attached to a particular event to a logical level, we begin to notice how illogical our feelings attitudes and beliefs can be. Examining our experiences in a conscious way will give us the ability to observe the instinctive nature these emotions possess. Let's take a look at the protective nature of some of our uncomfortable emotions.

Anger

Anger is one of the most misunderstood, misused emotions in our survival system. Anger occurs when someone or something has crossed our personal boundaries or goes against what we have structured to be true.

The physiological response to anger is an instant surge of energy to the upper portion of our bodies, giving us a temporary sense of power, and the energy needed to attack.

There was a time in human history when this type of energy was an essential tool for survival. However, in today's world, anger is often improperly directed. Some will scream to be heard, while others bully to gain "respect." In the moment, there is a feeling of complete satisfaction and control. But, when the moment has passed, the impact of anger will leave one feeling justified, disappointed or misunderstood.

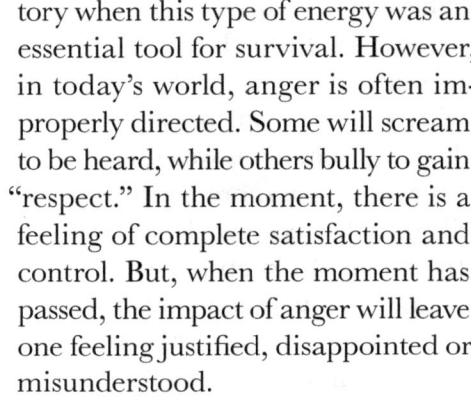

Yet, when channeled effectively, anger is an amazing motivator. It can assist us in standing up for ourselves and in making changes necessary to create more peace and happiness throughout our lives.

Yet, when channeled effectively, anger is an amazing motivator. It can assist us in standing up for ourselves and in making changes necessary to create more peace and happiness throughout our lives.

Guilt

William Shakespeare once said, "Suspicion always haunts the guilty mind." I've also heard it said, "The guilty flee when no one is pursuing." Guilt is designed to make us feel uncomfortable.

Guilt is a natural emotion that occurs when we go against our values and structured beliefs. In writing about guilt, Paul Coughlin, author of *Unleashing Courageous Faith*, described Viktor Frankl's opinion regarding guilt, saying, "Through guilt, [Frankl] wrote people have the potential to change for the better. Healthy guilt is a gatekeeper and boundary-maker. It helps us discover where we shouldn't go in life, what we shouldn't do. And it helps us make amends when we cause others pain and related hardships. Guilt helps us find our way back toward what's right and repair the torn portions of our lives."[2]

Healthy guilt can be a positive force for change, as stated above. Guilt can help us know when we have forgotten our boundaries,

---

[2] Coughlin, Paul. Healthy Guilt vs. False and Harmful Guilt, 2008. Accessed Nov. 8, 2013, www.focusonthefamily.com

strayed from our values and are off track. When we make a mistake, guilt can encourage us to make amends by bridging the gap between what we value and our misplaced thoughts and actions.

However, guilt is not always healthy. Some guilt is attached to detrimental beliefs. These beliefs keep us in a powerless place, where we try to control things outside of ourselves or seek the approval of others, in order to avoid perceived criticism. Unhealthy guilt can become extremely damaging, interfere with self-acceptance and limit our emotional growth.

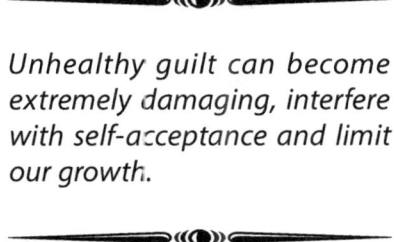

Unhealthy guilt can become extremely damaging, interfere with self-acceptance and limit our growth.

To rid ourselves of unhealthy guilt, we need to realize that the feelings we are experiencing is just helpful information telling us that something about our current reaction is out of alignment with the way we want to live. Then, we can take the necessary action to realign the choices we are making to fit with what is truly important to us.

Sadness

Sadness occurs when we experience loss: loss of a loved one, loss of a job, loss of a dream. Giving ourselves permission to feel sadness is an essential part of emotional growth and will promote proper healing. As we slow our lives down to process our loss, we gain the wisdom needed to progress in a new direction.

Sadness will withdraw when we have allowed enough time to heal and we feel in control of our lives again. If we fail to give enough time to grieve our losses, our sadness can turn into depression.

Sadness is a mood that can be lifted when we acknowledge our loss, give ourselves time to heal, embrace change and focus our attention on moving forward. Depression, on the other hand, is a clinical disorder that creates an overwhelming feeling of despair and, in many cases, requires professional intervention to regain balance in life again.

Depression

If you feel desperate or are experiencing depression in your life, you are not alone. I encourage you to reach out to those who love you and share the burdens you carry. Depression is much more than sadness; it includes feelings of deep despair and hopelessness that don't seem temporary, but seem overwhelming and permanent.

If your pain feels overwhelming and you don't know what to do, consider getting help from an outside source. Therapy will give you tools that can help you approach life differently. If you are not quite ready to openly express your challenges to a therapist, begin by writing your disparaging thoughts and feelings down on paper. Getting your feelings out can help release the pressure you are feeling. When possible, find a trusted friend who will not judge your current emotional state, but will give you the freedom to talk about your feelings. Feelings are not facts; they are just indicators that something in your current emotional state is out of alignment and some adjustments need to be made so you can feel better again.

Note: Therapy will feel uncomfortable, but if approached with the right attitude and knowing that a therapist is there to assist and support you as you move through your feelings, the benefits can be tremendous. Do not attach uncomfortable feelings to the one who is counseling you. Growth is change and change is uncomfortable, but we do not have to suffer alone. There are people who want to help us be happy.

Giving up on the Challenges of Life

Sometimes life can change so suddenly that one's ability to cope with the unexpected pain seems too much to bear. As pain increases, all track of reason is lost and feelings of despair take over. Life seems out of control and some begin to believe that the people in their lives would be better off without them.

In times of extreme sadness, overwhelming feelings like these have the power to influence even the most stable of people. Many years ago, I remember hearing a story of a good man in a small town who made a poor decision that ended his life. The circumstances around his death left a deep impression on me. The man involved was a quiet, well-respected person. He wasn't known to be a drinker, but when his wife of 14 years took his children and left him for another man, he lost all reason and began drinking.

While he was on his drinking binge, an officer confronted him. In a panic, the man began shooting, and the officer went down. Although the officer was not badly hurt, a frenzy of fear took over and the man got in his truck and drove away as fast as he could. After a 30-mile chase, he was forced off the road. He frantically ran into the woods, where he shot and killed himself.

Growth is change and change is uncomfortable, but we do not have to suffer alone. There are people who want to help us be happy.

My heart broke for this desperate man and for those he left behind. I know the intense feelings of loss and the years of pain that losing someone to suicide causes.

Suicide is a heartbreaking way to end a life and is becoming more and more common. The Centers for Disease Control and Prevention (CDC), citing a 2013 report from the World Health Organization, noted that in 2009 suicide was the 10th leading cause of death in the United States. Each year, more than 39,000 Americans end their own lives.

That is approximately 105 people every day on average. The report went on to say that suicide is the second leading cause of death in young people ages 15 to 24.[3]

---

[3] Centers for Disease Control and Prevention, "Understanding Suicide" fact sheet—United States, 2014. Available at: http://www.cdc.gov/violenceprevention/pdf/suicide_factsheet-a.pdf and CDC, Youth risk behavior surveillance—United States, 2011. MMWR, Surveillance Summaries 2012;61(no. SS-4). Available at: www.cdc.gov/mmwr/pdf/ss/ss6104.pdf. Accessed 1/25/2015.

It also stated that men were four times more likely to end their own life. I wonder if that is because, from childhood, men are taught to "Man up," or are told that "Big boys don't cry," so they really don't give themselves permission to acknowledge or deal with their pain.

Those who commit or even consider suicide are not crazy. Their emotions have taken control, dominating their logic and diminishing any realm of hope.

Even if you are in a situation where you believe a person is seeking attention by saying they have suicidal thoughts, keep in mind how misunderstood they must be feeling. Suicidal behavior in any form is a desperate cry for help.

In times of extreme sadness, overwhelming feelings like these have the power to influence even the most stable of people.

About 75 percent of those who actually commit suicide had prepared to do so months before their death. The frightening thing is that many people who take their own lives feel so desperate they don't ever talk about it. If a person you know is having thoughts of suicide, this is a sign that they are experiencing deep depression and need help. If caught early enough and treated in the right way, even deep depression can be transformed. If you know someone who is deeply depressed or has thought about suicide, take it seriously. Let them talk about their feelings and encourage them to get the help they need.[4]

Remember, any time we are in a heightened emotional state, our emotions will override our logical mind. The best thing you can do to help someone in this mental state is to let them talk about whatever they want. Don't push them to tell you how they feel, just do everything you can to listen to their thought process even though their thoughts may very likely be illogical. It is very important that you create a safe place by acknowledging that their pain is real.

Don't try to talk them out of their feelings; just listen to them, let them know they are loved. Be sincere and do what you can to convince them that you truly care about them and that you want to help.

---

[4] More about suicide risk factors and prevention available at: www.cdc.gov/violenceprevention/suicide/riskprotectivefactors.html and "Suicide Prevention: a global imperative" at www.who.int/mental_health/suicide-prevention/world_report_2014/en/."

Never agree to keep their situation a secret. Keeping these kinds of secrets can be deadly. When they are in a highly emotional state, more than ever, they will need emotional support. They are being driven by panic, fear and doubt, so you may not get the chance to engage them in a rational conversation before getting help.

It is very important to remember that when an individual is in a highly emotional state, their thoughts and feelings are intensely illogical. Don't take things they say or do personally or make them feel wrongly for any thoughts or feelings they may be experiencing.

> *It is very important to remember that when an individual is in a highly emotional state, their thoughts and feelings are intensely illogical. Don't take things they say or do personally or make them feel wrongly for any thoughts or feelings they may be experiencing.*

Stay with them until they feel safe and their emotional guard comes down enough to release some of the pressures they are feeling.

Enroll others to assist you in providing them with the emotional support they need. Medication may be required, so make sure you get them help from a professional that can prescribe medications.

Abuse

If you have been a victim of emotional, physical or sexual abuse, and you are too ashamed to talk about it, I am so sorry for your pain and suffering. You didn't ask for or deserve the deep wounds or heavy burden you are now expected to bear. I know it doesn't feel like it right now, but you are going to be okay. I am glad that you are reading this book and, even though I have never met you, my heart truly goes out to you and your struggle, and I hope to help you heal.

The experience of abuse, anytime in life, can make it hard to move forward. It can be even more traumatic if the abuse has come from a person who was supposed to love and support you. In this case, you not only have your own feelings to deal with, but you may also worry that telling someone may cause pain and sorrow to the ones you love.

All too often these types of fears occur not only from the shame that is encountered but also from threats of secrecy. Some perpetrators may threaten the ones they abuse, convincing the victim that it was their fault the abuse occurred. By increasing their victims' shame, the perpetrators feel assured their victim will not talk.

According to Elizabeth Smart, the beautiful woman who, as a child, was abducted from her bed while sleeping, "Threatening words can be stronger than steel chains or cords in stopping someone from trying to escape, especially when the safety of their loved ones is threatened."

> "Threatening words can be stronger than steel chains or cords in stopping someone from trying to escape, especially when the safety of their loved ones is threatened."

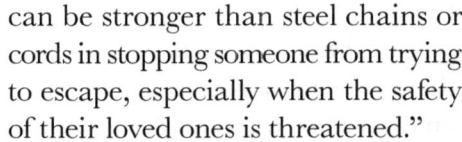

People caught in abuse often fall into the habit of keeping terrible secrets. They become so confused by all the suppressed emotions that they don't even know how to trust themselves. Yet, when they can't trust themselves, it makes it very difficult to trust anyone, even those who are trying to help. There are times when carrying this type of burden can be overwhelming, and they may feel like there is nothing left to live for.

Sexual abuse can be particularly challenging because the abused feel so violated that they don't want anyone to know what has happened to them. It is very common for them to take many showers and not feel clean. Feelings of worthlessness set in and all hope of future happiness diminishes.

If you struggle because you have experienced any type of abuse, please know your worth has never changed; reach out and find support. When possible, find a support group with others who have had similar experiences. Find a setting where you can listen to others express the same types of feelings you are going through. Even if you don't share anything, it is important to attend so you know that you are not alone.

You may be afraid or not know how to let go of all the pain. Sometimes this occurs because you have guarded your pain to the point that it has become a normal part of your life. The illogical fear becomes, "Pain is part of who I am, and without it I would be lost not knowing who I am or how I'm supposed to feel."

There is power and happiness on the other side of pain. You must be willing to take the first step. Find the courage to to step through your pain and share your feelings, so you can let go of your experiences and consciously process your pain in a way that will allow you to feel safe again.

You have everything you need to heal from your tragic experiences. If and when you feel safe enough, begin sharing your feelings. Give yourself all the time you need to heal, let yourself cry and don't rush the process.

If you are working with a counselor or therapist, or have other support, make sure you are honest. Rather than telling them what you think they want to hear, be sure to let them know what you are thinking and how you are really feeling.

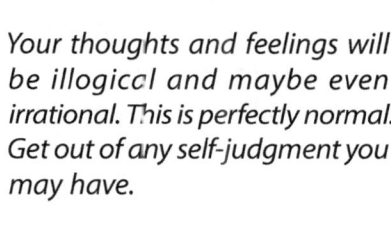

Your thoughts and feelings will be illogical and maybe even irrational. This is perfectly normal. Get out of any self-judgment you may have.

Remember, your thoughts and feelings will be illogical and maybe even irrational. This is perfectly normal. Get out of any self-judgment you may have, and share your feelings anyway. If you are angry, get it out! This type of honesty with yourself and others will open the door so that you can release the pain and get the help needed to process any detrimental feelings and put the trauma behind you.

Did you know that statistical reports show that one in every eight people has experienced some type of emotional, physical or sexual abuse?

There is absolutely nothing wrong with the way you feel about what has happened to you. Even if you are angry, you have every right to feel angry. It is better for you to talk about how you are feeling than to repress or act upon your feelings and do something that may destroy your life or the lives of others. Don't give another minute of your precious life to the one who has hurt you. Forgive yourself and let go of the pain they have caused.

There is hope on the other side of physical, emotional and sexual abuse. I know because my childhood and youth were filled with these types of events.

I was born into and grew up in a world full of addictions, where multiple types of abuse were part of my everyday life. I often felt worthless and unlovable. Yet, the lessons I have learned from my painful experiences have given me eyes to see what others may not, ears to hear the anguish of an unspoken word, and a heart that feels sorrow that the eye cannot see and the courage to write a book that leaves me feeling completely exposed and vulnerable. Yet, I love the person I have become. I had a friend say to me once, "You have such a sweet, innocent, childlike quality about you." With everything I have been through, I should neither be sweet nor referred to as innocent. But I have given myself permission to let go of the shame and talk about my abuses, so I finally feel comfortable enough to get beyond my fears. Because I have been willing to talk about my experiences and insecurities, my feelings no longer have the power to control my life.

Feelings are less intense and lose much of their power when they are brought up to the surface where they can be analyzed.

I have learned that I am in charge of the way I choose to feel. I have truly forgiven myself and others, and that forgiveness has released me from the power that my abusers once had over my life. As I stand on the other side of these tragic events, I realize how much they have changed me for the good.

If you have suffered abuse, please don't give up on yourself. Your experiences can help you find a strength that you never knew existed. Then, when you have the courage, you will be able to release the past, reach out, and create a whole new future.

Emotions are Powerful Motivators

By processing our pain, we can transform our heartbreaking experiences into powerful motivators.

Feelings are less intense and lose much of their power when they are brought up to the surface where they can be analyzed. Once our feelings are analyzed, we can consciously direct our thoughts, feelings, attitudes and beliefs in a way that encourages growth.

Journaling your feelings will help clarify your thoughts and direct your perceptions. What you write may not make sense, but don't let that stop you. The emotional mind doesn't have the capacity to make sense, so you are just fine. It is enlightening to notice some of the irrational and illogical thoughts that fuel our perceptions.

If you need help, don't be afraid to reach out. What you are going through is only temporary. Once you get past the struggle, you will recognize how resilient you are. This experience will then strengthen your life and enhance your ability to contribute to the lives of others in a powerful way.

Emotions are essential, yet some of us have never learned how to understand or express how we really feel. Expressing our feelings is important if we are to live a well-balanced and fulfilling life.

THE PROCESS OF UNCOVERING UNRESOLVED EMOTIONS

The purpose for this process is to bring unresolved emotions to a conscious level where they can be understood, analyzed and released.

- What problems do you encounter from the unresolved anger issues that occur in your life?
- If you have experienced loss, have you given yourself adequate time to heal so that you can let go of the past and have the emotional energy to create something new?
- How is unresolved guilt using up your emotional resources?
- Have you experienced overwhelming feelings of depression or thoughts of suicide? Do you know someone who has been depressed or has talked about taking their own life? If so, is there something you can do to help?
- Identify the best ways to resolve any issues you may have around anger, guilt or depression so you can move forward in a peaceful and effective direction.

Journal any thoughts or ideas that will encourage growth and promote change.

THE PROCESS OF IDENTIFYING EMOTIONAL PATTERNS

The purpose of this process is to assist you in identifying the intensity of unresolved emotional patterns.

At least three times a day for the next week, track the intensity of your emotional responses. Include any irrational thoughts, feelings, or reactions. Wait until the emotions have calmed before you begin the evaluation process. Use a scale of 1 to 10, one being least intense and ten being extremely intense. Rating the intensity of your emotional responses will give you a better understanding of when you are logically dealing with facts versus when you are simply reacting on emotions.

Example

You are driving in your car and see lights flashing behind you. You look down and notice that your car is going faster than you had realized. Define what you are feeling and the intensity of that feeling.

Journal any thoughts or ideas that will encourage growth and promote change.

Chapter 6

Beliefs

"Your beliefs become your thoughts, your thoughts become your words, your words become your actions, your actions become your habits, your habits become your values, your values become your destiny."

~ Mahatma Gandhi

Beliefs

The third wall that keeps us in our Emotional Safety Zone is our **Beliefs**.

Once events are structured and established in the emotional mind, that structure will attach to some type of emotion that creates a belief. Depending on the experience, the resulting belief will either enhance our self-worth or limit our ability to progress.

Scientists say our core belief system is completely established around age six. They further indicate that our primary caregivers significantly influence the belief system that guides us throughout our lives.

One day, as I was contemplating the process that forms our belief system, I became very curious about the beliefs of the children in my life. So I began asking them what they believed to be true.

My granddaughter said she believed in the tooth fairy. I asked her if she had ever seen the tooth fairy. She said, "No." She did not need to see the tooth fairy to know that she was real. All she needed to see was her tooth gone and money under her pillow.

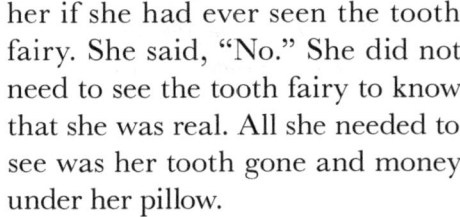

Essentially, it is our primary care providers that supply the emotional code for our basic perceptions.

I told my daughter-in-law of this experience, and we both giggled. Then I asked her what she believed to be true. She said she believed biology is hard. I asked her why she held that belief, and she said, "Because I have flunked biology three times." I guess she had enough evidence to know that, at that time in her life, biology was hard.

The most precious response came from my youngest son, who was seven at the time. I asked him what he believed to be true, and he told me that he believed that tigers are our friends, and we should not be afraid of them.

I smiled and asked him why he believed this. He said he saw how nice tigers were on the "tiger on the boat" movie, "The Life of Pi."

I asked, "What else do you believe?"

He said, "I believe bears eat fish." I told him he was very smart and asked him why he believed that, and he said he saw bears eating fish in the Disney movie, "Brother Bear."

Then he asked, "Mom, can people really do that?"

"Do what?" I asked.

"Can people really turn into animals?"

"No," I told him, "people cannot turn into animals."

Before he asked me the question, he had no idea what to believe. It was only when he asked, and I gave him an answer, that he developed the belief that people cannot turn into animals. This conversation made me realize that when we are young, our belief system is taking in all kinds of information and forming the opinions of what we believe to be true in the world around us, and many of those innocent beliefs stay with us throughout our lives.

Forming a Belief System

When we are in environments in which our primary care providers have under-developed emotional skills of their own, it can have a major effect on the way we handle emotions and establish our beliefs. Essentially, it is our primary care providers who supply the emotional code for our basic perceptions.

When I was young, my parents had many addictions and were caught in their own despair. I grew up abused, neglected and felt heartbroken and alone much of the time.

My father was a very angry man who never learned how to control his temper. Because of his violence towards me, I felt that he didn't love me and I tried to stay out of his way as much as possible. Growing up in this kind of world, one where I felt abandoned and lonely, made a perfect environment to establish many detrimental beliefs about myself.

When I married, I married someone who treated me insignificantly, in much the same way that I was treated as a child. Because these feelings were typical of the way I experienced the world and I already felt bad about myself, I thought I was the cause of this mistreatment. Without even realizing it, I gravitated toward a relationship that would ultimately produce the same loneliness and pain that was familiar to me. Because these types of feelings felt so familiar, I had no idea that the way I was filtering my circumstance was the deeper cause of my suffering and pain.

This loneliness and pain magnified other detrimental beliefs, such as, "I am not lovable," "I am not good enough," or "I am not worthy of love or attention, because I am unimportant." These types of feelings dictated my unconscious perception of the world and I tolerated things that perpetuated my insignificances. Unknowingly, I felt like I deserved to be mistreated, and I didn't stand up for myself or seek to be treated any differently. I didn't have the expectation that I was worthy of love.

With "I am unlovable" unconsciously running in the background of my mind, how easy do you think it would be for me to feel loved or accepted?

In my younger days, it was easy to validate the unconscious belief "I am unlovable," because I felt unlovable. That is how I perceived the world, so everything I experienced served to validate that feeling.

When we feel unlovable, it really doesn't matter if others love us. We don't feel worthy of love and have a hard time feeling loved. The reality is when we don't love ourselves, it is hard to accept or receive love from others.

In my case, I married a person who had his own set of childhood challenges and had structured a detrimental belief system of his own. During our marriage, we blamed each other for the lack of love we felt. This blame not only supported but also validated and increased our beliefs, feelings and insecurities.

I was married for twenty-eight years, and one of my biggest regrets is that I tolerated things I shouldn't have. With more knowledge, I could have put my childhood insecurities behind sooner. If I had confidence in who I really was, I could have stood up for myself, and for him, too, and inspired him to become a much better man. The saddest thing of all is we had everything we needed to live a happy life, but by the time I was conscious enough to change things, it was too late.

Detrimental beliefs have the power to control our self worth. However, because these beliefs are unconscious, discovering them so we can change can be very challenging.

Not a Burden

When my husband of twenty-eight years left, I had a very hard time coping. The divorce brought back intense feelings of fear, insecurity and pain. At times, the heartbreak felt almost overwhelming. I worked very hard in my marriage because I didn't want to be abandoned or alone like I was as a child. When my husband left, my heart was screaming, "I'm alone, unwanted and unimportant again."

I thought I had worked hard and had done a good job of working through my past, but here were all my fears and insecurities crashing down on me. I felt embarrassed, ashamed and guilty. Even though I had done my best, I had failed in the most important relationship of my life.

I remember having to call my husband's secretary to request some documents for the divorce. While I was on the phone with her, she was impatient with me. I noticed that my heart started to beat faster, and it was hard to breathe. My chest felt like it was being crushed, while tears rushed to the surface.

> *If you are conscious of a detrimental belief controlling you, remember that releasing controlling beliefs is a process that takes time.*

I got off the phone immediately, and the tears began to fall. I thought to myself, "Why am I having this reaction?"

An immediate voice in my head said, "It's because you are a burden."

A burden, I am a burden! The tears began to pour, as I rehearsed in my mind all the times I had failed and felt like a burden.

After pondering this belief that had unconsciously dominated my life, I discovered that under the "I am a burden" belief was "I am not worth it."

And, I had plenty of irrational and highly emotional "evidence" that validated that this "I am not worth it" belief was true.

Once I noticed and acknowledged my unconscious beliefs and emotions, I could reason with myself by saying things like: "This is not who I am, this is just how I am feeling right now."

I made a list of all the important ways I had touched the lives of others. I read cards from people who had thanked me for things I had done to remind myself that I do make a difference. Focusing my attention on the difference I had made did not take away the pain or keep out all the fears and insecurities that I was feeling, but it did help me remember who I am and what I have to offer. Reading the cards also helped me challenge my beliefs with real evidence that I am worth it and loved. I was also able to comprehend that feeling like a burden had led me to acquiring many strengths. Some of them include being strong, independent, kind, compassionate, understanding, thoughtful and caring about others in a non-judgmental way.

The moment I noticed the unconscious belief, "I am a burden," I surrendered and allowed the tears to flow. I was grieving in a way that gave me permission to feel whatever I was feeling without making my feelings wrong which was very healing.

Once I acknowledged the emotions that came along with the "I am a burden" belief, I was no longer controlled by my unconscious insecurities, and the conscious mind could then step in and help me restructure habits that would productively support my new life.

For me, releasing detrimental beliefs has been a powerful process that has given me control over many of the beliefs that used to sabotage my happiness. If you are conscious of a detrimental belief controlling you, remember that releasing these beliefs *is* a process that takes time. Once you notice an unconscious belief and have acknowledged the associated triggers and emotions, you will likely have *habits* attached to the belief that will require restructuring as well. For example, with the "I am a burden" belief, I formed an attitude that "If I call someone when they were at work, I would be a burden to them," so my habit was to wait until after business hours to call. Even if they had asked me to call, I would wait.

Now, with my conscious mind in control, when the insecurity of never calling someone during work hours arises, I can consciously get beyond my fear and call without feeling like a burden.

It has been helpful to find a saying or quote to remind me of my worth and encourage the change I want to make. In the case of "I am a burden," I think of a quote from Oprah, when she said, "You get in life what you have the courage to ask for." This quote energizes me and gives me the courage to ask for what I want and create something new!

THE PROCESS OF NOTICING DETRIMENTAL BELIEFS

The purpose of this process is to open the door of awareness by noticing the emotional beliefs that direct your behaviors.

To understand more about your structured beliefs, take time to consider areas of your life where you struggle. Ask yourself if there are any fear-based beliefs limiting your ability to perform.

- Look at the fear based stories you tell yourself. Example: "I have to make a certain amount of money before I can socialize, get married, have a child…" Now determine the belief that is limiting your growth.
- Identify some of the ineffective habits you have formed throughout the years.
- Match a logical fear-based belief for each habit.
- Determine how your habits and beliefs prevent you from moving forward.
- What logical evidence can you produce to override your fear based beliefs and create something new?

Journal any thoughts or ideas that will encourage growth and promote change.

Our emotional structures are the foundation of our belief system, and our belief system determines the way we perceive the world and fuels the habitual actions that result.

This cycle, driven by the unconscious mind, forms our perceptions and influences our reality.

Chapter 7

Perceptions

"The way we perceive the world is always going to come from the way that we feel and the way we feel will always be constructed from what we have established to be true. This creates the foundation for the reality in which we live."

~ Victoria Lee Carlyle

The **fourth** wall that keeps us in our Emotional Safety Zone is **Perceptions**.

Be Yourself

"Ever since I was a little kid, I didn't want to be me. I wanted to be like Billy Widdledon, and Billy Widdledon didn't even like me. I walked like he walked; I talked like he talked; and I signed up for the high school he signed up for.

Which was why Billy Widdledon changed. He began to hang around Herby Vandeman; he walked like Herby Vandeman; he talked like Herby Vandeman. He mixed me all up! I began to walk and talk like Billy Widdledon, who was walking and talking like Herby Vandeman.

And then it dawned on me that Herby Vandeman walked and talked like Joey Haverlin. And Joey Haverlin walked and talked like Corky Sabinson. So here I am walking and talking like Billy Widdledon's imitation of Herby Vandeman's version of Joey Haverlin, trying to walk and talk like Corky Sabinson. And who do you think Corky Sabinson is always walking and talking like? Of all people, Dopey Wellington—that little pest who walks and talks like me!"[1]

We are emotional beings who innately learn by following the example of others. These examples, along with our distinctive emotional structures, will help us sustain a realistic view of the world, or they will distort our perceptions and leave us feeling powerless, blaming others for our disappointing results.

Emotional Filters

Because we are influenced by emotions, everything is filtered through the way we feel. Our feelings originate from the distinctive way we have structured emotions and beliefs around certain events. Sometimes the way we filter certain elements in our lives can make it easy to take things personally or get offended without even looking at the facts. Understanding emotional filters can give a new perspective as to why people think, act and feel the way they do.

The way we filter our experiences can skew our interpretations and perpetuate pain. When I was younger, I felt so unlovable and insecure that I would often take things personally. I would feel hurt, and then I would make up my own self-destructive conclusions and silently shut down without clarifying the facts.

I remember a conversation I had with my children's father about our children attending community college. He expressed his disappointment with their study skills and felt that if they would have spent

---

[1] Canfield, Jack and Mark Victor Hansen. *A Second Helping of Chicken Soup for the Soul: More Stories to Open the Heart and Rekindle the Spirit*, "Be Yourself," author unknown, submitted by Scott Shuman.

more time studying, they could have gone straight into a university with better chances for a successful life.

After this conversation, I was mad because I felt like he was always blaming me for things he didn't like about our children! We argued, and he left for the day. Throughout the day, I noticed that little things irritated me.

When I finally realized that I was in a bad mood, I stopped and wondered why. It took me a while to pinpoint the source of my mood, but then I remembered the irritating conversation earlier in the day.

> *Sometimes the way we have structured certain elements in our lives can make it easy to take things personally or get offended without even looking at the facts.*

This was the first time I had consciously stopped myself and looked at a situation in a neutral way. I tried to recall the exact verbiage we used, how I felt, and the conclusions I had made.

I started the conversation with the attitude, "Here we go again! Another lecture on how the children and I are not good enough." When he said he wished our children had better study skills, I heard, "You're a bad mother because you didn't make them study hard enough!"

After this realization, I called and apologized, only to find out that he was angry with me. He didn't understand why I got so mad when all he was trying to say was that he wished he would have been more attentive as a father.

This was the first time I consciously realized that what I was thinking and how I was feeling about a situation was perpetuating some of the contention that I felt in my relationship with him.

THE PROCESS OF EMOTIONAL FILTERS

The purpose of this process is to assist you in taking a neutral look at the emotional filters that perpetuate attitudes, miscommunication, and unwanted contention in your life.

This process is designed to help you separate emotional reactions from facts.

Start by playing an experience over in your mind as if you were an observer. Observe any thoughts, feelings, attitudes, or beliefs that you currently associate with the interaction. Give yourself time to release any feelings you may have experienced before you begin.

Now, separate yourself from your emotions and view the situation as if you were viewing a movie on a screen. From a neutral place, take a look at what occurred.

- What did you observe about yourself?
- What did you observe about others?
- How did your feelings influence your perception of the situation?
- What was actually said?
- What meaning did you add?
- What were your physical reactions (i.e., body language, facial features, and posture)?
- What assumptions did you make based on others' physical or emotional reactions?
- Did others involved seem to come from a place of feeling hurt, offended, blame, frustration, or anger?
- If they did, did this stimulate or intensify an emotional reaction from you?
- How did your thoughts, feelings, attitudes, or beliefs add to the conflict?
- Did you delete the facts and unconsciously make up a story that validated that how you were feeling was right?
- How has observing this situation from a neutral place changed your perception of the situation?

- How will this type of observation enhance your relationships and help you move forward in a productive way?

Journal any thoughts or ideas that will encourage growth and promote change.

Processing the ineffective interactions you experience in life without adding your own emotion-based story, will give you the power to shift your perspective in a way that will create productive relationships and lasting change.

Behavior

Another area where our Emotional Safety Zone can distort our reality is through our behaviors.

Consider the conversation I had with my children's father, for example: I was very insecure about my intelligence. As a child, I didn't always attend school, so I didn't feel I had the foundational academic skills to help my children with their homework. I felt stupid, so I would get hurt and defensive when anyone did anything that would trigger this insecurity. What I didn't realize was how my defensiveness affected the relationships I had with others.

I became a martyr, and it seemed easier to walk away and not say anything than to face my fears or stand up for myself.

It was hard to create the kind of loving relationships I wanted when my unconscious mind was associating relationships in the present with past relationships that were full of insecurity and pain.

When we feel uncomfortable, our unconscious mind will distort our reality by linking our current situation to other situations that seem emotionally similar. Then in an attempt to protect us from feeling uncomfortable or experiencing pain, the emotions and physiological responses from the past immediately surface, which redirects our attention to our feelings and immediately alters our perception. This is how we get caught in ineffective emotional patterns. Even if we are aware of unproductive behaviors and want to change them, without the conscious ability to understand why we think, feel or act the way we do, our behaviors will remain the same.

For example, you may notice things like: "I get angry when people challenge me," or, "It hurts, and I go silent or walk away when I feel others are being critical of me." Even if we are somewhat aware of our behavior, but fail to recognize the emotional patterns that are perpetuating our thoughts, feelings, attitudes and beliefs, no matter how hard we try we cannot change.

We may handle situations in our life by getting angry. Anger feels empowering in the moment and can seem like a good way to express ourselves and get what we want. To justify our anger, our attitude could be: "Well, someone needed to put them in their place." Then, what will ultimately occur is that anger will prevent those around us from feeling emotionally safe which will cut us off from the respect, love and intimacy we desire most.

We may think going silent or walking away is a peaceful way to avoid conflict, but silence has its own controlling power and can be just as destructive in relationships. When there is no response to communication, others have no idea where our mind has gone, what we are thinking or how we will respond. Those being ignored have no resolution to the conflict. They are left to draw their own conclusions, which could validate their own set of fears and insecurities.

Our Emotional Safety Zone can distort our reality to the point that we begin to believe that the way we handle emotional situations is helping, not hurting, others.

The problem is, if we are not consciously sorting out our Emotional Safety Zone, our feelings will validate and support our distorted reality, making it challenging to create anything new.

Our emotional structures make it easy to create distortions. My daughter grew up feeling as if her father never had time for her. When she married, she married a man with the same ambition and drive for success as her father. Her husband is always busy trying to figure out new ways to advance his company. He spends a lot of time at his office and consulting with his employees.

During his down time, he forgets the world by playing video games with his younger brother, who serves in the military.

Consciously, she can see that he wants her to be happy and is working hard to provide her with all the nice things this world has to offer. But unconsciously, my daughter often connects his behavior to her feelings of abandonment from her father, and she ends up being hurt and pulls away by keeping busy to avoid more pain. Her husband, seeing that she is busy, does things that he wants to do, which produces more evidence to validate her *"feelings"* that her husband never has time for her.

This is how our current reality gets distorted: We have an emotional experience, and we automatically associate it with a past experience. Instant feelings of fear, pain, frustration or anger will stimulate a flood of chemicals into our system which will intensify our need to react. This rush of emotion will convince us that the intense feelings we are experiencing pertain to our current situation.

As we begin to comprehend how our Emotional Safety Zone affects our thoughts, feelings, attitudes and beliefs, it becomes easier to understand why there are times when we unconsciously protect ourselves from perceived danger and inadvertently give our power away.

THE PROCESS OF RECOGNIZING EMOTIONAL TRIGGERS

The purpose of this process is to recognize the triggers or emotional reactions that direct your thoughts, feelings, attitudes, and behaviors and get in the way of your happiness and growth.

- Take time to identify the factors in your environment that typically trigger an emotional reaction.
- What is the intensity of your emotional reaction?
- Describe how your triggers affect your mood and change your perceptions?

Gaining a true understanding of what triggers an emotional reaction is a treasure that will guide you to deeper self-awareness. It will also open the door to personal growth better than anything else you could ever do.

Journal any thoughts or ideas that will encourage growth and promote change.

The Ways We Give Our Power Away

Every time we give our power away, we victimize ourselves through the things that we tolerate, as what we tolerate affects the way we perceive the world. I have a son who, when he was in high school, started using drugs. When he turned 18, he got in trouble with the law. I remember taking him to court and listening to each person tell their story of what led to their arrest. I was amazed at how the legal system not only tolerated the reasons, stories and excuses of each defendant, they encouraged, and even exaggerated, their victim mentality.

One man in his early 50s had stolen a car. As his lawyer shared a few traumatizing events from his childhood, I could tell, based on this man's story, that he saw himself as a complete product of bad parenting. At age 54, he was still blaming his parents for the choices he was making. Because he was blind to the way he had structured his perceptions, he became an unconscious victim and was caught up in powerless, unaccountable blame.

He was not aware of the power that his Emotional Safety Zone had over his current situation, and the way he filtered these events made him feel blameless, as though there was nothing he could do about his current circumstances.

Every time we give our power away, we victimize ourselves through the things that we tolerate, as what we tolerate affects the way we allow ourselves to be treated.

The sad thing is, some people die without ever knowing how much personal power they could have had over their own lives. It took me a long time to understand that I had the complete power to change the way I felt about myself.

As I became more consciously aware of the emotional structures that had been creating confusion in my life, I began to realize that there were changes I could make that would help me gain more confidence to create a happy life. During this time of change, I read a beautiful passage by Nelson Mandela that was printed on the back of a funeral program. The words had a profound impact on my life.

They said, "Our deepest fear is not that we are inadequate. Our deepest fear is that we are powerful beyond measure. It is our light, not our darkness that most frightens us. We ask ourselves who am I to be brilliant, gorgeous, talented, fabulous? Actually, who are you not to be? You are a child of God. Your playing small does not serve the world. There is nothing enlightened about shrinking so that other people won't feel insecure around you. We are meant to shine, as children do. We were born to make manifest the glory of God that is within us. It's not just in some of us; it's in everyone. And as we let our own light shine, we unconsciously give other people permission to do the same. As we are liberated from our own fear, our presence automatically liberates others."[2]

Years after I first felt the impact of this passage, I discovered that Marianne Williamson was the original author of these beautiful, life-changing words.

Plato once said, "We can easily forgive a child who is afraid of the dark; the real tragedy of life is when men are afraid of the light." Who knows why those words touched me so deeply, but what I was beginning to realize was that I had been afraid of the light that resonated within me. I began to get curious about my insecurities and, from that point forward, I took my life on in a completely different way.

I stopped the blame and started looking at all the ways I gave my power away and how all my reasons,stories and excuses were just adding to and supporting my miserable, powerless state.

I was in my early 40s when this transformation began to occur. It took many years after that to comprehend the full impact my Emotional Safety Zone had over my life and to restructure new habits and beliefs that would support a happy and productive life.

It has been valuable for me to understand the implications my fear-based beliefs have had over my thoughts, feelings and attitudes. I also realize that in times of intense vulnerability and sorrow, like I felt during my divorce, these types of beliefs may still have the power to impact my emotional life and temporarily influence the way I feel about myself. However, because I am aware of how my childhood

---

[2] Williamson, Marianne. *A Return to Love: Reflections on the Principles of a Course in Miracles.* New York: HarperCollins, 1996, pp. 190-191.

beliefs take control to protect me from more pain, I have the power to move through insecure times in my life a lot more quickly.

In addition, understanding that the emotional mind is stronger and faster than the rational mind gives me the conscious ability to override the feelings that come along with the, "I'm not good enough" belief. Now I look for and create evidence that supports who I am and the direction I want to go.

Until we understand the strength of the emotional mind, we are completely blind to the ways we give our power away, and we never look at the choices we make that create our unhappiness. I love the saying "It is never too late to have a happy childhood." When we consciously restructure our childhood events, our lives change for the good.

Until we notice and consciously restructure our emotional reactions the emotional mind will stay in control of the choices we make, and we, in turn, blindly use reasons, stories and excuses to validate, justify and blame others for our current circumstances and the misery that accompanies them. When this happens, our emotional validation is busy forming a false reality that transposes us into an emotional victim. This victim blinds us to the ways we perpetuate our own sorrow.

Detrimental Emotional Patterns

Let's face it, no one ever wakes up in the morning and says, "I wonder what I can do to feel uncomfortable or experience pain today."

Even those who are caught up in emotional circumstances of life don't want to feel the way they feel. In fact, most people who are overly emotional would do anything for the ability to control their feelings and emotional reactions.

The opposite is true as well.

There are those who only handle emotions when they know what to do with them. When they don't know how to handle their feelings, they stuff them away and forget about them. This behavior can be frustrating in relationships and will stop them from establishing the intimate connections they truly desire.

In fact, those who don't know how to process their own emotions feel very uncomfortable in emotional situations and may become impatient with emotional people. The attitude that runs this ineffective pattern is: "If I do not know how to take care of my own emotions, there is no way I can take care of, or even want to handle, others who are being emotional."

Some may have had experiences that are so painful that they try to shut off the emotions they don't want to feel. The problem with ignoring painful emotions is that we also compromise other more effective emotions that will enhance the happiness and joy we truly desire.

In fact, those who don't know how to process their own emotions feel very uncomfortable in emotional situations and may become impatient with emotional people.

Our childhood structuring and lack of education on how to handle, understand or process our emotions contribute to our emotional confusion. This confusion will also blind us to the ways we give our power away and deprive us of the power to change.

Gaining a deeper understanding of the unconscious ways we avoid our emotions and give our power away to habits and behaviors that lead to The Victim Addiction will give us the ability needed to control our emotional responses and move our lives forward in a productive way.

Unconscious Emotional Victim Patterns

If someone is unconsciously caught in The Victim Addiction, it is easy for them to:

- React to feelings because they do not like to feel uncomfortable.
- Give their power away to disappointments and unrealistic expectations.
- Blame others for the unproductive circumstances in their lives.
- Feel limited in the choices they can make.
- Fail to see how their victim mentality can victimize others.
- Choose to blame others, rather than face and resolve their own guilt or pain.

Powerless Victim language sounds like:

- It wasn't my fault.
- How dare they?
- Well, I've never.
- I didn't do it.
- What else was I supposed to do?
- It's not my problem.
- It was an accident.
- That's not what I meant.

The Victim Addiction steals your ability to perceive or utilize your own power.

THE PROCESS OF NOTICING THE VICTIM ADDICTION

The purpose of this process is to notice where you unconsciously give your power away to feelings, attitudes, and beliefs that position you in a victim state of mind. This process will also help illuminate the victim state of mind and powerless reactions those around you have as well.

It is typically easier to identify victim patterns in others than in yourself. For the next few days, notice victim language and other patterns of those with whom you encounter. Note how easily they unconsciously give their power away to emotional situations. Be sure to document any time a judgment is made.

The information you gain from studying others will prove useful as you analyze your own perceptions. When possible, determine who in your childhood has influenced your attitudes and judgments. Example: You may be irritated by someone you feel is lazy then recall how, as a child, when you didn't do what you were asked, one of your parents would call you lazy.

The questions below will assist you, when you are ready, to look at ways you give your power away. Remember to be curious, not critical. Avoid self judgment. It will get in the way of the shifts that must occur to experience lasting change.

- Notice where you blame your emotional reactions on others.
- Observe your comfort level with your own emotions and anything you make up about the emotions of those around you.
- Listen for victim statements around you, such as, "It wasn't my fault", "I didn't do it", "What else was I supposed to do?" etc.
- Notice your own victim statements.
- Observe how people behave when they feel attacked.
- Notice how you behave when you feel like you are being personally attacked.
- Notice when others fight to be right, blame, or justify their position.
- Notice when you fight to be right or feel the need to justify your position.

Journal any thoughts or ideas that will encourage growth and promote change.

The more aware we are of the influence The Victim Addiction has over our thoughts, feelings, and our emotional reactions, the more equipped we will be to consciously process and change our automatic emotional responses. With this change, our confidence will increase, which will support us in moving in a more productive direction. We will also gain a deeper understanding for others who have emotional struggles.

When you exercise courage and take a realistic view of the ways you have created your own misery, stop beating yourself up for the unconscious ways you have given your power away. You Have The Power to Change.

Tier II
The Power to Change

*"Change happens when the pain of staying the same
is greater than the pain of change."*

~ Tony Robbins

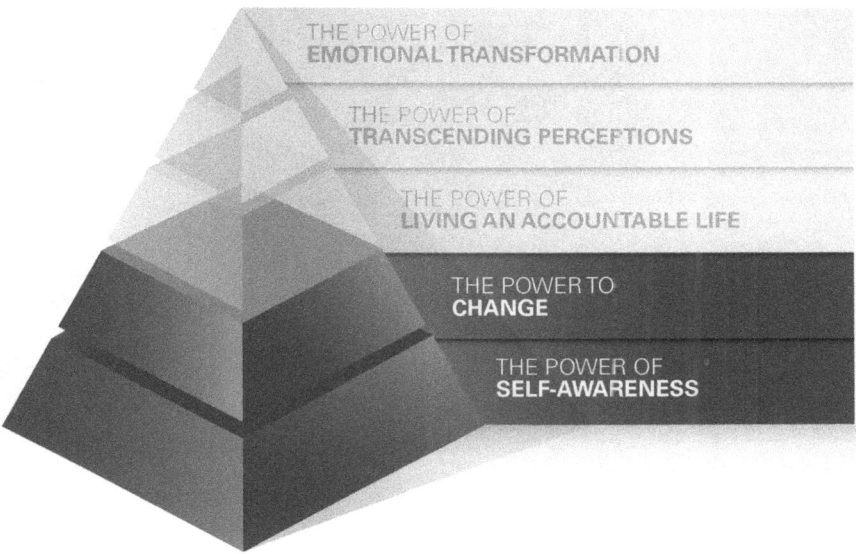

Tier II, The Power to Change, will introduce you to exciting principles that will assist you in going from powerless to powerful.

You will continue your self-awareness journey by gaining a deeper understanding of the biological functions of the rational and emotional minds. This discovery will highlight how the strongest part of the mind is literally wired to avoid the uncomfortable nature of change and what you can do to get beyond the self-imposed limits of your Emotional Safety Zone.

Most of all, you'll discover how to step into your own personal power and how to use that power to create the beauty, balance and freedom that will ultimately generate the inner peace and personal satisfaction to create a rich and fulfilling life.

Chapter 8

Change

*If we don't change, we don't grow.
If we don't grow, we aren't really living.*

~ Gail Sheehy

    The ability to change our lives will come as we actively and consciously change the way we view the various situations in our lives.

    One of my favorite stories about changing our view is a personal story told by Dr. Stephen R. Covey about himself. He describes quietly sitting on a bus one early Sunday morning when a man and his five children entered the bus and proceeded to sit near him.

    The children seemed out of control and were very disruptive, yelling and fighting with each other and even pulling the newspaper out of the hand of an elderly gentleman.

    Dr. Covey was getting impatient with the father who took absolutely no notice of his children's disruptive behavior.

    Finally, he couldn't take it anymore and leaned over and said, "Sir, your children are really disturbing a lot of people! Could you please do something to calm them down?"

    The man looked at Dr. Covey with a blank stare, as if he really did not comprehend what had just been said. Then, he quietly replied, "Oh, I am so sorry. We just left the hospital, they lost their mother and I don't think they know how to handle it. And, to be honest, I'm not sure I do either."

    Dr. Covey explains that in an instant his attitude toward the situation changed as his judgments melted away and he wanted to do what he could to help this father and his young family.[1]

    So what is change?

---

[1] Covey, Stephen R. *The 7 Habits of Highly Effective People: Restoring the Character Ethic.* New York: Free Press, 2004.

The Merriam-Webster dictionary defines change as:
to make or become something different: to give a different position, course, or direction;
to undergo transformation, transition, or substitution.

When we really think about it, change is the ability to adapt and grow which, in all reality, is a crucial part of living a well-balanced and productive life. Yet sometimes, even when we know that change would be good for us, we resist change and continue to stay in the familiar safety of what feels normal.

Did you know that it is human nature to experience a reluctance to change?

This occurs because change is uncomfortable and you are biologically wired to avoid uncomfortable feelings. Anytime you feel uncomfortable or experience pain, the brain will send out a warning that automatically shields you from potential danger. Your senses will heighten and feelings of reservation and fear will immediately increase.

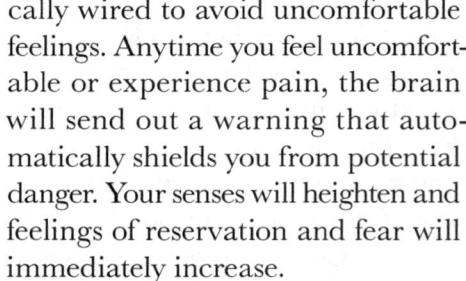

This sense of normalcy and safety will occur even if what is familiar is not productive or safe.

Feelings of reservation and fear produce a reluctance to change. Can you think of a time when you have been afraid to do something new? Or a time when you were excited about making a change, but when the action you needed to take was inconvenient or challenging, your commitment went out the window and you automatically fell into familiar patterns of the past?

The reason we revert into familiar patterns is we feel comfortable in our ability to manage and control the situation. What's familiar seems normal because this is the way we have always felt and the reaction we have always had. That feeling of comfort will create a sense of safety. This sense of normalcy and safety will occur even if what is familiar is not productive or safe. In other words, anything that feels unfamiliar, and thus uncomfortable, will instinctively be associated with danger, and we will automatically want to avoid it.

Our instinctive fear of change can keep us in the familiar boundaries of our Emotional Safety Zone and deprive us of the power to change.

Perpetuating Fears

Our emotional structuring can hold us back by perpetuating our fears. Fear has been defined as False Evidence Appearing Relevant.

Instead of looking at what is factual, we operate out of fear, which is often linked to other familiar feelings such as anger, frustration, and even abandonment. Unconsciously, we are connecting our present situation to other times in our lives when we have felt those same types of emotions. When we are caught in this victim cycle, we hide who we really are because the feelings running our thought process distort the perceptions we have of ourselves and the way we view the world around us.

Trusting our abilities will renew our confidence and give us the power to take the necessary risks required to step out of our fear, experience growth and create the happiness we desire.

This is why, when we are in an emotional situation, we often feel walls of trepidation and fear go up. These walls rise to protect us from things the emotional mind has predetermined could be painful.

The end of my second marriage was a good example of this. I felt like a complete failure. I honestly never thought I would get divorced from my first husband—and then, a short time after I remarried, I was divorced a second time.

Because my husband suffered from an anxiety disorder, he couldn't handle living with someone in his home environment. I know he loved me, but the anxiety he had was overwhelming and he feared the thought of change. On a conscious level he knew he always had a hard time with people in his environment, but he rationalized his feelings and blamed others for his anxiousness.

His compulsions and daily rituals were part of how he established peace and he realized he had to make a decision—change the way he handled daily life or change his relationship with me. He chose to stay in the familiarity of his Emotional Safety Zone.

I was devastated! I grieved and grieved over my failure, even though I knew there was nothing I could have done. My feelings once again were validating my core beliefs of, "I am not good enough," and, "I am not lovable."

On a conscious level, I knew I was good enough and very lovable, but the fear of more pain and the thought of encountering even more painful evidence hurt so badly that creating a new loving relationship felt too risky—and I wasn't sure I could handle another failure.

Fear truly is False Evidence Appearing Relevant. Rather than letting fear hold me back, I gave myself time to heal and then was able to trust myself enough to open new possibilities.

Trusting our abilities will renew our confidence and give us the power to take the necessary risks required to step out of our fear, experience growth and create happiness.

It seems our greatest opportunities for growth occur when we recognize our fears and exercise the ability to change and adapt. At times, this may require adapting in unfamiliar ways. Adapting, when you have no idea what to do, can inadvertently throw us into our Emotional Safety Zone.

I have a child who, due to her situation at birth, has some sensory issues and sometimes she will become extremely nervous and agitated. I tried all kinds of naturopathic remedies to assist her with her anxieties. After two years of watching her struggle, I finally determined it was time for a change and placed her on anxiety medication.

She seemed to respond well to the medication and began to calm down and happily enjoy life. Then one day, she had her feelings deeply hurt and, out of frustration, she pulled out all of her eyelashes and brows.

When she looked in the mirror, she felt very insecure and worried what people were going to say. I found some information on the Internet to help her know that this type of behavior was a common coping mechanism and everything was going to be all right.

I wanted her to understand that sometimes we feel emotional pain that we don't know how to control, so we inflict physical pain upon ourselves. Some people feel calmer when they control their physical pain, as this gives them an overall sense of control. Inflicting physical pain redirects focus off the emotional pain and, thus creates a sense of comfort. Yet helping her understand this did not ease her anxiety or change her behavior.

Then one night, she jumped off the bed, her hand hit a picture frame and she began to scream. I took a deep breath as feelings of impatient anger rose to the surface. Immediately, judgmental thoughts ran through my head: how ridiculous she sounded screaming like a two-year-old and how stupid she looked having pulled out all her lashes and brows. I asked her older sister to take her downstairs to get her a Band-Aid. I knew I needed a little time to deal with my emotions.

At first I was angry and I blamed her for bringing on her own misery by throwing fits and pulling out her eyelashes and eyebrows. I was so irritated that, in the moment, I didn't even care that she had actually hurt herself.

As I began to notice my thoughts, another voice said, "You are the stupid one. She is just a child and you are supposed to be the adult." Over the next few days, I began to wonder why I was so frustrated with her. I finally realized that much of my anger stemmed from the fact that I had never encountered anything like this before and I didn't know what to do.

I began to cry as I thought of her struggle, realizing that she would not be acting out of control unless she felt out of control. Examining what I was really feeling gave me the opportunity to release my fear and frustration and actively work on finding a solution.

I realized I was in unfamiliar territory and felt completely unskilled on how to manage, handle or control the situation. I was completely focused on myself, which blinded me to the fact that I could do anything differently. This type of resistance, even to the point of being paralyzed to move forward, will commonly occur when we face the unknown and will obstruct our ability to seek solutions.

THE PROCESS OF STEPPING OUT OF OUR FEARS TO CHANGE

The purpose of this process is to notice where unconscious fears get in the way of creating changes that will bring balance and peace.

- Name the areas of your life in which you feel you are unable to manage, control, or handle a situation.
- List things you know you want to change.
- What are the benefits you want from these changes?
- What are the long term consequences you will face if you don't change?
- Where have you tried to change and failed?
- How have similar failures made you question your ability to change?
- What current fears hold you back from the change you desire?
- What factual fears are you facing (i.e., fear of loss, loneliness, or illness)?
- Are those facts relevant to your current life?
- If all of your fears were to come true, what is the worst thing that could happen? Would you survive?
- How has fear influenced the decisions you have made? How has it altered your happiness?
- If you were able to get past your fears, what would you create?

Journal any thoughts or ideas that will encourage growth and promote change.

Chapter 9

The Convincing Influence of the Emotional Mind

"Many can argue that reality is as it is, but my experience is that the opposite is exactly true. Reality is ours for the making."

~ Asara Lovejoy

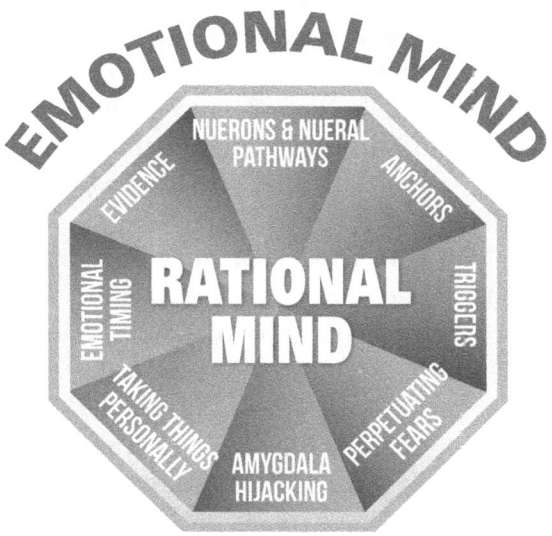

When we experience change that is unfamiliar, or when we fear the unknown, it can place the mind on high alert, and we can get trapped in a state of emergency that blocks out all reality. That is what happened to over 3 million people in our country in 1938.

In the early 1900s, a series of tragic events occurred that primed the citizens of the United States to have the fright of their lives! Twenty-three-year-old Orson Welles, who produced a regular radio program, thought that the science fiction novel about a Martian invasion of earth, called *The War of the Worlds* by H.G. Wells, would make an interesting radio play. Soon after Welles wrote the radio version, it was pre-recorded by the Mercury Theater Group for him to listen to before it was scheduled to be aired.

As he listened, he determined that the production would be dull and uninteresting. Welles knew he needed to make some drastic changes to liven up the program. While pondering a new approach, he was listening to Archibald MacLeish narrate "Air Raid," which was performed on the radio as though it were a live news broadcast. This inspired Welles and he decided to rewrite his script. In his new version, the Martian invasion would be reported as if the invasion was actually happening.

After ten hours of revisions, he reviewed his new plan with the cast. He asked each member to study the script and make their character and the events they were portraying as realistic as they could.

To prepare for his role, the man chosen to be the reporter for the play prepared to enhance his performance by listening to the recordings of the Hindenburg disaster, which had occurred the previous year. "War of the Worlds" aired live on CBS on Sunday, October 30, 1938, the eve of Halloween.

The play began with what seemed to be a broadcast of string instrumental music. The reporter then broke in, stating, "We interrupt this program to bring you a special news bulletin." The cast then acted out an alien invasion.

The plot was genius. As what seemed to be a CBS musical program continued, it was interrupted repeatedly by the increasingly alarming news of the mock invasion. More and more members of the cast began to portray panic and terror, as they gave so-called eyewitness reports of the devastation. Then, Welles had the cast take an abrupt six-second pause, as if something had interrupted the airwave. The gripping pause only increased the panic and fear the listeners were already experiencing.

Massive hysteria began to spread throughout the listening audience. People began to bombard news agencies, police stations and radio shows, asking for the safest way to flee the city and escape the poisonous gases that the Martians had reportedly released.

Thousands put all they could carry into their cars and just drove out of town not even knowing where they were going. Some even suffered pain and misery from non-existent gas.

In their minds, many people converted what they heard—"Martian invasion"—to a "German army invasion," and they were completely convinced that the world was coming to an end.

Why did the listeners act so irrationally?

This confusion could have been attributed to the fact that many listeners had been tuned to the Chase and Sanborn Comedy Show, so they had missed the first ten minutes of the broadcast, which stated that this was a play performed by the Mercury Theater Group. However, in addition to the initial announcement, the fact that this was a play was repeated several times throughout the performance. Even though this had been announced repeatedly, those glued to their radio were in such a state of fear that the announcer's words didn't even register. They ignored the facts and swallowed the whole story—hook, line and sinker.

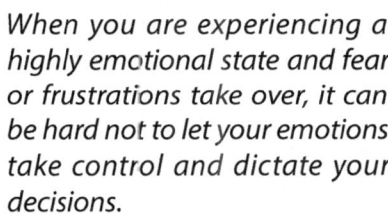

When you are experiencing a highly emotional state and fear or frustrations take over, it can be hard not to let your emotions take control and dictate your decisions.

Approximately 6 million people were listening to CBS radio that night and heard Orson Welles' rendition of "War of the Worlds." Of that 6 million, an estimated 1.7 million people actually believed the story to be true and an additional 1.2 million were frightened enough to take action. That means almost 3 million U.S. citizens allowed their emotions to override their rational thinking and sabotage reality. To them, the invasion (what they heard) felt real, so it was real.

How could so many people believe such an unreasonable, illogical and irrational idea as an actual alien invasion from Mars?

To better comprehend how this could occur, it is important to understand the conditions of the world they lived in at the time. It was a time of unprecedented change for our nation. Just eight years before, the country had entered into the Great Depression, and millions were still out of work and struggling to get by. People in general felt a sense of powerlessness, the world seemed out of control, and many felt like they had nowhere to turn.

Other tragedies had recently been reported. The Lindbergh baby had been kidnapped and people had reeled at the shocking news. The disastrous Hindenburg accident, as well as a hurricane that killed 800 people, had been reported in great detail. People were used to hearing tragic events on the radio. It was a time of tremendous fear. To make matters worse, in the weeks just prior to Welles' broadcast, ongoing reports flooded in regarding Hitler's invasion of Europe.

So, how did all these incidents cause 3 million radio listeners to alter the facts? The emotional mind has no comprehension of reality. Instead, our emotional mind is prewired for survival and is always on the alert for danger.

The Talmud says, "We don't view the world as the world is; we view the world as we are." Well, I believe that, as human beings, we actually view the world the way we feel about it.

When our mind is already in a heightened state of fear, fear itself will throw us into an instinctive, protective mode that validates our perception that what we feel is "real."

For example, at a certain place in the radio program, one of the actors was introduced as Secretary of the Interior. However, in their heightened sense of fear, some of the listeners perceived the voice to be that of their president, Franklin D. Roosevelt. People heard the president's voice warning them of impending danger, which validated their fears of a real invasion.

This is a documented historical event that frightened millions of people. Many well-educated and otherwise intelligent people irrationally acted upon their fears, completely believing that they could see and smell the poisonous gas.[1]

Their current reality had been influenced by tragic, unexpected and unprecedented global events. This triggered their fearful perceptions and irrational behaviors.

In similar ways, unexpected events in our lives can impact our fear-based perceptions, which will then influence our attitudes and

---

[1] Hand, Richard J. (2006). *Terror on the Air!: Horror Radio in America*, 1931–1952. Jefferson, North Carolina: Macfarland & Company. p. 7.
Stefan Lovgen for National Geographic News June 17, 2005 *"War of the Worlds": Behind the 1938 Radio Show Panic* http://news.nationalgeographic.com/news/2005/06/0617_050617_warworlds.html
Source: Franklin D. Roosevelt, Inaugural Address, March 4, 1933, as published in Samuel Rosenman, ed., *The Public Papers of Franklin D. Roosevelt, Volume Two: The Year of Crisis*, 1933 (New York: Random House, 1938), 11–16.

behaviors. Intense feelings of fear trigger our perceived danger response, which has the power to completely block out logical thought. One of the most challenging things we face as human beings is the ability to think and act clearly when we are in situations of panic, fear, and doubt.

Recognizing how your fearful perceptions influence your thoughts, feelings, attitudes and beliefs will allow you to have patience when an emotional state is triggered. This will not only assist you in your emotional growth, it will give you a new understanding of how to assist others in their growth as well.

When you are experiencing a highly emotional state and fear or frustrations take over, it can be hard *not to* let your emotions take control and dictate your decisions.

Keep in mind that the emotional mind *feels* and communicates to us through *feelings*, not logic. In fact, the emotional mind does not even know the difference between what *is real* and what it *perceives to be real*.

Phantom Pain Study

A physical example of how illogical the mind can be is demonstrated in a study that was performed by the neuroscientist Vilayanur S. Ramachandran, Director of the Center for Brain and Cognition.

Doctor Ramachandran wanted to understand, and also to assist, amputees who suffered from phantom pains. Phantom pains are pains that occur in a region of the body where a limb has been removed. These pains can consist of aching, throbbing, stabbing or burning from the nonexistent limb.

One of the things Dr. Ramachandran discovered was that the mind holds the body as whole and complete, even when a body part is missing. To relieve the phantom pain, Dr. Ramachandran designed a mirror box that would create an illusion of restoring the missing limb.[2]

This is how the illusion worked. Let's say I lost my left hand just above the wrist and felt constant pain in the missing hand. To relieve the pain, I would put my right hand in the mirror side of the box and my left arm in the side of the box with no mirrors. When I looked down at the mirrored side of the box, I would see two whole

---

[2] Rawlence, Christopher. *Nova: Secrets of the Mind*. PBS. Season 29, Episode 3, 23 Oct. 2001. Television.

and complete hands. My mind would see evidence that the missing hand was restored and moving to try to relieve the pain, so the pain would be released.

The above is a physical example of how the mind will create a false reality.

Just like phantom pains occur with a missing limb, we can also experience emotional phantom pains because of our childhood structures and fear-based beliefs.

Again, it is that **FEAR** factor, with False Evidence Appearing Real, or *childhood reality appearing relevant in our adult life.*

Because your emotional mind does not have the capability to analyze or express logic, it does not realize that some of the ways you have structured your reality are no longer relevant to your current life. In the same way that the mirror box creates visual evidence that a missing limb has been restored, you too can create evidence that will restore your conscious ability to succeed.

Creating the ability to succeed can only occur on a conscious level, so it is important that you recognize how you have structured uncomfortable events throughout your life. You can do this by analyzing the things in your environment that trigger an emotional response. The intensity of the trigger will determine how long it will take before you are calm enough to actually explore your reactive thoughts, feelings, attitudes and fear-based beliefs. If your feelings are intense, you may feel too uncomfortable to think rationally enough to analyze your automatic reactions. What makes our reactions so unfortunate is, the protective nature of our survival system can get in the way of even our best intentions.

Our Survival System

When we comprehend the power our survival system has and how the rational and emotional minds work together to support this system, we gain deeper insights as to why we think, feel and behave the way we do.

Consider the following scenario:

You step out in front of a car, and the driver begins to honk. Your body's automatic response engages. Your nervous system accelerates, releasing adrenalin that causes your breathing and heart rate to increase, and you move quickly out of the way.

Now that you have had that experience, the mind will generate similar physiological responses whenever it senses a similar threat, whether that threat is real or not.

The rational mind reacts to the physiological surge of energy associated with the highly charged emotional state by looking for anything in the current environment that could validate the danger, like an oncoming car.

> Sometimes it doesn't matter what your rational mind knows to be true, what feels more relevant is what the emotional mind believes to be true.

The emotional mind continues to send signals until the conscious mind either validates or negates the danger—confirming that what we are feeling is real, or reassuring the emotional mind that there is no danger and it is safe to cross the road.

Just as it does with physical threats, the emotional mind reacts to emotional pain in a similar manner. When you experience extreme emotional pain, like the death of a loved one, loss of a job, a breakup of a significant relationship, or abuse, your emotional senses take on a heightened level of protection. Extreme emotional events will also place the emotional mind in an over-protective role and unconsciously get stuck in a constant state of fear.

In order to maintain safety and reestablish stability, you must evaluate your feelings. Yet, when your emotions heighten, evaluating your feelings can be challenging and will take conscious practice.

Because your emotional mind has the power to override your logical thinking, consciously evaluating your emotional situations can be challenging. Sometimes it doesn't matter what your *rational mind knows to be true*, what feels more relevant is what the *emotional mind believes to be true*. "If I *feel* unsafe, my unconscious perception of the situation becomes that I *am* unsafe and will act accordingly."

The emotional mind will not let down its protective shield as long as you are merely "going with the flow" of your emotions. The shield will remain in place until rational evidence is gathered and you feel safe. Until that shield goes down, you will feel the need to protect yourself, even if you are actually safe in your current environment.

Feelings Bridge the Gap

Even though our uncomfortable feelings can be difficult to handle they can be extremely helpful in accessing our personal power. Our feelings create an important bridge that goes from the emotional mind to the conscious mind and helps us to recognize the automatic reactions that get in the way of our personal growth. Our feelings are also the foundation of our inner knowledge or intuition.

Our inner knowledge is like a personal compass that gives us the reassurance and guidance to move forward. Trusting our inner knowledge will increase our confidence to make productive decisions and increase our ability to succeed.

Developing that trust requires deciphering between impulsive feelings and deep reassuring feelings that guide the choices that we make. Learning to trust our feelings and the inner knowledge or intuition that accompanies them will assist us in trusting ourselves.

Have you ever had a conversation like this?

"Wow, I'm so excited you got the job. What made you apply?"

"I had a feeling to just go for it." Or, "It just felt right!"

Can you recall a time in your life when you just knew something was right, so you took a chance and everything turned out just the way you wanted? That's a great feeling!

What about a time when you followed a prompting and took action before something bad happened?

One night while driving in a snowstorm, I had a strong feeling to pull off the freeway. Just as I was exiting, I saw a semi-truck that had lost control and was heading straight for the lane I had just been traveling. If I had not followed my intuition to get off the road, my children and I would have been killed.

When making a decision, notice how often you rely on your own instincts to guide you.

1. Pay attention to times when you automatically question or second guess yourself.

2. Acknowledge any fear that might hold you back from trusting your inner knowledge.
3. Notice times when you override your impressions or ask for the validation of others before you act on your insights.
4. Recognize areas in your life where you experience confidence in your ability to succeed.
   - Determine what it is about those areas that make it easy to trust your judgment.
   - How can you apply the confidence from these successes to areas in your life you want to improve?
5. How can you apply the insights you have learned, trust your own inner knowledge and create the inner motivation to succeed?

Much of the time we lack the confidence we need to rely upon our own senses. This often occurs because we have had reoccurring results that make us question our ability to make decisions.

When we fail at something that is important to us, we lose the ability to trust ourselves. For example, I have met many wonderful single people who are actively seeking the right companion. But because they have been hurt multiple times, they don't trust their judgment. This attitude has sabotaged many opportunities to create the kind of loving relationship they desire. When they find a relationship that they enjoy, the fear of getting hurt sets in, and they pull away. They may even encourage the person to move on, and when they find out that the other person is indeed dating, they convince themselves that the relationship would never have worked anyway.

There are even some who have determined that unless they are knocked off their feet by love at first sight, they will never take a chance at love again. The sad part is, deep down, their greatest desire is to love and to be loved in return.

Trusting your instincts is an important element that will increase your emotional stability and enhance your life.

Now, let's take a look at how the distinct differences of the rational and emotional minds can help us create the happiness we desire.

Chapter 10

The Rational and Emotional Minds

"Our emotional mind will harness the rational mind to its purposes, for our feelings and reactions-- rationalizations-- justifying them in terms of the present moment, without realizing the influence of our emotional memory."

~ Daniel Goleman,
Emotional Intelligence

Distinctions of the Rational and Emotional Minds

Our *Rational, Logical Mind,* operates in the cortex or prefrontal lobes of the brain and is where our consciousness lives. This is the processing center of our mind and is the part of the system that will reason, rationalize, analyze and process our thoughts, feelings and experiences, and logically connect us to the world around us.

The *Emotional Mind* operates in the amygdala, or the limbic system of the brain, and is instinctive and unconscious. This part of the system processes pleasure and pain and emotionally connects us to the world around us.

Because the rational and emotional minds have distinct functions, each will store the experiences that occur in our lives in its own distinctive way. The rational mind will record the logical details of the event, or in other words, what happened, who was involved, and when and where the event occurred.

The emotional mind takes in all the senses and records not only what it sees, but what it hears, how it feels, any physical touch, smells or tastes associated with the event.

It also records any physiological and psychological responses—such as panic, fear or desperation—and physical reactions such as a rush of joy, racing heart, heavy chest, sweaty palms or nausea. The emotional mind will also attach our current emotional experiences to other interactions we've had in the past where similar reactions have occurred.

Now let's take a practical look at how the rational and emotional minds store information.

Let's say you are in New York City and you just left the hotel to meet a friend for lunch. On the way to the restaurant, a man in a grey sweatshirt grabs you and demands your money. Your heart begins to race and you start to struggle and fight back. The man puts a gun in your gut and demands that you give him your money. The smell of garlic on his breath makes your stomach turn as you pull out your money and give it to him. He pushes you aside and runs away.

Your rational mind has recorded the details of your experience, and you are able to give the police a good description of the man and the details of the robbery. The emotional mind has unconsciously recorded all the things you were not focused on or consciously thinking about, like the pounding of your heart and the churning of your stomach.

Because the emotional mind is reactive and cannot consider facts, we end up acting out of our emotions without even realizing what we are doing.

Now, let's say months later, you are enjoying a basketball game with your friends and all of a sudden your mind is taken off the game due to a sudden rush of anxiousness. You have no idea why you unexpectedly feel the way you do, so you excuse yourself and go to the vendor to purchase a drink. You feel a little calmer and return to your seat.

When you get back to your seat, a feeling of uneasiness returns and you try to shake it off. What you didn't realize is that your unconscious mind has noticed a man in a grey sweatshirt sitting a couple of rows behind you. Even though you did not consciously register the grey sweatshirt, your emotional mind has associated the grey shirt with danger, and has taken you back to the emotional recording of the previous traumatic event involving a man in a grey sweatshirt.

Then a week later, you are in the mall and as you pass an Italian restaurant, once again your anxiety level rises as your stomach begins to turn and you feel nauseous. The smell of garlic has once again triggered an emotional reaction of the event in New York City.

The Rational and Emotional Minds

As shown here, the emotional mind is vigilant in trying to keep you safe from potential harm. Unconsciously, your emotional mind diligently does its job, warning you of threats and perceived dangers in your environment that appear similar to past painful experiences and then attach these feelings to your current situations.

Once the emotional mind has anchored something like a grey sweatshirt, traffic noises, or the smell of garlic from one traumatic event, the emotions of that past event can govern your present interactions and reactions.

But because the emotional mind cannot make a distinction between what it sees and what it remembers, its efforts to protect usually cause more confusion than protection as the stronger, faster emotional mind can and will override our logical thought process.

Because the emotional mind is reactive and cannot consider facts, we end up acting out of our emotions without even realizing what we are doing.

As mentioned previously, the emotional mind is wired to protect by illuminating reoccurring emotional patterns that keep us "safely" in the familiarity of our Emotional Safety Zone.

When we move out of what is familiar, a physical reaction occurs. The emotional mind releases chemicals into the somatic system that will initiate a sense of anxiety, which will automatically trigger fear.

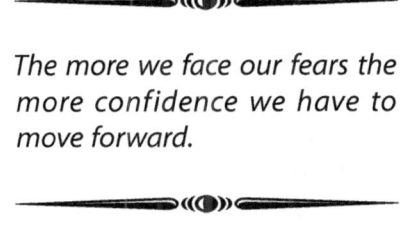

The more we face our fears the more confidence we have to move forward.

It happens like this: Let's imagine that we can hear the thoughts of a shy man who wants to have dinner with an attractive young lady.

He thinks to himself: "I would like to ask that young lady to have dinner with me."

The faster, stronger emotional mind kicks in and the first thing he feels is anxiety. That anxiety triggers fears that not only ignite but also reinforce his stored feelings of past failures, both real and imaged.

It all happens so suddenly that he doesn't even realize what is going on. In the moment of panic, he retreats into familiar patterns of safety and convinces himself that he wouldn't be good enough for her, and may be rejected. A victim of his fear-based beliefs and faulty thinking patterns, he unconsciously decides that he will fail. So without even trying, he moves on with his day, disappointed as he leaves the opportunity behind—again.

The emotional mind is the force behind all of our motivation. That's why, at times, we can logically plan, strategize and prepare to create effective results and yet, in the moment of action, the emotional mind sends us back to what we are familiar with and stifles our ability to think or act clearly, which can sabotage our success.

In order to break the cycle, we must acknowledge our emotional patterns, bring our feelings up to a conscious level, restructure them, and release the hold they have had on our lives. This is where the rational mind can help, as the rational mind is the processing center of the brain and will help us analyze our past experiences in a logical way.

Have you ever been subject to a random act of violence or faced a traumatic event, such as a car accident, and felt overwhelming panic and fear for days or weeks and sometimes even years thereafter? When unexpected events cause us to feel unsafe, or we experience pain, the emotional mind goes into protection mode, and we temporarily lose our ability to feel peaceful.

As we face our fear by getting back into the proverbial car in the days and weeks ahead, our rational mind slowly begins to accumulate evidence that we are safe. The more we face our fears, the safer we feel to move forward.

Being able to collect enough evidence to create safety after a traumatic experience has occurred will require conscious diligence and may involve additional gentleness while we give ourselves proper time for healing.

As we consciously reason, analyze and restructure our thoughts, feelings and emotions around our uncomfortable events, we are able to re-establish a sense of safety, taking the lessons we have learned and applying them to our future success.

Interaction of the Two Minds

Even though the roles of the two minds are different, they are always working together. While the emotional mind is feeling the

The Rational and Emotional Minds

details of an event, the rational mind is filtering and analyzing those details in an effort to make sense out of them. There are times when events can seem illogical or feel so uncomfortable that we have trouble "wrapping our brain around them." When emotions are heightened, the rational mind's ability to reason is limited. To make sense out of the illogical way that we feel, the rational mind will find ways to justify our feelings. It may even twist the details or rearrange the truth to make sense of our unconscious perceptions and beliefs. The goal is to create an illusion that makes us feel better.

We will feel angst or excitement until we find a justification that aligns with the way we feel about our current situation. This could even occur, for example, when we get caught up in the excitement of a purchase that we really can't afford. Our emotions cause us to completely overlook the logical facts of the pressure we will face as we attempt to pay off the debt. Still, when we are in an emotional place, our rational mind works to justify those emotions, focusing our attention on all the exciting benefits of the purchase.

Often we believe that we are making completely rational decisions, but when we are caught up in our emotions, the emotional connections become the driving force behind everything we see, feel, and do.

Emotional Anchors

We can learn a lot by taking a deeper look at how the emotional events in our lives have been emotionally anchored.

Ineffective anchors are those that hold us captive, sabotage our relationships and keep us from enjoying the benefits of living a happy, well-balanced life.

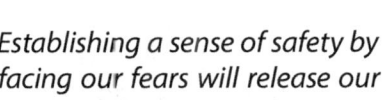

Establishing a sense of safety by facing our fears will release our emotional reactions.

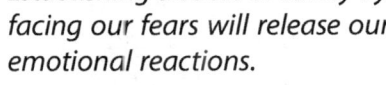

There are a few ways these types of anchors can be set.

One way an anchor is set is when we experience something that is incongruent with our values or conscious beliefs.

Let's say today is my eighth birthday and my dad said he was going to take me to lunch to celebrate. I wait on the porch for him to come. Mom tells me that he had an emergency at work and will take me out on Saturday instead. I don't believe her. I still believe he is coming because he promised. Besides, he took my sister out on her birthday, so I continue to wait on the porch for the rest of the day.

When my dad doesn't come home to get me, I feel really bad because I love and trust my father and I want to spend special time with him. Consciously I believe, "Dads who love their children keep their promises." Because I am hurt I may anchor the belief that, "Because my dad didn't take me out on my birthday like he did my sister, my dad must not love me." If I have had other broken promises or experiences similar to this one, I will link this experience to other times where I have been hurt, which will only intensify my insecurity.

Consciously, I may know that my dad loves me, but he broke his promise and it hurts. Therefore, my fear-based belief and automatic response is, "My father must not love me." Even if my father comes home and sees my disappointment and takes me out that night instead of waiting until Saturday, it will not change the emotional anchor or the unconscious belief that the situation has established.

I cannot change the belief until I become conscious of it. It will affect my attitudes and behavior not only toward my father, but also toward others. I will then look for and create ways to validate the feeling of: "I must not be lovable." Even though I know that I am loved, this belief and the lack of trust I now feel will generate feelings that will distort the truth. Unconsciously I will find evidence that will validate and strengthen the way I feel.

Another way an emotional anchor can be set is through a significant experience. If I get in a car accident, my emotional mind will record the panic and fear that I experienced in the accident. Until my emotional mind can gain a sense of safety, every time I get in a car, or pass the area where the accident occurred, I will feel the same panic and fear I felt when I was in the accident.

Even though I still have fears and anxieties, making the decision to push through those fears and get back into the car will help me to reestablish safety. Those fears may continue to show up, but each time I challenge them I am gathering evidence that, "I am safe," until eventually I have enough evidence that those uncomfortable feelings no longer prevent me from enjoying my life. Establishing a sense of safety by facing my fears will release the emotional reactions.

A third way anchors are set is through repetition.

Let's pretend that when I was a child, my brother excelled at sports and I was very good academically. Now imagine that my grandparents loved sports, and I would always hear them talking about how great my brother was and bragging about his natural athletic abilities. Yet, they never praised or even acknowledged how hard I worked in school. I could easily grow up feeling like my grandparents love my brother more than they love me. This might cause me to feel unimportant and to anchor a fear-based belief that I am "less than" others.

These unconscious emotions and beliefs would then be consistently running in the background of my mind, affecting my self-esteem and unconsciously controlling my thoughts, perceptions and behaviors. I may even associate myself with people who will validate this belief by treating me as if I didn't matter.

Throughout our lives, we have unconsciously anchored many misperceptions about life based on the way we felt in a particular moment. If we are not consciously aware of the power these unconscious events have, they can quietly sabotage our happiness.

THE PROCESS OF DISCOVERING EMOTIONAL ANCHORS

The purpose of this process is to discover unconscious events that distort your perceptions and consume your emotional energy.

We can become more educated regarding our emotions when we are hurt, irritated or upset, because, at these times, our thoughts, feelings, attitudes, and beliefs will present themselves and become easier to decipher.

As you ponder an emotionally charged event from your past, contemplate your reaction. Analyze any thoughts, feelings, attitudes, and beliefs anchored to this event. When possible, contemplate the first time you had this feeling or thought. Consider various consequences this emotional anchor has caused and how it has formed some of the illogical ways you view the world.

If you are having a hard time pinpointing the original event, consider the following actions:

- Think about your current situation. Acknowledge any physical and emotional reactions you are experiencing.
- Address the way you feel. Study any emotional pain.
- Examine the intensity of your feelings. Acknowledge any fears.
- When you spot a fear, question the logic of that fear. How relevant is it to your current situation or life? Can you pinpoint how long have you had this fear?
- Try to determine the protection you have received from this fear.
- Ponder your reaction and consciously link your feelings in this situation with other times you have felt this way.
- Can you identify the common factor for the trigger?
- What beliefs are attached to this anchored event?
- Ponder how these beliefs create safety.

Journal any thoughts or ideas that will encourage growth and promote change.

Locating emotional anchors can be difficult. It takes practice and requires lots of curiosity. However, the process does get easier the more you make a conscious effort. If you find yourself struggling to pinpoint an anchor, it may help to go through several scenarios in your mind and repeat the details out loud until you feel some type of connection with the aspects surrounding the original anchor. Again, remember that this process will get easier the more you do it.

Now let's explore how, once an emotional anchor is set, it can be triggered by the things we see, hear, smell, taste, touch or feel.

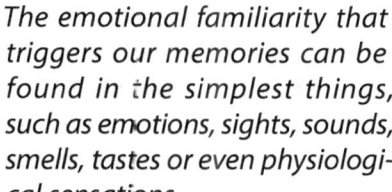

The emotional familiarity that triggers our memories can be found in the simplest things, such as emotions, sights, sounds, smells, tastes or even physiological sensations.

Anytime the emotional mind connects to something that has been emotionally anchored—such as a phrase, a song, a certain smell, or a type of car—you will be triggered to experience the emotional details of that past event. What you are feeling will unconsciously be connected to your present event, which will either enhance your happiness or distort your perception.

Emotional Triggers

An anchor is like an emotional outlet and a trigger is like a plug. When something in our current environment seems familiar, or even similar to a time when we have felt uncomfortable or experienced pain, the brain will plug into that memory and trigger electrochemical shocks throughout the body to stimulate action. The emotional familiarity that triggers our memories can be found in the simplest things, such as emotions, sights, sounds, smells, tastes or even physiological sensations. Every time we are triggered, it reinforces and, at times, will even intensify our emotional reactions.

Every experience that we encounter will branch out and establish logical, emotional and physiological anchors throughout the brain. This means that throughout our lives we have established billions of anchors. Each anchor has its own emotional charge that will stimulate different types of psychological and physiological responses. Because each event we encounter has formed many different types of anchors, becoming triggered by something in our current environment can be fairly easy.

Often our triggered reality has nothing to do with reality itself. In our triggered reality, we make inadequate judgments of situations and of others without even realizing that how we feel about a situation is not based on facts from the present moment.

A trigger will produce intense emotions that will place the rational mind on alert. The rational mind then looks for something in the current environment to validate our feelings. When our emotions are on high alert, the rational mind will focus on substantiating or negating the warning. When we don't stop to consciously analyze our triggered experiences, the inadequate judgments we make will become our current reality. Once our perceptions change, it becomes very challenging to reverse the effects.

The following example illustrates this point:

Years ago I met a wonderful man who was interested in pursuing a dating relationship. We began talking, and he started sending me text messages every morning, which I really enjoyed. Every once in a while, he would text the phrase: "Hey, sexy thang, wass up," and it would really irritate me. But I dismissed it without saying anything.

After several irritating texts had gone by, I finally asked him not to use that phrase with me. He justified his actions, which intensified my feelings of irritation and I started to truly dislike him.

I began pondering why my feelings had changed when he had not. After I asked him not to use that phrase he never used it again. Yet my feelings of disdain toward this wonderful man were still the same.

What I discovered was, the phrase that irritated or triggered me was tied to reoccurring interactions with another person where I felt I was not respected or appreciated.

I realized that every time I was triggered by that particular phrase, I felt disrespected by this wonderful man, which was not his intention at all. However, my feelings of disdain were so strong that even recognizing why I was being triggered did not change the feelings I had come to associate with this man.

Our perception, history, emotional state and, at times, the type of trigger that is activated, will determine if our triggered events will become a simple annoyance that can be tolerated or, as in the case above, a deal breaker.

Every time we are triggered, we strengthen the emotional and physiological feelings associated with that trigger. We then take those feelings and imprint them onto the person whose actions have triggered our reaction.

Triggering Memories that Enrich Our Life

Understanding how to recognize and restructure your ineffective triggers will be a powerful part of living a life full of peace and happiness.

Ineffective triggers may have the ability to sabotage your happiness, but you also have enriching memories that, when utilized, will connect you to your personal motivation to succeed. Enriching anchors have the ability to trigger hidden motivators that create extremely powerful differences in your life.

These memories not only have the ability to override your ineffective anchors, they also have the power to generate the energy you need to excel to greater heights in every area of your life.

When you consciously connect your desired success to successes you have already accomplished, the confidence from your previous success will transfer to your desired result and give you more excitement and energy to succeed.

It all starts with identifying energizing experiences that you have already encountered. When you consciously connect your desired success to successes you have already accomplished, the confidence from your previous success will transfer to your desired result and give you more excitement and energy to succeed. As children, many of us learned to ride a bike. For some of us it was a painful balancing act, where others learned much quicker. As we grew, our ability to ride a bike grew with us and, even if we went years without riding a bike, the belief that we knew how to ride a bike stayed with us.

Earlier in the book, we talked about pushing through emotional fears over and over again, until we feel comfortable in what once was an uncomfortable situation. That same principle applies to success; we must push past all our doubts, fear and pain over and over again until we experience a feeling of success. This process becomes much easier when we connect the energy and motivation of previous successes to our current dreams and desires.

Just think about the areas in your life where you feel successful; in most cases, you have had many successful results. The repetition of productive results builds your confidence and, if you feel successful, you are successful, right?

We will actually explore more about the concept of utilizing your energizing experience to create the life you want a bit later. Right now, let's look a little more at powerful emotions you can use to enhance your ability to achieve effective results.

Love is one of those emotions that miracles are made of. You've heard the saying, "The crazy things we do for love." The reason this occurs is that love is emotionally powerful and can easily blind us from obvious facts. Love is also an influential motivator that can usually get beyond any boundary. In fact, most people have strong emotional events anchored around love, such as their first kiss, memories of romance or even a lost love.

I'm sure you can think of at least one song that will automatically bring up fun-loving memories of childhood.

In the Disney movie "Ratatouille," Ego the restaurant critic tasted Remy the rat's rendition of the dish called Ratatouille, and was transported back to a loving childhood memory, instantly changing his initial harsh view of Gusteou's restaurant. When our desires are connected to love, nothing seems impossible!

THE PROCESS OF EMOTIONAL TRIGGERS

The purpose of this process is to consciously notice emotional triggers and analyze the physical and mental reactions that sabotage your emotional wellbeing.

As your awareness increases regarding what triggers an emotional reaction for you, it will become easier to change the ineffective patterns that have silently sabotaged your emotional wellbeing.

The next time you are triggered, consider the following:
- Who or what initiated the triggered reaction?

Analyze your response.
- How appropriate was the reaction to the current situation?
- Can you identify the connection between what triggered your emotional reaction and the anchored event or events from your past?

When you are triggered, how do you react?
- Do you blame yourself or others?
- Do you feel powerless?
- Do you feel anxious?
- Do you get angry?
- Do you feel attacked or attack others?
- Do you withdraw?
- Do you blame?
- Do you justify your actions?
- Do you cry, eat, or self-medicate?

As we recognize the mental and behavioral patterns which we hand over our power to, we create a conscious ability to override our automatic reactions. We become more empowered to respond in a way that will encourage personal happiness and growth.

Journal any thoughts or ideas that will encourage growth and promote change.

The amount of pain anchored by an emotional event will determine the intensity of the trigger. The intensity of a trigger indicates how many times the feelings and beliefs have been accessed. Understanding the intensity will give you an idea of the amount of consciousness and time you will need to process the fear and release the pain. Just remember, there is an amazing life waiting for you on the other side of fear.

Fear is one of those emotions that, when triggered, has the ability to take complete control of our rational thoughts. Sometimes these fears can trigger experiences that are so unexpected and so painful they overwhelm us and blind us from our normal ability to cope. Our emotional mind takes complete control and we are transported in time as we lose all touch with reality.

Chapter 11

Amygdala Hijacking

"When we question our emotions and discover our fear-based beliefs, we gain a better understanding of why we give our power away. This understanding will increase our ability to direct our choices and to create the happiness we desire."

~Victoria Lee Carlyle

Amygdala Hijacking

Virtually every fear-based trigger raises some type of protective defense. Yet, some anchored events can trigger such a strong emotional reaction that all sense of time and reason seem lost. In an instant, the world feels like it is crashing down and there is nothing you can do.

Some of us have times in life when the triggers we experience connect us back to an extremely painful, unresolved event. In these instances, our emotional mind doesn't just remind us of potential danger; instead it completely takes over and we are immediately filled with feelings of life threatening danger as we are consumed with panic, fear and confusion.

An amygdala hijacking happens when you are overwhelmed by such intense feelings of fear, pain or sadness that your rational mind is incapacitated and you are unable to act reasonably or even maintain your composure.

In this state, strong emotions instantaneously override the logical mind, and all of our thoughts, feelings and beliefs from a painful event are brought forward. In essence, it is as if we are reliving the traumatic event or events over again. This is called an *Amygdala Hijacking*.

An amygdala hijacking happens when you become so overwhelmed by intense feelings of fear, pain or sadness that your rational mind is incapacitated and you are unable to act reasonably or even maintain your composure.

Many people have experienced an emotional hijacking without even realizing it.

Recently, I met a man who was extremely distraught over the fact that he might lose a job that he was very good at and absolutely loved. Confused, I asked why he was so concerned. He said that once a month he had to give a presentation explaining the progress he and his team had made on their current projects. As he described, it didn't matter how hard he prepared or how many notes he wrote, when he was in front of the room he felt that "deer in the headlights" sensation. He would freeze and no matter how hard he tried, he would forget everything. In essence, he would experience an amygdala hijacking.

My son recently shared how he has a similar experience anytime he has to confront someone. He said he can go over exactly what he wants to say a thousand times, but when it comes time for him to communicate something he is unhappy about, his mind goes blank and he can't do anything but simply agree with what is being said.

My daughter, who is one of the hardest workers and best employees I know, had a breakdown during an interview for a new job and was unable to answer even simple questions. She had worked very hard to familiarize herself with the company. Yet, when the interviewer began asking questions, she became so nervous she forgot everything she had worked so hard to learn. The interviewer could see how nervous she was. He began to talk calmly to her about something one of her references had said. He continued having a casual conversation until she felt comfortable and safe. Once she calmed down, she enjoyed her interview and got the job.

These examples show how an amygdala hijacking can dramatically limit our ability to succeed. For these individuals, the emotion of fear literally takes over the rational mind and paralyzes their ability to perform.

In an amygdala hijacking, our perceptions are skewed because we are basing our reality on the panic, fear and doubt going on within us, not on what is really happening around us.

Amygdala Hijacking

I had an experience that illustrates this. As a young mother, I was struggling with an eight-year-old child who could completely bully me. I wanted to be a good mother, but I felt utterly helpless; so, I attended a workshop to gain new parenting tools.

On the second night of the workshop, the homework assignment was to identify someone in your past that you had hard feelings toward and write a letter, make a phone call, go see them, or, in other words, do whatever it would take to ask for their forgiveness.

> *In an amygdala hijacking, our perceptions are skewed because we are basing our reality on the panic, fear and doubt going on within us, not on what is really happening around us.*

The next morning, one man came back to the workshop and, with a great deal of enthusiasm, wanted to share his experience. He was extremely animated when began to speak. He said, "I F-n can't believe how F-n good I feel!" (He actually said the "F" word, but I don't think I need to repeat it here for you to get the idea.) Then he began sharing his experience from the night before. He said he was so angry when he left because he knew that he needed to forgive his father, but he didn't want to. His father had treated him so badly when he was a child that he had vowed he would never be in a relationship with the man again. When he thought about the assignment and considered contacting his father, he said he stomped around the house, thinking of all the ways his father had done him wrong.

Then, he decided he did not need to forgive his father at all. Instead, he could forgive someone else and still fulfill the assignment. But, he stomped around his house for another 30 minutes, thinking about how much he really hated his dad. Finally, he decided that he would just get it over with, found his father's number, picked up the phone and called. When his dad answered the phone, the man quickly hung up. He thought, "What am I doing? I have hated my dad my whole life. Even if I wanted to forgive him, I don't know how."

As he thought, the man remembered a time when he saw his father at a family reunion. At the time, he had derived great joy in degrading his father in front of family members his father respected. It had felt great in the moment, but now, remembering the sadness on his father's face, he regretted what he had said. Even though he still felt like his dad completely deserved the comments that were made, he decided he would call his father and apologize.

He picked up the phone and when his father answered, he quickly spit out his apology.

The man's voice boomed with excitement as he continued to share his experience, "You wouldn't F-n believe what happened next. My dad started to cry and apologized to me. I hung up the phone and went right to his house. He opened the door and my F-n dad hugged me. I don't think my dad has ever hugged me! Then we were both standing on the porch, crying like sissy girls. It was amazing. I love my F-n dad!"

Watching him describe his experience, my mind began to wander to thoughts of my father, and I began to cry. All of a sudden, I was jerked out of my thoughts as a woman in the back of the room stood up and started screaming at the man because of his language.

The facilitator got a twinkle in her eyes and said, "Oh, you don't like the F word?" Then the facilitator began screaming, "Well, FF FF FF FF FF FF FF." The woman was furious and started screaming back.

I was confused and couldn't comprehend what was going on. I started to shake, and my chest felt heavy. I literally had my knees pulled up against my chest to stop myself from having a complete breakdown. I had broken out in a rash, and my heart was beating so fast I could hardly breathe. I knew I had to get out of the room—right then. It was everything I could do to make my legs cooperate so I could move enough to get out.

I somehow reached the hallway, even though my panic was so intense that I didn't know what was going on or what I needed. I managed to make it to the safety of my car. I climbed inside and began to sob.

When you're having a severe emotional reaction, it has nothing to do with what's going on in the present. In that moment, your feelings are screaming so loudly that the emotions take over, you're immobilized and you lose the ability to think or act rationally.

When that happened to me, even after reaching the safety of my car, it still took about 45 minutes before I was able to calm myself down enough to go back into the room and finish the day. Even then, I felt extremely anxious and it was challenging to set aside the experience and concentrate on the class.

When I got home, I had time to look back at what happened. As crazy as it sounds, it took me a while to remember what actually triggered me. I remembered the man who had shared his experience and his use of the "F" word.

When I recalled that part of the experience, I didn't feel any emotion of panic tied to that; and I thought, "No, that didn't trigger me." As I continued to think about the experience, the fear hit me again. Then I remembered the two women screaming at each other and realized *that* was the trigger. But why? It took me a while, but I finally pinpointed the reason I had an amygdala hijacking. The man's story brought up feelings of sadness, reminding me of my own pain of never experiencing my father's love. I was already feeling sad and to some degree, a bit lost when the woman in the back of the room started to express her disapproval of the man's language. When the two women started screaming at each other it sent a shock into my system, connecting me even more fully to my frightful past.

My father was a very angry man and, even into my adult years, I was still terrified of him. Anytime I witnessed a display of anger, I was transported back to the childhood fears that were created by his violence.

One of the illogical fears I had emotionally structured in my childhood was that if there was enough anger around me, I was going to die. Anger was the trigger that produced the feelings of overwhelming fear that had caused the reaction. This governed my behavior, so I automatically did whatever it took to avoid anger.

Anyone who has had an amygdala hijacking knows how confusing this kind of an experience can be, because you feel like a painful event from the past is actually occurring in the present time. Painful memories you have tried to avoid are brought to the surface making you feel extremely unsafe.

You may have witnessed similar unconscious behaviors in someone who is extremely angry or in a person who is drunk. In these situations, it is obvious that the conscious, more rational mind is literally turned off. When the rational mind is off, there is no chance of having a logical conversation. The emotional mind is hypersensitive and seeking validation or safety.

The only thing the emotional mind will listen to at this point is, "I Am Right!" When you encounter a person who is in a heightened emotional state, in order for them to calm down, you must listen to them and make them feel like you understand their point of view. It is only when the emotional mind feels safe that it will let its protective guard down and logic will return. When they are able return to logic, you can then have a rational conversation. The mind becomes hypersensitive when large amounts of chemicals are released into the system, so it will be hard to think logically.

It also takes a while for the effects of these chemicals to wear out of the system. Therefore, patience is needed. If you have an amygdala hijacking, it is important to allow yourself time to calm down in a place where you can feel safe. Once you're calm and can think logically, it is important to become conscious of the elements that triggered you. Then, take time to process your emotional thoughts, feelings, attitudes and beliefs so that the same experience will not completely sabotage you again.

As we have the courage to get curious and not critical with our emotional reactions and begin to understand the patterns we have established, we become consciously aware of the influence these patterns once had.

To do so, consciously think of the memories the hijacking brought back, and then try to figure out how the things you saw, heard and felt in your current environment connected past memories to the present moment. It may be challenging to fully comprehend the different aspects of your encounter. Your emotions will feel intense and it will be uncomfortable to face them, but don't give up. Also, be gentle and give yourself all the time you need to process and heal.

The thing that helped me was to first identify the trigger, which was anger. Once I could logically see how anger not only triggered an emotional reaction, but also was the source of the physical and mental reaction. It was only when I became conscious of the disabling ways the past events controlled my behavior that I could then restructure my thoughts, feelings and attitudes and, thus, create a different result.

For me, part of this logical restructuring included noticing patterns in which my flight response automatically took over my behavior. I remembered being in the mall watching two people yelling at each other. My heart began to race, my chest became splotchy and red, and I quickly left. In the grocery store, I saw a mother's impatience with her child, and I realized that I had the same reaction with the same immediate response. Any time there was anger around me, even when it didn't involve me, I would have an emotional and physiological reaction and flee!

Acknowledging my fear of anger, and validating that I had a good reason to feel fear around anger, evoked a lasting change that has given me the ability to control and eventually stop my physical and emotional reaction involving anger.

I'm not going to tell you that after I processed my *fear* of anger, I never had another *emotional reaction* to anger again. I had a lot of anchors attaching fear to anger but, up until the time I had the amygdala hijacking, I was completely blind to the power and control anger had over my life. It wasn't until I was stuck in a situation where I couldn't run but came face to face with my fears that I realized the hold anger had over my life. Only then could I consciously restructure my experience so that the fear of anger no longer had power over me.

Now, because I am consciously aware of my fear, I am able to look at a situation involving anger and automatically question my feelings. Am I really in danger, or are my childhood structures trying to protect me?

As we have the courage to get curious and not critical with our emotional reactions and begin to understand the patterns we have established, we become consciously aware of the influence these patterns once had. This knowledge will give us the power to override our ineffective structures and, instead, choose a response that supports the kind of life we want to live.

THE PROCESS OF AN AMYGDALA HIJACKING

The purpose of this process is to shift extremely emotional experiences to a conscious place where you can release the sorrow and involuntary power these sad experiences have had over your life.

Here are some helpful tips on restructuring an amygdala hijacking.

After an amygdala hijacking has passed, identify specific things in your environment that triggered your emotional state.

To do this:

- Think about the memories, feelings, or beliefs you may have experienced.
- Try to connect any details of your present situation to the triggered event. In order for you to move on, it is important to recognize that any time emotions from a past event surface they will skew or even exaggerate feelings in your current situation.
- Because the details may not make logical sense, it will be up to you to stay curious until you pinpoint the details of the different connections.
- Once you have identified the triggers, write as many details as you can remember from the traumatic event. Make sure you pay special attention to your detrimental thoughts and feelings. They will help you process your pain more quickly.
- Once you have uncovered the details, imagine yourself at the age of the event then consider the scenario from that perspective.
- Forgive yourself for the pain you have carried.
- Forgive others so you can release from the freedom they have taken.
- Give yourself time to heal and then forgive yourself for any pain you have carried. When you truly forgive yourself, you open the door to releasing the emotional hold others have held.

When you transfer detrimental actions back to the one who has caused the pain, you can let go of any emotional energy they have had by forgiving them..

It is challenging to face painful memories. You will need to be patient with yourself. After an amygdala hijacking has occurred, the emotional mind will sense the danger that comes from the overwhelming emotional reaction and immediately go into an overprotection mode. While you are working to restructure the experience the mind may throw you back into panic and fear several more times. It may take several months before you completely work through your feelings and feel at peace. Yet, keep in mind how long you have been carrying this emotional burden. The freedom you gain and the things in your life that will change is worth facing your discomfort.

To gain full power over your life, you must analyze as many of the details as you can remember, even if it makes you uncomfortable. By identifying the environmental triggers that have sent you into automatic fight or flight mode, you can more easily sort out the damaging details of the painful event.

Start questioning your reactions by asking these questions:
- Specifically, what did I react to?
- What emotions did I feel?
- What coping mechanism did I use to calm myself?
- Is there a specific person to whom the reaction was tied?
- What is my relationship with that person now?
- Was this reaction tied to one event or multiple events?
- What fears and emotions were running my reactions?

Notice any automatic behavioral patterns that occur with different types of emotional reactions.

Journal any thoughts or ideas that will encourage growth and promote change.

Processing an amygdala hijacking can be very uncomfortable. Remember, the key to experiencing the freedom that comes with personal power is shifting fear-based structures by consciously deciphering and directing your thoughts, feelings, attitudes and beliefs.

Emotional Timing

One of the reasons an emotional hijacking can override our logic is because emotions have no sense of time. Any time our emotions are triggered and offenses or hurt feelings occur, we will experience the same type of logic and emotional reactions that occurred when the triggered event was originally anchored.

If an emotional experience was anchored when I was three years old, my ability to think logically when triggered remains at the level of a three-year-old. Three-year-olds are too young to understand logic, so if someone is triggered to an event that happened when they were three, their current thoughts, beliefs and emotional reactions could look and sound like the actions of a three-year-old.

If an emotional experience was anchored when I was three years old, my ability to think logically when triggered, remains at the level of a three-year-old.

For example, one of the first things I did when I experienced my amygdala hijacking was to pull my legs up to my chest and rock back and forth to calm myself. The illogical belief that I would die if someone was extremely angry, was established when I was very young. When the women in the seminar were really angry with each other, I happened to be in the middle of the room. I felt unsafe, trapped and helpless. I didn't feel like I could escape. I was overwhelmed with the same sense of helplessness that I had felt as a very young child. These types of feelings will remain at a very young age as I continue to grow.

This is why some people have a hard time understanding what they are feeling and why they always end up feeling so insecure. These types of feelings can carry over into adult life.

For instance, if as a teenager, I had many experiences where I didn't feel accepted or like I fit in, I may experience times as an adult, where certain social interactions will trigger those feelings of unacceptance. Then my current situation will feel that uncomfortable familiarity of the past, so I will feel unaccepted or like I don't fit in. My feelings will validate the reality that I don't fit in and my thoughts will start thinking about all the things that I must get home to do. Unconsciously, I want to go home where I feel safe and am not going to be rejected. My thoughts will comfort my fears, and my actions will create a temporary feeling of relief, but illusion of relief will perpetuate my lonely reality.

This is how our past reality continues to appear relevant in our current lives. Because our emotional mind has no capability to analyze, and knows no time, it doesn't realize that when we are triggered, we remain in a mindless state where our triggered events have the power to confuse our perceptions. It then becomes very easy to get offended or take things personally.

Chapter 12

Taking Things Personally

Taking Things Personally

I really like this quote from Eleanor Roosevelt. She said, "No one can make you feel inferior without your consent." I like to take that statement a bit further by saying, "No one has the power to hurt your feelings or even offend you without your consent."

Yet, many of us get offended or have our feelings hurt on a regular basis. We feel slighted, left out or ignored. We may take a co-workers comment as a personal affront. We hear people laughing together, and wonder if they are talking about us. We take offense at what people do and even what they don't do.

"No one has the power to hurt your feelings or even offend you without your consent."

Sadly, these are all signs that we are caught in The Victim Addiction. Any time we take things personally, are offended or get our feelings hurt, it is because we are letting our emotional perceptions overrule the facts and influence our thoughts, feelings, attitudes and beliefs.

In fact, anytime you get your feelings hurt or are offended, you are just connecting to an emotional anchor, and whatever is going on in your current environment has just triggered the emotions of that event.

I'm not saying that every person you encounter will have good intentions. You may have occasions where someone in your life will go out of their way to purposely cause emotional pain, but even in situations where someone is trying to hurt or offend, you always have the power to accept or reject their offence.

As stated previously, an anchor is like your own personal, emotionally charged outlet on a wall. The event is neutral until something triggers it. Just like an outlet only releases energy when something that "fits" is plugged into it, our personal emotional anchors will only release energy when something that "fits" our past experience triggers those anchors. *Our triggers connect us to an uncomfortable experience from the past and charge our reactions.*

When an emotional anchor is triggered, the emotional mind sets off a physiological and emotional cascade of signals. These signals generate panic, fear or doubt and we feel anger, angst, sadness, or misery. And, "If I *feel* miserable, I *look for reasons that will validate my misery*."

Each time we are triggered, we continue to gather evidence, creating an even stronger case to justify our miserable feelings and finding even more excuses to blame others for the offenses that we feel are heaped upon us.

As mentioned earlier, emotional anchors don't have to be true, they just need to have an emotional connection and *feel* true.

When I take things personally, I am unconsciously victimizing myself by giving my power to an emotional anchor that was set long before the current interaction occurred.

So, while our feelings, thoughts and reactions may not be a true representation of what is occurring at the moment, they are true for us based on our past experience. We wholeheartedly believe that our co-worker really is talking about us, that our friend purposely tried to hurt us, or even that the universe itself is out to get us.

We believe the offense is true because, unconsciously, what is being said resonates with something we have already experienced before. As an example, if I was having a conversation with my athletic friend, Dustin, and I said, "Dustin, I really don't like your green feet," do you think Dustin would be upset? No. Why? Because it isn't true! He doesn't *have* green feet.

Now there are some who feel so bad about themselves that their unconscious reality is "I'm not good enough." Sadly they would feel attacked, get offended or take something personally even if what you said had no factual basis, like, "I really don't like your green feet."

Taking Things Personally

Most often, however, we are hurt or take offense at comments or actions that are similar to something we have experienced before. So, what if, shortly after my friend Dustin had showered, I jokingly said, "Man, Dustin, put your shoes on. Your feet smell terrible!" Knowing Dustin, he would probably stick his feet in my face so I could enjoy the aroma, but if he was in a bad mood he could have a different reaction. If Dustin had been criticized, left out or rejected before because of his stinky feet, he might connect to a time he felt rejected and hurt and automatically react as if I was personally attacking him. When he feels attacked, his defense mechanisms go up, and he reacts by getting angry, embarrassed, or offended. He may even blame me for his reaction.

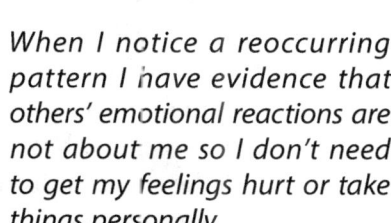

When I notice a reoccurring pattern I have evidence that others' emotional reactions are not about me so I don't need to get my feelings hurt or take things personally.

Just like plugging into an electrical outlet, when something that was said connects to one of my outlets, it will release an emotional charge and then I react by feeling attacked, taking things personally, getting my feelings hurt or being offended.

When we take things personally, it reinforces destructive thinking patterns, validates our distorted perceptions and will deprive us of the personal power we need to consciously get out of The Victim Addiction.

The only way to regain our personal power is to realize that we are influenced by emotions and when this occurs we become "meaning making machines." It's not what people do or say to me that hurts, it's the feelings I have and the meaning I attach to the interaction that determines my actions.

When we take things personally, it's easy to "make meanings" that are not based on truth but on a skewed perception.

Unfortunately, some people get offended by others and, instead of talking to the person with whom the offence had occurred, they seek out allies who will agree with them and validate what a victim they have been. This validation will only intensify the "emotional charge" of the meaning they have created.

The most important thing we can do for our personal growth is to look at the ways we are hurt, offended or take things personally and get downright curious. It is also helpful not to take others reactions personally either, but approach emotional situations with understanding. Now I am not talking about ignoring their behavior; I am talking about being present with them in an emotional situation and trying to understand the situation from their perspective. Consistently turning our backs on someone's emotions will create mistrust, while trying to understand their perspective will create a trusting environment that will encourage emotional growth.

The more ownership we take for our ineffective thoughts, feelings, attitudes and beliefs, the easier it becomes to separate ourselves from the emotional patterns of others. When we have the ability to notice others' emotional patterns, we can reason with ourselves when an emotional reaction occurs by looking for patterns that show up in other relationships. When we notice a reoccurring pattern, we have evidence that their emotional reaction is not about us so we don't need to get our feelings hurt or take things personally. We also have the conscious ability to either point out the pattern that we notice, or decide if we want to remain in that relationship. Now if we have inadvertently hurt someone, the best way to handle that is to acknowledge and apologize for our actions. For important relationships, such as with family members or in working with a boss, it is best to remain present and supportive; if you choose to point out the emotional pattern, be very sensitive. Use specific examples, so they can notice the patterns they have been blind to. When you address the emotional patterns in others, they may feel attacked and go into protection mode. Be careful that the language you use does not sound like it comes from a place of blame, but is specific and comprehensible. Do your best to complete the conversation in a way that will enlighten their perspective and encourage their growth.

THE PROCESS OF UNDERSTANDING WHY WE TAKE THINGS PERSONALLY

The purpose of this process will assist you in realizing why you get offended or take things personally.

Consider:

- How have things you have taken personally affected relationships in your life?
- What types of things offend you?
- When you are offended or take something personally, how do you typically react?
- Are there certain subjects in which you are more sensitive?
- When something offends you, what do you interpret to be the other person's intent, connotation, implication, etc.?
- What underlying belief is stimulating the offense?

When you feel offended, do you:

- Blame others?
- Try to "be right" and justify your actions?
- Talk to someone to get them to side with you and enroll them in your drama?
- Lash out?
- Transfer your irritation to someone else not involved in the situation (i.e., spouse, children, neighbor's dog)?
- Withdraw or sulk?
- Act out to draw attention to yourself?

As an experiment this week, notice what offends you. Notice body language, tone, pitch of voice, or facial expressions that trigger you. How does that trigger affect your mood? Figure out why certain things bother you. Go back in your history and determine who in your past has used those same types of gestures. The more conscious you become of your reactive behaviors, you move from powerless to powerful.

Journal any thoughts or ideas that will encourage growth and promote change.

As you begin to recognize the ways in which you take offense or get your feelings hurt, you will start to find empowering ways to free yourself from this limiting practice.

Emotional Validation

Sometimes it is hard to refrain from getting offended or taking things personally because we are always making meanings based on the way we feel.

The Reticular Activating System is held in the thalamus portion of our brain and acts like a bodyguard.

The ongoing activity of assigning meaning and validating the way we feel is largely a function of the part of the brain known as the Reticular Activating System. The Reticular Activating System is held in the thalamus portion of our brain and acts like a bodyguard. As human beings, we are subjected to all kinds of stimuli. The job of this bodyguard is to filter outside information and determine what is relevant to the structures that form our particular reality and what is not. That is why we don't view the world the way the world is. Instead, we view the world the way our Reticular Activating System filters and validates the experiences and interactions around us.

Let's return to some of the amazing discoveries made by Dr. Ramachandran, the inventor of the mirror box, and look at a man he refers to as David. David was thrown through the windshield of a car, and was in a coma for several months. When he awoke, everyone was glad that he appeared to be conscious and able to function well.

When David returned home, he struggled to reconnect to his world. He would say to his parents, "You look like my parents, but you are impostors. This looks like my home, but it is not. I want to go home." When his parents really wanted to connect with David they would go outside and call him on their cell phone, and then David would talk to them and express his concerns. His situation became even more disconcerting when he began to disassociate from himself, talking about himself in third person.

What Dr. Ramachandran discovered was that the neural pathway that connected David's visual cortex to the amygdala had been disrupted in the accident, so David could not emotionally connect to his world through the things that he saw.[1]

Our emotional connections play an essential role in connecting our world to reality. Because David did not emotionally connect to his parents, when he saw them, his perception was, "You are not my parents. You are impostors."

We will distort evidence so that it will fit our feelings, making sense out of things even when they're not true. The emotional mind is always looking for a familiar connection that will validate the meanings we have assigned. A familiar meaning will help us feel safe and adapt to our current environment. However, we must keep in mind that there are times when what is familiar is not going to be particularly safe or productive or true.

---

[1] Rawlence, Christopher. *Nova: Secrets of the Mind*. PBS. Season 29, Episode 3, 23 Oct. 2001. Television.

THE PROCESS OF VALIDATING OUR REALITY

The purpose of this process is to notice the areas in your life where you validate familiar things that blind you from the facts and, consequently, distort the truth and perpetuate unhappiness.

This week, notice the way you make meaning of the things around you.

- In what areas of your life do you distort the truth to fit the way you feel?
- What do those distortions validate?
- How do you formulate your thoughts when validating your feelings?
- How do your thoughts affect your mood?
- How do your feelings affect self-judgment or attitude toward others?
- How do your attitudes affect your behaviors?
- How do your attitudes and behaviors inhibit positive relationships?
- Choose one relationship in your life that you would like to improve. Now look at your perceptions and behaviors towards this person. Name one valuable change you will make to start the process.

Journal any thoughts or ideas that will encourage growth and promote change.

Because our Reticular Activating System filters and validates the familiarity of each emotional experience, giving our personal power away is one of the most common practices of those who are caught in the Victim Addition. The problem is, anytime we are caught in this destructive cycle, we feel powerless to manage, control or change our circumstance. In the next chapter, we will explore more about the powerless feelings that come from two types of victim patterns, and in the chapters ahead we will learn how to overcome them.

Chapter 13

Victim Behavior

"Our greatness lies not so much in being able to remake the world as being able to remake ourselves."

~ Gandhi

I want to emphasize that any time we demonstrate victim behavior, such as when we are hurt, offended, giving in to our fears or fighting to be right, WE ARE GIVING OUR POWER AWAY!

However, we typically don't give our power away because we want to play victim. We are unconsciously giving our power away because we rely on the emotional structures that have served us throughout our life, even when the perceptions we have formed are no longer relevant.

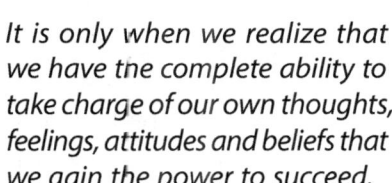

It is only when we realize that we have the complete ability to take charge of our own thoughts, feelings, attitudes and beliefs that we gain the power to succeed.

When we are caught in The Victim Addiction, we give our power over to our circumstances or to others by blaming them for our results. When we make others responsible for our results, we place ourselves in a powerless state, perceiving that others have control over the choices that we make, and limit our ability to progress or change. Similarly, we may blame our circumstances, as if we are subject to what happens to us and have no choice in those matters.

It is only when we realize that we have the complete ability to take charge of our own thoughts, feelings, attitudes and beliefs that we gain the power to succeed.

When an emotional event happens, our unconscious mind throws us into our Emotional Safety Zone to protect us. In this heightened state of survival, we feel victimized, and believe we do not have the power to control the situation. Panic, fear and doubt shield us from having a realistic view of the unconscious ways we give our power away.

In order to take our power back and to be in control of our lives, we must acknowledge that our emotional structures and detrimental beliefs have created an unconscious guardian that distorts our view and victimizes our thoughts, feelings and perceptions. It also limits our ability to form fulfilling relationships.

Remember, any victim behaviors you may resort to were formed many years ago and are natural, fundamental responses that automatically come up when you feel threatened or uncomfortable.

But, we do have a choice. We can identify the thoughts, feelings, attitudes and fear-based beliefs that feed The Victim Addiction. This acknowledgement will assist us in removing our blinders and allow us to move forward in a more energetic, healthy and happy way.

In Tier I, you were introduced to some basic concepts of how The Victim Addiction creates the illusion that we are being victimized. Now, we will dig a little deeper and explore the thoughts, feelings, attitudes and beliefs of two types of emotional victim patterns.

Those are the Faultless Victim Patterns and the Helpless Victim Patterns. A faultless victim unconsciously ignores their feelings and then believes they have the ability to handle their emotions better than others. Their "Reactive" behaviors are always justified, so they feel right in the way they treat others. Because they feel justified in the way they handle things, it is very hard for them to notice their victim patterns. Patterns of a faultless victim will prevent deep emotional connections from occurring.

A helpless victim believes others have control over their happiness and there is nothing they can do about it. Their reactive behaviors come from a place of insecurity and fear. Most helpless victims know they have problems, but feel overwhelmed, and don't know how to manage, control or change their situation. Insecure patterns of a helpless victim will prevent deep emotional connections from occurring.

The following descriptions are not meant as a judgment, but as a tool to help you identify some of the ways you unconsciously give your power away. You may also recognize certain patterns in others,

Victim Behavior

as well. This awareness can be useful in relationships, as it gives you insights into their emotional perceptions.

As you read the descriptions, notice any emotional charge you feel. Be objective with any reactions you may experience. An emotional reaction indicates that there is something you should take a look at. Remember that any one of our ineffective thoughts, feelings, attitudes or beliefs can affect our behavior, so stay curious with the patterns that keep you stuck in an ineffective place.

The following table shows a few examples of how we transfer our personal power outside of ourselves when we are caught in the emotional behaviors of Faultless or Helpless Victim Patterns.

As you read the descriptions in the following categories, do not be concerned if you notice patterns on both side of the spectrum. Just do your best to identify which of the descriptions fit your reactive behavior or trigger an emotional reaction. It is important that you reserve any type of judgment. Remember, any victim behaviors you may resort to were formed many years ago and, at that time in your life, were very useful. Many reactions automatically come up when you feel threatened or uncomfortable, without conscious effort to do so. Often, these protective reactions become habits and have a prominent presence in the way you view the world. Be careful to not make yourself wrong for your behaviors. Instead, simply recognize the ways that you have structured your perceptions have limited your ability to establish the deep connections that form secure loving relationships.

It is only by examining your patterns without judgment that you find the power to change.

THE PROCESS OF FAULTLESS/ HELPLESS PATTERNS

The purpose of this process is to assist you in observing the unconscious reactions that automatically occur when you are caught in the emotional patterns of a Faultless/Helpless Victim.

	Faultless Defensive Patterns	Helpless Defensive Patterns
Behaviors	Seeks power and control Goes into fight/reactive mode Independent Creates win/lose scenarios Is focused on flaws in others Blames others Demands respect Doesn't communicate needs	Seeks acceptance and approval Flees or withdraws Dependent/co-dependent Compares Is focused on own flaws Blames self Never says "no" Always apologizing
Thoughts	It's not my problem If others would just listen to me… You should have done it my way I do what I want My way or the highway Others are incompetent I don't care what they think	I shouldn't have Why don't they support me? I can't do anything right I don't know how What was I supposed to do? If I were more…. I wonder if I offended them.
Feels	Blameless Justified Angry Defensive Resentful	Feels sorry for him/herself Afraid to try Defeated Accused Unworthy
Attitudes	Arrogant Demands respect Competitive (win/lose) Superior Self-righteous	Powerless to circumstance Needy Doormat Inferior Silent martyr
Beliefs	I'm right, you're wrong I am owed I am perfect I am better than…	I am less than I am not good enough I am unworthy I am a burden

To determine which patterns create an uncomfortable emotional charge, ask yourself the following questions:

- Which descriptions triggered an emotional reaction in you?

- How have these emotional reactions influenced your perception of yourself?
- Have they changed the way you view others?
- Where do you give your power away to these types of patterns?
- How have these victim patterns affected your relationships?
- Is the way you perceive certain things in your current environment keeping you in these victim patterns?

Journal any thoughts or ideas that will encourage growth and promote change.

Giving your power away to The Victim Addiction is an unfulfilling, powerless place to live. Because The Victim Addiction is unconscious, some people live their whole lives never feeling truly loved or accepted by others and have no idea why.

We can only love and accept others at the level we are willing to love and accept ourselves.

Acknowledging and consciously processing the subtle ways we unconsciously give our power away to The Victim Addiction will give us the ability to implement the necessary changes to move forward and create the life we desire.

Let's now look at the other side of giving our power away to The Victim Addiction, where we have the freedom to create what we want through Living an Accountable Life.

Tier III

The Power of Living an Accountable Life

"The moment we take accountability for the choices we are making that have led to our results is the moment everything in our lives can change."

~ Victoria Lee Carlyle

The Power of Living an Accountable Life

In Tier III, we learn to experience the Power of Living an Accountable Life.

We saw in Tier I the value of becoming curious in order to develop Self-Awareness. In Tier II, we explored how to start applying that awareness to achieve the Power to Change.

Now, in this tier, we gain an understanding of the freedom that accompanies living an accountable life and how it will serve us as we take another step toward greater personal power.

Some have misinterpreted accountability to mean we are responsible for every event that occurs in our lives. but, accountability is not about guilt or self-blame. Instead, it is about getting out of the powerless feelings that come from blame and justifications. When we do so, we take ownership for our lives and have the complete power to direct our thoughts, feelings, attitudes and beliefs and become the master of our emotions.

Chapter 14

Accountability

The Triple-Filter Test

In ancient Greece, Socrates was reputed to hold knowledge in high esteem. One day an acquaintance met the great philosopher and said, "Do you know what I just heard about your friend?"

"Hold on a minute," Socrates replied. "Before you talk to me about my friend, it might be good idea to take a moment and filter what you're going to say. I call it the triple-filter test. The first filter is Truth. Have you made absolutely sure that what you are about to tell me is true?"

"Well, no," the man said, "actually I just heard about it and..."

Accountability is not about guilt or self-blame. Instead, it is about getting out of the powerless feelings that come from blame and justifications.

"All right," said Socrates. "So you don't really know if it's true or not. Now, let's try the second filter, the filter of Goodness. Is what you are about to tell me about my friend something good?"

"Umm, no, on the contrary..."

"So," Socrates continued, "you want to tell me something bad about my friend, but you're not certain it's true. You may still pass the test, though, because there's one filter left—the filter of Usefulness. Is what you want to tell me about my friend going to be useful to me?"

"No, not really."

"Well," concluded Socrates, "if what you want to tell me is neither true, nor good, nor even useful, why tell it to me at all?"[1]

This story represents the stark difference between a person who lives an accountable life and one who gets caught in the powerless patterns of The Victim Addiction.

---

[1] Socrates' *Test of Three*.

When we are caught in The Victim Addiction, we compromise our integrity and the integrity of others through gossip. We also place ourselves in compromising situations as we fight to be right and blame others for our attitudes and behaviors, which ultimately limits our ability to change.

The good news is, we can take a more effective stance by choosing the freedom that comes as we adopt an accountable lifestyle.

What is accountability and why is it so important?

Accountability is having the skills and determination to take ownership for the choices we make and, in so doing, direct the results we produce. When we take full accountability for our lives and our choices, we gain power over the situations we encounter and are no longer a victim of circumstances.

As we become increasingly more accountable, we also have more respect for the fact that others have stewardship over the choices they make as well. This understanding will help us realize that we only have the ability to influence, not control others' thoughts, feelings, attitudes, actions or beliefs.

When we take full accountability for our lives and our choices, we gain power over the situations we encounter and are no longer a victim of circumstances.

We then gain the ability to powerfully move from the *Unconscious Victim* to being *Consciously Accountable*, as we perceive life in an entirely new way.

An accountable person recognizes that they have the conscious ability to produce the results they want in every area of their lives.

Accountability includes looking at effective and ineffective choices we have made, then taking that information and using it to produce results that will create a happier life.

Effective Choices are those that create peace and happiness in our lives and in the lives of those around us.

Ineffective Choices are those that produce angst, frustration or discouragement in our lives and in the lives of those around us.

If an accountable person is dissatisfied with their job, they will define exactly what it is that they are not satisfied with. They will then take ownership for the choices that they have made and take the necessary action to create the results they desire.

For example, an accountable person named Joe may decide a mere attitude shift on his part is all it will take to create the work environment he seeks. This attitude shift might show up as he steps out of his comfort zone, while encouraging and uplifting others with a simple smile, words of praise or a helpful hand.

Or for Jane, who is also acting accountably, taking ownership may mean stepping out of fear by asking those in charge of the position she desires what type of education she would need to advance. She would then follow their advice, taking the required certification course or additional schooling. Victims remain stuck in their circumstances because they feel unable to alter the choices they are making.

Becoming accountable for the choices you make will give you the power to change your life. When you take full accountability for the choices you make, you ultimately create better relationships.

As an accountable person, you know that others' reactions are not about you, and you do not need to own or react to their ineffective emotional patterns or accept their blame.

Accountability gives you the choice to fully love, trust, and forgive yourself. It also gives you the ability to love, trust and forgive others as well. This freedom allows you to experience the inner peace and happiness that comes from living from your own personal power.

Let's contrast the patterns of those who allow themselves to unconsciously feel victimized, and those who choose to be accountable for their actions and results.

Unconscious Victim Language	Conscious Accountable Language
It wasn't my fault.	I made a mistake.
I didn't do it.	What choices did I make that added to this circumstance? What have I learned that will help me in future choices?
It's not my problem.	Let's work together to figure this out
What was I supposed to do?	Thank you! I'll do things differently next time.
It was an accident.	What can I learn?
That's not what I meant.	I have not communicated properly.
This is too hard.	I am equal to the task.
I'm lost. I don't know what to do.	I have all the resources I need to do this.
I don't know what to say.	Let's look at alternatives.

Accountability is taking ownership for all the choices you make that create your results.

The following list helps to clarify accountable behavior even further.

An accountable person is:

Character	Solution-oriented. Interdependent / involves others to accomplish their goals. Open and honest. Looks at the whole picture. Stays neutral. Accepts their worth and values others. Stays out of the blame game. Is willing to engage in uncomfortable conversations, when needed for clarification and solutions. Can honestly express feelings and opinions, even when they differ from those of others'.
Feel	Balanced Confident Empathetic
Thoughts	"This is not personal." "What is under the reaction?" "Why am I feeling this way?" "Are my feelings in alignment with my values and beliefs?"
Attributes	Takes ownership for past, present, and future results. Consciously deciphers facts from feelings. Knows they have the ability to create what they want. Has the sense of confidence to move forward.
Behaviors	Is present and interested in others. Generates positive action. Demonstrates the ability to identify and direct their own emotional responses. Separates themselves from others' behavioral patterns. Does not take the reactions of others personally. Is kind and compassionate to human frailties. Chooses to feel and express gratitude and appreciation.

THE PROCESS OF ACCOUNTABILITY

The purpose of this process is to increase your understanding of how to take personal ownership for the choices you make that directly affect your emotional life.

During a challenge or when you're upset, ask yourself:

- What choices did I make that contributed to the problem?
- Am I honestly expressing what I want others to hear or are my emotions clouding my communication?
- In what circumstances can I be a better listener?
- Am I open minded to the perspectives and ideas of others?
- Do I need to forgive or ask for forgiveness?
- What considerations am I overlooking?
- Am I open to the feedback of others?
- How can I inspire people to be their best?
- How can I successfully achieve my goals?
- What is working with the way I approach the situation?
- Where in my life am I generating positive results?
- What opportunities can I create?
- How can I inspire growth in my life and the lives of others?
- What can I learn?
- What do I appreciate about this situation?

Journal any thoughts or ideas that will encourage growth and promote change.

Chapter 15

Conscious Choice

"Greatness is not a function of circumstance. Greatness, it turns out, is largely a matter of conscious choice."

~ Jim Collins

Through the help of brain-imaging techniques, neuroscience has proven that, following any kind of stimulus, we have six seconds before our brain's automatic responses take effect. This means that many of our decisions occur several seconds before we are consciously aware of our choices or the resulting actions.

In *Man's Search for Meaning*, Viktor Frankl states: "Between stimulus and response, there is a space. In that space is our power to choose our response. In our response lies our growth and our freedom."

It is during that pause or gap that our conscious choice can occur.

What is Conscious Choice?

Conscious choice is the ability to override our automatic emotional reactions and our current emotional state, and instead respond in a productive manner.

The six-second space occurs between the time we are triggered and the chemical release in our brain that activates our physical and emotional response. It is only when we control those six seconds that we have the conscious ability to direct our thoughts and emotions that ultimately create our results.

That pause or gap is where our freedom lies; this is the place that conscious choice can occur.

True growth and freedom come when we gain the conscious ability to choose the emotional life we want to live. The following story reminds us that mastering our emotions is a lifelong choice worth making.

The Wolves Within

A young man, who was angry after a friend had offended him, went to talk to his grandfather about it.

"Let me tell you a story," the old grandfather said. "I, too, at times, have felt a great hate for those who have taken much, with no sorrow for what they do, but hate wears you down and does not hurt your enemy. It is like taking poison and wishing your enemy would die. I have struggled with these feelings many times," he continued, "It is as if there are two wolves inside me. One is good and does no harm. He lives in harmony with all around him, and does not take offense. He will only challenge others when it is right to do so, and in the right way."

"But the other wolf, ah! He is full of anger. The littlest thing will set him into a fit of rage. He fights everyone, all the time, for no reason. He cannot think because his anger and hate are so great. It is helpless anger, for his anger will change nothing." "Sometimes, it is hard to live with these two wolves inside me, for both of them try to direct my life."

The boy looked intently into his grandfather's eyes and asked, "Grandfather, which wolf will win?"

The Grandfather smiled and quietly said, "The one that I feed."[1]

There are times when giving into the emotional behaviors of others is easy, but what we don't realize is, every time we mindlessly react, we pay a price. When we give in to our triggers and let our emotions control our actions, life can seem confusing and, at times, may even feel out of control. In fact, when we are in this unconscious place and feel hurt, abandoned or betrayed, it is hard not to give our power away to the biological urge to react.

The sad thing is anytime we are caught in these types of reactions, we lose sight of the choices we could be making that would change our course for the better.

I understand how living your life in constant reaction can feel. When I was growing up, the thought that I could choose the way I felt about myself or my circumstances was inconceivable. I viewed myself as broken and needing to be fixed. In fact, because I was

---

[1] Cherokee Indian Legend: *The Two Wolves Within*.

Conscious Choice

treated so insignificantly, I lived most my life afraid of the world and afraid of myself. I felt insecure and, at times, needed someone—anyone—to say, "Victoria, you are okay"—because I didn't feel okay. I felt powerless and hopelessly alone. Unknowingly, I had given my happiness over to this powerless feeling, to the point that I didn't even realize how I had been placing myself in positions and tolerating things that only validated how insignificant I believed myself to be.

Freedom came when I realized I wasn't, and had never been, broken or powerless. No one was taking my power from me; I was giving my power away to my feelings and circumstances.

> *Freedom came when I realized, I wasn't—and had never been broken or powerless. No one was taking my power from me I was giving my power away to my feelings and circumstances.*

All the blame, justifications and denial I used to cope with my situations perpetuated this powerless state, and I honestly believed that I didn't have a choice. What I have come to realize is that I didn't need to be fixed. The power to change the helpless way I felt was always within my reach.

I finally understood that I had a choice, I could either continue to feel powerless or I could go inside, face my fears and change my life for the better. I discovered that underneath all that fear and pain was the inner strength I needed to rise above my circumstances and create a peaceful, well-balanced life.

Processing the way I had structured events in my early childhood has given me the capacity to view all the heartache and pain I have experienced as a teaching tool—guiding me to the courage I needed to access my personal power. I now know I can set boundaries around the way I want to be treated. I get to choose who and what enters my life, the home I live in, and the people I love. I also have the ability to create a rich, fulfilling and happy life.

The power to access the inner strength needed to succeed is not just in me, it is in every one of us! We simply have to realize that there will be times when life will not be easy or fair, but we will always have the power to make things better.

Even when the emotions of our circumstances cloud our perspective and override our ability to cope.

I experienced circumstances like that when Tristan and I divorced; I was totally devastated. Because my feelings were so intense, I spent a lot of time concentrating on the "all too familiar" evidence of my childhood belief system. I had a hard time moving on.

I allowed myself to get into a mindless place, where my emotions would inadvertently control my thoughts, feelings, attitudes and beliefs. The pain I felt only perpetuated the cycle.

> I look at this situation in my life as priceless. I have consciously chosen to concentrate on how he loved me, and the beautiful memories that we created, and not how he left me.

To stop this self-defeating pattern, I had a choice to make. I could spend a lifetime mourning the loss of a love I thought would last forever, or I could consciously choose to look at the experience in a way that would allow me to move forward.

I now acknowledge how Tristan's tender love healed me in ways that may not have occurred without his deep, if only temporary, love for me.

Even though this relationship did not last very long, healing from the loss of something I had waited so long to find took time. Now I look at this situation in my life as priceless. I have consciously chosen to concentrate on how he *loved* me, and the beautiful memories that we created, and not how he *left* me.

There are many beautiful moments in life that are worth holding on to, but when we are hurt we unconsciously focus on the pain. If we face the pain and give ourselves permission to mourn, as well as time to process and heal from our losses. We can hold on to what we want and let go of the rest. Treasuring these precious moments can give us the strength and motivation, and even excitement to move on to create something new.

As I have chosen to view this experience with a fresh perspective, everything has shifted and my confidence in creating another relationship that includes what I had with Tristan has increased.

Now I find joy in the fact that his love for me was real. In addition, I know that because I created that kind of love before, I have the ability to create that kind of love again.

One of my favorite sayings is: "Gratitude turns what you have into enough." I am grateful for the power I have to effectively choose a perspective that will support a revitalizing transformation as I move in an exciting new direction.

Effective and Ineffective Choices Defined

When we make effective choices, we will produce a life filled with benefits that we enjoy.

With ineffective choices, we will pay the price and remain confined to our circumstances. Consider the following consequences to the following choices:

Effective: If I work as an equal partner to create a loving relationship, I will enjoy the benefits of that relationship.

Ineffective: If I concentrate more on getting my needs met than on being an equal partner in a relationship I may feel lonely and unsatisfied in virtually every relationship I encounter.

Effective: If I eat right and exercise, I will enjoy the benefits of healthy living.

Ineffective: If I don't care what I eat or put harmful things into my body, sooner or later it will affect my energy, mood and eventually my health.

Effective: If I pay my bills on time and save money, I will enjoy the benefits and security of financial wellbeing.

Ineffective: When I buy what I want when I want it, even when I don't have the money I will create anxiety and stress that will affect every area of my life.

Effective: If I dedicate myself to working hard in my career, I will enjoy many benefits, including confidence, security, respect, etc., which come from being successful.

Ineffective: When I take my job for granted or rationalize lazy work habits because the company isn't very fair to my anyway, or I believe that others are always getting promoted ahead of me and getting all the breaks, so I don't even try—I will make it hard to find and keep a job. These habits will also affect my financial security and emotional wellbeing.

We must remember that emotional patterns show up in every area of our lives. If we are happy with our lives, it will reflect in the way we interact with those around us.

The opposite is true as well. We can continue on the path of unconsciously giving our power away to helpless emotions that will take much and give nothing in return, but by so doing, that energy will transfer into other areas of our lives.

> *No matter what kind of trials we face, exercising our power to choose our thoughts, feelings, attitudes, behaviors and beliefs will give us all the resources we need to live a happy and productive life.*

No matter what type of circumstances you face or are born into, gaining an understanding of the power to consciously choose your results will generate greater confidence in choosing the direction of your life!

To create the life that you want, you must look at the choices you have made that have gotten you to this point. When you refuse to take accountability for the choices you make, you lose the power to manage, control or change your situation.

Accepting the choices you have made will give you the opportunity to celebrate the things in your life you enjoy while acknowledging the results that you wish to change. Accountability gives you the power to create something new.

Even if the circumstances seem out of your control, such as a terminal illness that is affecting you or a loved one, controlling your overwhelming emotions can be helpful. Plus, the feel good chemicals that will be released can reduce your pain and give you hope. Do your best to get out of your fears and focus on what you can manage and control. You don't have to face your trials alone; reach out and let others comfort and love you through this time in your life.

No matter what kind of trials we face, exercising our power to choose our thoughts, feelings, attitudes and behaviors will give us all the resources we need to overcome our fears and live a happy life.

Chapter 16

Accumulating Evidence To Conquer Our Fears

"Ultimately, we know deeply that the other side of every fear is freedom."
~Marilyn Ferguson

As discussed in the previous chapter, developing the ability to consciously choose the direction you go will yield many wonderful benefits. As you fine tune the ability to consciously intervene in your emotional reactions, the rewards will increase and you will find even greater strength to surpass your fears and step into your personal power. Below is a simple four-step process that will assist you in redirecting your emotional energy and overcoming your fears.

The four simple steps are: Notice, Interrupt, Question, and Analyze.

1. Notice your emotional reaction.

2. Interrupt the reaction by using a statement that will redirect your focus. An example might be: "Up until now I would have given my power to anger, feeling hurt or frustrated, etc., but I don't want to let my emotions run me anymore so I choose to take a breath and go for a walk." Remember, you have six seconds of conscious thought before the chemicals in your brain override your ability to think or act clearly. By consciously directing your energy, you can change the types of chemicals being released into your system, giving you the power to stay calm and create the results you desire.

3. Once you have redirected your energy and feel calm, question the validity and relevance of your reaction.
   - What triggered my reaction?
   - Was I hurt or offended? Did I take something personally?

- How have the thoughts I interrupted been perpetuating my reactions?
- How would I normally react to situations like this?
- How have I justified my reactions in the past?
- In my reaction, how did I view myself and what was my view of others?
- What am I afraid of?
- How has my reaction altered the facts?

4. Once you have a good understanding of your reaction, realistically analyze your thoughts, feelings, attitudes and beliefs and consciously decide how you will think, feel, and act in the future. Remember, it is essential that, when triggered, your initial focus be on stopping the past event from altering your perspective. This is an important concept that will empower you with the ability to choose how you will interact with those around you. It's an important concept to master if you want to live a well-balanced life. Take some time to ponder the kind of impact you are going to have and what you are going to represent in your life.

I recently spoke with a young man who, while incarcerated, began to apply the principles from the four steps described above.

He shared some of the discoveries he had made. He noticed that anytime he felt criticized, judged, attacked or disrespected he would feel angry and would fight back. Anytime he felt rejected or treated like he was stupid, irrelevant or inferior, he experienced deep feelings of insecurity and would feel lost.

Once he noticed his emotional reactions, he was able to apply step three and ask himself why he was feeling and acting the way he was.

This made it possible for him to identify experiences in his life that led up to the choices he had made, that had contributed to his angry reactions and feelings of rejection.

The awareness he received gave him the capacity to intervene, and he did so with determination.

Whenever he noticed his anger stirring, or if he felt like he was being rejected, he interrupted his thoughts with statements such as, "I can understand why I felt that way as a child, but I'm not a child and I don't have to feel that way anymore;" or "No one is forcing me to resent everyone and everything. My feelings come from the way I was treated as a child, my parents did the best they could with the background they had;" or, "The anger I am feeling is not about what is going on right now. It is tied to the past and holding on to that is only hurting me."

By repeating statements like these and looking at the choices he had made that produced his misery, he was able to have a realistic view of his circumstance and of the situations that had occurred in his life. This view changed the way he felt about himself.

He replaced his blame and justifications with self-trust, self-worth and self-confidence.

Consciously choosing how he wants to respond has completely changed his outlook on life. His heart not only changed, but he felt others around him were treating him differently, reinforcing the positive direction his life was headed. This change also gave him the desire to do something productive with the remainder of his time in prison. He enrolled in a course and is learning a trade that will help him create a successful life.

This young man had the courage to face the painful truth that he was the one creating his challenges. He became accountable for his outcomes.

He has now replaced his blame and justifications with self-trust, self-worth and self-confidence. He says, for the first time in his adult life, he has confidence in his ability to succeed and has true hope for the future.

This young man gave me permission to use his story, but with one condition, and that was that I include one important point. He says he was in the worst place he had ever been in. He hated the world and he hated himself. He felt abandoned and was angrily blaming everybody for everything. He had given up all hope and got to the point that he was fighting to die. Then one day he was too tired to fight and began questioning the detrimental way he talked to himself. The more curious he became to learn about himself, the easier it became to see the ways that he had created his own misery. Every time he noticed himself reacting, he pondered why it seemed he had always felt the way he did. At first, it was frustrating to try to stop his overwhelming thoughts, but the more he questioned and intervened with his emotional reactions, the easier it became. Journaling his thoughts made it easier for him to see how illogical his perceptions had become. He started by listening to his self-talk and noticing how the different thoughts made him feel and react.

Then he began to question his thoughts and contain the automatic urge to fight back. The more he did this, the easier it became. As his confidence grew, he became better at looking for what was right in his life instead of what was wrong. This shift ignited a desire to be happy and do what he could to encourage others' happiness.

Most importantly, he praises God for the emotional shift that has occurred. He says if God can love and forgive him after all the mistakes he has made, then it is okay for him to love and forgive himself. Now that he truly loves himself, it has become much easier to love and forgive others. He has become a positive force for good as he serves those who are discouraged around him.

Evidence for Change

Interestingly enough, when the emotional mind perceives that something will make us feel good or that something resonates as "more true" for us than our current beliefs, an emotional shift can occur in an instant.

While I was working toward my psychology degree, I studied a story about a motivational speaker named W. Mitchell. His story describes how instantaneous an emotional shift can be.

Mitchell was one of those silent military heroes who worked to defend our country. When a motorcycle accident left him badly burned, it was hard for him to face the world. Children were afraid of him and called him a monster. Mitchell moved to the small town of Butte, Colorado. Being the humorous guy that he is, people were drawn to him and he made friends quickly in his new home.

He piloted his own plane and, occasionally, he would take morning flights with his friends.

One morning, just after takeoff, he noticed that the engine didn't sound right. He turned the plane around and made an extremely rough landing. When the plane came to a stop, he shouted for his friends to quickly get out of the plane. When they were all safe, they began to encourage him to get out as well. It was then that he realized he couldn't move.

He was rushed to the hospital where he learned he had broken several vertebrae in his lower back and would never walk again. He had a choice to make.

He decided to see his circumstance not as a setback, but as a starting point and he began physical therapy so he could learn to maneuver in his new life.

> *He had a choice to make. He decided to see his circumstance not as a setback but as a starting point.*

As he tells the story, "Every day, Beverly, my physical therapist, would be waiting for me. She would have her clipboard, with five impossible things for me to do that day. Every day, I would leave her room feeling a little more confident about my abilities."

He continued, "One day, after I had accomplished my five tasks for the day, Beverly wanted me to learn how to transfer from the wheelchair to the couch. Now I could understand the value in transferring from the wheelchair to the bathtub, or from the wheelchair to a plane seat, but to transfer from the wheelchair to the couch made no sense." He said, "I thought, 'This is stupid! I am not going to do it! *I already have a comfortable place to sit!* I don't need to sit on the couch!'"

The wheelchair-to-couch transfer is one of the hardest transfers. The couch is always lower than the wheelchair, so you can fall onto the couch. However, when you try to transfer back to the wheelchair, the couch cushion gives so much, it is difficult to get enough leverage to lift yourself high enough, to get back into the wheelchair.

The next day after his five tasks were completed, Beverly put her arm around his shoulder and said, "Mitchell, let's work on transferring to the couch."

Mitchell said, "Beverly, I'm not going to do it. This is stupid and you can't make me!"

Beverly said "Mitchell, calm down! You have discussed a special relationship you have formed here in the hospital. I know you hope to continue this relationship when you go home. The way I see it, there will be two places you will get close to your sweetheart. One will be in bed and you already know how to do that, the other will be on the couch. I suspect the couch will come first."

"Five minutes! It took me five minutes! On the couch, off the couch, on the couch, off the couch, I don't know if you saw me, I was the one in the Special Olympics wearing the gold medal for the wheelchair-to-couch transfer."[1]

Once the emotional mind makes a shift and connects to a stronger emotional reality, phenomenal change can happen in an instant.

More often than not, the mindless way we go about life ultimately gets in the way of shifts that will change these familiar patterns. We run on automatic pilot, never even questioning why we do some of the illogical things that we do. A simple example of this can be found in a silly story about the young mother who, every time she cooked a ham, would cut the ends off before she placed it in the oven. One day, her little girl asked her why she did that. She said she had no idea. She supposed it was because her own mother used to do it. Now curious, the young mother called her mother to ask why she cut the ends off the ham before cooking it. Her mother thought about it for a moment and responded that she didn't know why either, but that's what her mother had done. In turn, she called her mother to ask why. As she posed the question, her mother began to laugh and said, "I always cut the ends off so the ham would fit into the pan I had to cook it in."

This young mother did what she saw her mother do without even thinking. She only questioned her actions when her child asked why.

This kind of blindness and the ability to "go with the flow" is valuable when we are children because it leaves us open to exploring

---

[1] *"W Mitchell - International Keynote Speaker Author National and Business Leader Triumphant Victor."* N.p., n.d. Web. 2012.

a variety of new things and different ways to approach life. Yet, as discussed earlier, we soon begin to experience hurt and disappointments and we anchor to various painful events. Our fears increase, and we cautiously structure our worldview accordingly.

When we become mindful of the ways our ineffective structuring has affected our approach to life, we gain the ability to direct our thoughts, feelings, attitudes, and beliefs in a way that will support the life that we want to live.

Because we are wired to avoid feeling uncomfortable, we let fear hold us back, and we retreat into the familiarity of our Emotional Safety Zone.

As we attempt to restructure things from our past, some anchors will release in an instant, while others will require time. We can manage and hasten the change process by consciously intervening and applying reoccurring evidence for change to occur.

It bears repeating here that the natural effects of change can be uncomfortable because we are seeking to restructure anchors that, more often than not, have been reinforced thousands of times. These anchors were also established at times in our lives when we were feeling uncomfortable or experiencing pain. When we are triggered, we are reminded of that recorded frustration and pain which has been reinforced over and over again.

Because we are wired to avoid feeling uncomfortable, we let what we are feeling hold us back, and we unconsciously retreat into the familiarity of our Emotional Safety Zone. It is more comfortable to live with what is familiar to us rather than facing the temporary discomfort of change. Fear stops us from exploring new options that would accelerate our growth; it is also what stops us from taking chances.

Remember, part of the reason we experience ineffective results in our lives is because the unconscious emotional patterns directing our behaviors are so familiar that we do not notice them. Even when are conscious of destructive behaviors such as having a bad temper, the familiarity will make our perception of our behaviors seem normal.

These justifications will keep us blind to the ways we could change our behavior.

In order to create lasting change in our lives, we must shift our emotional perceptions.

Once the emotional mind has sufficient evidence, it will surrender. In fact, with sufficient evidence, it becomes more uncomfortable to remain the same than it will be to change.

We literally have the power to create anything we want. The key is to consciously notice our triggers and become aware of our ineffective patterns. One of my first realizations of this power came after the emotional hijacking I described earlier, when the two women in the seminar with me were angry with each other.

After I was triggered, I took the opportunity to question my fears and reactions to the anger in the room. When I began to sort out my feelings, I realized emotional and behavioral patterns from childhood fears were influencing my behavior and limiting my security and growth. In that seminar, I was reacting more to my fear from unsafe environments of the past, than to what was actually happening at that moment. I perceived imminent danger and reacted accordingly, even though I was perfectly safe. I was only able to create lasting change by noticing my triggers and becoming consciously aware of all the evidence I had gathered throughout my life. Once I understood the impact my childhood fear of anger had on my adult life, I was able to realistically separate my fears from other events in my life involving anger. Restructuring the fears around anger allowed me to question the evidence involving anger in a realistic way. Once I could consciously question my reactions, I was able to logically find evidence that I was safe and had nothing to fear. Although my fear of anger had been obstructing my emotional growth for years, my fears were so familiar they seemed normal and my automatic reaction caused immediate avoidance so I never noticed them. Questioning how childishly frightened I became around anger was the beginning of accumulating evidence to conquer my fear. Because I had so many anchors structured around anger, it took a while of consciously interrupting the automatic effects before I was able to stop my physiological reaction enough to feel comfortable in situations involving anger.

Accumulating Evidence to Conquer Our Fears

Have you ever noticed the automatic effects that occur with things you tend to avoid? Why do we have to experience discouraging results over and over again before we feel the urge to change?

Most of the time, as in the example above, the effects have to be extremely blatant for us to notice them and for emotional change to occur. Many of our emotional shifts will require repetitious evidence before the shift actually takes place, but once an emotional shift occurs, there is no going back.

An episode of "Law and Order" demonstrates the concept of how evidence must be repeated to achieve the conscious awareness needed for an emotional change to occur.

In this particular episode, the detectives were trying to convince a woman to cooperate with them so they could lock an influential cult leader behind bars. He was very intelligent and used others to do his dirty work so he could never be implicated.

Many of our emotional shifts will require repetitious evidence before the shift actually takes place, but once an emotional shift occurs, there is no going back.

For years, the leader had been extorting the woman out of millions of dollars and was now trying to gain access to her daughter's inheritance.

The investigators tried everything they knew to get this woman to cooperate but the woman was completely convinced that the cult leader was a good, loving man and all the evidence they had against him was a lie.

She explained that when her husband had an affair with another woman in the convent and left 10 years earlier, this "loving" cult leader took her and her young daughter in and, for all these years, had loved them both and raised her child as his own. The child, now 14, was carrying this so-called "good man's" child. The mother seemed fine with it. The cult leader had an ulterior motive. He knew pregnancy before age 21 meant the daughter would be eligible to collect her inheritance and he figured, with that money, the mother and daughter could continue to generously pay him for his kindness toward them.

Through their investigation, the team found her husband's body. He had been shot execution-style 10 years earlier. They told her of their findings and showed her a picture of his remains. She still did not believe what they were saying was true. The cult leader had told her the police would say things to set him up, and she was determined they were not going to use her to frame this man she had come to love and trust.

When they showed her the wallet they had found on the body, she began questioning her reality. *It was her husband's wallet,* and it was just as she had remembered it from 10 years earlier. Yet, the feelings she had for the cult leader were strong, and she still did not want to believe that what the detectives were saying was true, even with the evidence right in front of her.

Then the detective asked, "Why do you think your husband had an affair?"

She began to explain that before he left, he got real close to a woman, and she always saw the two of them doing things together. She didn't think much of it until the day they both disappeared.

The cult leader had told her he was sorry to be the bearer of bad news. He said her husband and the other woman had run off together and he didn't think they were coming back. The leader was very attentive to her needs and the needs of her child as she mourned the loss of her marriage. The leader became her new loving provider and she began to rely on him for emotional support and trusted him completely.

The detective explained that the leader had put her husband and the woman together on purpose, so she would believe the affair story when they disappeared. His motives were not loving or kind at all. He knew he could more easily access the millions of dollars he wanted if her husband was out of the way.

Then the detective said, "You think your husband had an affair? Your husband didn't cheat on you. He was faithful to you till the day he died. Your husband died with this on his finger," he added as he handed her husband's wedding ring to her. She held the ring she had given him on their wedding day. With all the evidence the detectives had presented to her, this final piece of physical evidence was enough to comprehend things as they really were and her devotions toward this man made an immediate shift. She could finally see how everything she had believed for the past 10 years was a lie.

Many emotional shifts take a lot of evidence which can happen over time, perhaps years.

In this example, the facts continued to be presented until there were enough logical facts to create a different awareness. Once we have enough evidence and comprehend how our current reality is skewed, an emotional shift occurs in an instant.

When I began to sort out my feelings, I realized emotional and behavioral patterns from illogical childhood fears were influencing my behavior and limiting my security and growth.

The woman felt so safe and secure she never once considered the fact that her husband and his new love never touched a penny of the money she and her husband had acquired throughout the years.

This woman's experience is a perfect example of how our feelings and perceptions can blind us from noticing facts that would otherwise assist us in our continued growth.

It can be painful when we have to face the realistic fact that some of the ways we have always viewed the world has been distorted. At first, this skewed reality can create confusion because we haven't determined the best way to move forward.

Because you feel uncomfortable, it may seem a little cumbersome to disturb the familiar patterns you have structured. Yet, once you get out of the confusion, you gain the freedom to consciously choose how you want to think, feel and act. When you take back your personal power, your energy will rise and it will become much simpler to structure a reality that feels empowering.

Your happiness and personal growth is worth the time and effort it will take to interrupt the automatic reactions that occur when you are triggered. After you interrupt your reactions realistically, analyze the facts, stop the distortions and consciously decide the kind of life you are willing to create.

Accumulating evidence to conquer your fears will open the door to endless possibilities.

Chapter 17

Restructuring

*"There is no passion to be found in playing small —
in settling for a life that is less than the one you are capable of living."*
~ Nelson Mandela

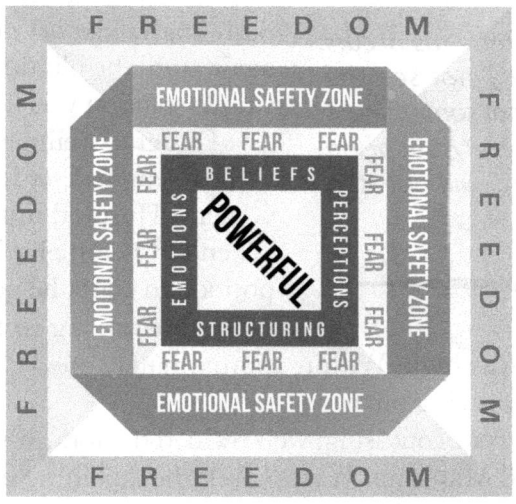

RESTRUCTURING

The Victim Addiction is an unconscious, invisible force that controls our behaviors and takes our power away. We've seen how this invisible force—also known as our Emotional Safety Zone—locks us in emotional structures and fear-based beliefs and how those structures and beliefs can distort our perceptions.

Taking down the self-imposed walls of our Emotional Safety Zone begins with restructuring a new, more empowering reality. Yet, as we discussed in the previous chapters, sometimes the warning signs we need to acknowledge are so familiar we don't even notice them.

When a computer virus occurs, you may or may not see the warning signs that something is not working properly, but being blind to the virus will not stop the damage.

Similarly, when faulty structures continue to run in the background of your mind, the entire system will be affected until you rigorously analyze, process and restructure the details of the ineffective patterns.

The following story illustrates how one man was faced with an invisible power that was creating catastrophic results, and rigorously analyzed every detail again and again until the blindness lifted and a simple solution was found.

> When a computer virus occurs, you may or may not see the warning signs that something is not working properly, but being blind to the virus will not stop the damage.

Dr. Ignaz Semmelweis was head of the research department at Vienna General Hospital in the mid-1800s. When Dr. Semmelweis acquired his position in 1846, he noticed the mortality rate among women in Maternity Ward 1 was high. Within approximately one year, 451 women had died after giving birth.

This was very confusing; well-trained doctors and resident physicians attended Maternity Ward 1. Yet, the adjoining unit, Maternity Ward 2, where the midwives practiced, had a lower death rate of only 90 during the same amount of time. Vienna General had such a frightening reputation women would actually give birth on the street to avoid going into Maternity Ward 1.

In the mid-1800s, there were many theories about medical science. They believed each symptom required a separate treatment. Inflammation meant there was too much blood, so they would perform a bloodletting procedure. They would treat fevers with leeches and would address breathing problems with more ventilation.

The problem was, in Maternity Ward 1, none of the theories they tried ever worked to lower the death rate. More than half of the women who gave birth there contracted "childbed fever" and died within days.

After some time, the agreed theory was that the childbed fever deaths were caused by "an invisible poisonous gas that only certain people are vulnerable to." This, to Dr. Semmelweis, was completely illogical.

He became obsessed with the problem and, trying to get to the bottom of it, standardized everything in both wards, including all aspects of the deliveries, from diet and birthing positions to how the rooms were cleaned. He even standardized the detergents used on the linens. Everything was exactly the same in both environments, but the mortality rates did not improve.

In the midst of this dilemma, Dr. Semmelweis took a four-month leave of absence to visit another hospital. Upon his return, he learned, in his absence, the death rate had fallen significantly. Feeling that he was part of the problem, he became even more rigorous in finding a solution.

The fact that the mortality rate had declined in his absence caused him to consciously look at his own practices.

He realized he spent far more time than the other doctors did doing research on cadavers. He began to link the possible significance of the lab research using cadavers, to the death rate. He immediately instituted a policy requiring all physicians to thoroughly wash their hands in a solution of chlorine and lime before leaving the laboratory. The death rate fell to 1 in 100.

At that point in history, conventional medical science was based on the knowledge and information available to them at the time. The doctors at Vienna General were doing everything they knew how, but were completely blind to the devastating effect tiny germs from the cadavers had on the new mothers in Maternity Ward 1.

Only through *consciously processing every element of his habits and behaviors* was Dr. Semmelweis able to stop the destruction and discover a solution. His discovery was a tremendous turning point for medical science.[1]

Dr. Ignaz Semmelweis was eventually credited for identifying the germ theory.

In a similar way, our perceptions and resulting habits have been influenced by the knowledge and information available to us at the

---

[1] *Leadership and Self-deception: Getting out of the Box*. San Francisco: Berrett-Koehler, 2000. 17-19. Print.

time we anchored our events. The problem is that most of the knowledge and information we used to structure our anchors are no longer relevant to the lives we now possess. But just because the knowledge and information is not relevant does not mean it has no power.

Our irrelevant structuring can work like an invisible power that destroys relationships, dreams, ambitions, health, vitality and even our lives. It is only through *consciously processing the elements that we are able to stop the destruction and restructure a solution that will reclaim our personal power.*

Restructuring is, essentially, training your brain to perceive life differently. In the image below you may perceive a frog sitting on a lily pad.

If you turn the illusion vertically your perception changes and the frog magically turns into a beautiful stallion.

The key to becoming conscious is utilizing our ability to shift our perceptions so we can see things differently.

Emotions that remain on an unconscious level have complete power to influence your thoughts, feelings, attitudes, and beliefs. The more you understand your anchors and triggers, the more power you will have to manage, control, and even change your perceptions. Your conscious ability to shift your response will give you the power to change your life.

THE PROCESS OF RESTRUCTURING

The purpose of this process is to enhance your awareness and open the conscious ability to release The Victim Addiction and engage your personal power.

Notice the rut of everyday life. You get in your car, go to work, come home, watch TV, go to bed, get up, and do it all over again. Everyday life can be fertile ground for The Victim Addiction. Identify familiar thoughts, feelings, and beliefs that change your perspective and trap you into unhealthy attitudes. Keep in mind that the more familiar it is the more difficult it will be to see.

When you find yourself in a heightened emotional state, the following questions will help illuminate the emotional patterns you are giving your power to.

- What am I feeling? Name an emotion.
- How does this feeling affect the perception I have of myself or others?
- Where am I stuck in pride, guilt, blame or denial?
- Do I fight to be right? If yes, define how.
- What thoughts keep me in The Victim Addiction? Examples: "Why does he or she always do this to me?" "I hate it when I get blamed! This is not my fault."
- Are there things I refuse to admit to myself or others? If so, what am I afraid of?
- Which of my thoughts, feelings, attitudes and beliefs draw me closer to others?

- Which cause me to blame others and push them away?

Our thoughts contribute to our feelings, which lead to the attitudes that make up our perceptions. When we allow mindless thoughts to direct our lives, we can feel trapped and hopeless.

When you notice such thoughts, ask yourself the following questions:
- What do I gain from such thinking? An example would be: "I gain a sense of control," or, "I feel accepted."
- What am I compromising? Feeling loved, experiencing peace, or happiness?
- What attitudes validate my current thought process?
- Is my perception realistic?
- Do I choose to see and feel others as wrong so I can be right?
- Do I choose to see and feel others as right, leaving me to feel inferior?
- Do I exaggerate my strengths to feel superior?

You do not have the power to change anyone but yourself; but the more you change yourself, the more you will notice the relationships around you change!

Journal any thoughts or ideas that will encourage growth and promote change.

Positive Solutions

I started this book with a brief reference to Mother Teresa. One thing that has always impressed me is the way she looked for solutions instead of focusing on challenges. When Mother Teresa set her mind on doing something, she would focus her energy on creating a positive solution that would be beneficial for all involved.

Mother Teresa never made a request or addressed a challenge without having a practical way to resolve it. She took time to clarify exactly what she wanted, why she wanted it, what the benefits to others would be and the action she would take to implement her plan. Whenever she made a request, she would start by addressing the severity of the problem, and then give practical solutions to solve it.

She wouldn't take "no" for an answer because, in her mind, she had resolved any obstacles so the problem was already solved. Mother Teresa was not the type of person to see an injustice and turn away. When she noticed how many of the poor in India were sick and dying with no refuge, she devised a solid plan, and then enrolled others to help her care for their needs.

Once she had the support she needed, she set out to find a place that would provide the shelter necessary to care for the sick. Her quest led her to an abandoned Hindu temple, and she carefully analyzed a plan that would lead to a solution. After enrolling Indian officials, she converted the abandoned temple into a free hospice for the poor and called the temple, Kalighat (Home for the Dying).

> *"Being unwanted, unloved, uncared for, forgotten by everybody, I think that is a much greater hunger, a much greater poverty than the person who has nothing to eat."*

Then, she enrolled others to help her bring those needing help to a place where they could be cared for. Soon after, she opened another hospice, Nirmal Hriday (Pure Heart), and a home for lepers called Shanti Nagar (City of Peace), as well as an orphanage she called Shishu Bhavan (Children's Home of the Immaculate Heart). I am always amazed at the impact one person can have.

One of my favorite sayings of hers is: "Being unwanted, unloved, uncared for, forgotten by everybody, I think that is a much greater hunger, a much greater poverty than the person who has nothing to eat."

Have you ever given much thought to the emotional refugees who live among us? Many of these people live secluded in the painful desperation of their own minds. These feelings separate them from feeling loved, which only increases existing feelings of loneliness. I think of all the loneliness that goes on in this world, especially when I see a homeless person or encounter people who are angry at life. Can you imagine how lonely and unwanted they must feel?

Others have developed feelings of unwanted loneliness because of the way they have been treated throughout their lives. To help them to heal, these refugees need a special kind of love and attention that promotes emotional safety.

The passion that drives this work has come from times in my life when I have felt like an emotional refugee. I have been abused, abandoned and homeless. I know what it's like to feel overwhelmed with loneliness, with nowhere to go and no one to turn to.

The problem is, when we get stuck in the emotional state of feeling unwanted, unloved, uncared for, or forgotten, it becomes our reality.

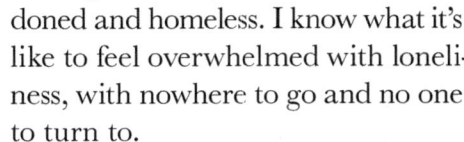

It is my deepest desire to extend a hand to those who feel lost in emotional poverty. I hope to help you see you have all the strength you need to apply these principles and create more peace in your life. This truly can be a turning point. You have the ability to access the love, healing, and peace you desire. You just need to believe you have the power to do so.

I wish people could understand how the choices they make because of the way they have structured some of their perceptions is what is creating the disappointments they face.

The problem is, when we get stuck in the emotional state of feeling unwanted, unloved, uncared for, or forgotten, it becomes our reality. Then, instead of resolving our pain, we fight to be right, push people away and then angrily blame them for our sorrow.

Imagine the ripple effect we could make if each one of us focused our emotional energy on positive solutions that not only created amazing results in our lives but also enhanced the lives of those around us.

THE PROCESS OF CREATING POSITIVE SOLUTIONS

The purpose of this process is to gain the ability to create solutions that will enhance your life and the lives of those around you.

Anytime you are facing an obstacle or needing an answer, apply the following process.

Clarify what you want by answering the following questions:

- What do you want?
- Why do you want it?
- Who will it benefit?
- What obstacles might you face?
- Who can you contact or enroll?
- What decisive action is required to meet your objective?

Write a detailed plan of action defining the steps you will take to create a solution to a challenge you seek.

Journal any thoughts or ideas that will encourage growth and promote change.

Having the ability to create *positive solutions* will enhance your life and strengthen the path to mastering your emotions.

Chapter 18

Mastering Our Emotions

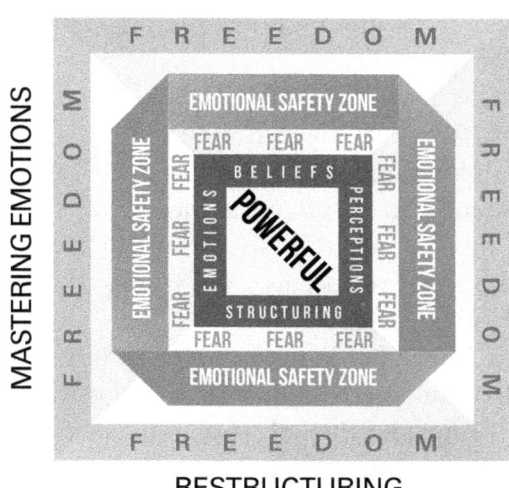

"The only person you are destined to become is the person you decide to be."

~ Ralph Waldo Emerson

One of the necessary adjustments we need to make if we are to get out of our Emotional Safety Zone and transform our lives is to master our emotions. When we master our emotions, we are no longer victims to our circumstances or reactions.

This emotional freedom enhances our ability to get beyond emotional reaction and see people as they are and view their behaviors in a very different way. This principle was taught in a powerful way many years ago to a young American on a rickety old bus in Tokyo, Japan. He tells the following story:

> A major turning point in my life came as an unexpected surprise one day in the middle of a quiet spring afternoon on a sleepy train in the suburbs of Tokyo.

It all started as the old train car was rattling over the rails. The train was comparatively empty. Then, as the train arrived at a stop and the doors opened, the calm afternoon was suddenly shattered. A man on the platform bellowed at the top of his lungs, yelling violent, obscene, incomprehensible curses. Just before the doors closed, the still yelling man staggered into our car.

He was big, drunk and dirty. He wore laborers clothing. His ragged shirt was stiff with dried vomit, his hair crusted with filth. His bloodshot eyes were bugged out, beaming scorn and hatred to all who caught his glance.

Screaming obscenities, he swung his big fist wildly at the first person he could reach, a scared young woman holding a baby.

The blow glanced off her shoulder, sending her spinning into the laps of an elderly couple. It was a miracle that she was not badly hurt and the baby was unharmed.

The frightened young woman ducked for cover, protecting her baby, and the elderly couple jumped up and scrambled toward the other end of the car. They were terrified.

The big laborer aimed a wobbling kick at the retreating back of the old lady. He missed, as the old woman barely scuttled to safety. This so enraged the wretched drunk that he grabbed the metal pole in the center of the car and tried to wrench it out of its stanchion. I could see that one of his hands was cut and bleeding, likely from an earlier scuffle.

The train lurched ahead, the passengers frozen with fear.

I stood up.

I was young then, and in pretty good shape. I stood six feet, weighed 225 and spoke fluent Japanese. I'd been putting in a solid eight hours of Aikido training every day for the past three years. I thought I was tough. Trouble was, my martial arts skill was untested in actual combat. As students of Aikido, we were not allowed to fight.

My teacher, the founder of Aikido, taught us each morning that the art was devoted to peace. "Aikido," he said again and again, "is the art of reconciliation. Whoever has the mind to fight, has broken his connection with the universe. If you try to dominate other people, you are already defeated. In Aikido, we study how to resolve conflict, not how to start it."

Yet in my heart of hearts, I was still dying to be a hero. A part of me still wanted a chance, an absolutely legitimate and justified opportunity to save the innocent by destroying the guilty.

"This is it!" I thought to myself, as I stood up tall and proud to confront this menace to society. "This cruel animal is drunk, mean and violent. People are in immediate danger. If I don't do something fast, somebody is going to get hurt."

Seeing me stand up, the belligerent drunk relished the chance to focus his rage. "Aha!" he roared. "A foreigner! You need a lesson in Japanese manners!" He landed a heavy punch on the metal pole beside him to give weight to his words. I puckered my lips and blew him a sneering, insolent kiss.

It hit him like a slap in the face. "All right!" he hollered. "You're gonna get a lesson." He gathered himself for a rush at me.

Yet just as he was about to lunge, a single-syllable shout pierced the air.

"Hey!"

I wheeled to my left; the drunk spun to his right. We both found ourselves staring down at a little old man. He must have been well into his seventies, this tiny gentleman, sitting there immaculate in his kimono. He took no notice of me, but beamed delightedly at the laborer, as though he had a most welcome secret to share.

"C'mere," the old man said in an easy Japanese vernacular, beckoning to the drunk. "C'mere and talk with me." He waved his hand lightly towards the seat next to him.

The big man followed, almost as if on a string. He planted his feet belligerently in front of the old gentleman, and towered threateningly over him.

"Talk to you!" he roared above the clacking wheels, "Why the hell should I talk to you?"

The old man continued to beam at the laborer. There was not a trace of fear or resentment about him. "What'cha been drinking?" the old man asked lightly, his eyes sparkling with interest.

"I been drinking sake," the laborer bellowed back. "Whatsit to you?" Flecks of spittle spattered the old man.

"Oh, that's wonderful," the old man said with delight. "Absolutely wonderful! You see, I love sake too. Every night, me and my wife warm up a little bottle of sake and take it out into the garden, and we sit on the old wooden bench that my grandfather's first student made for him. We watch the sun go down, and we look to see how our persimmon tree is doing."

He looked up at the laborer, eyes twinkling, happy to share his delightful information.

As the bewildered drunk struggled to follow the details of the old man's conversation, his face began to soften. His shaky fists slowly unclenched. "Yeah," he said slowly, "I love persimmons, too…" His wavering voice trailed off.

"Yes," said the old man, smiling and leaning slightly forward, "and I'm sure you have a wonderful wife."

"No," replied the laborer to this so strangely friendly man in a softer, sullen voice. "My wife... she died last year."

The suddenly changed drunk hung his head in heavy sorrow. Then, gently swaying with the motion of the train, this big, burly man, who was so threatening just a moment earlier began to sob. "I don't got no wife. I don't got no home any more. I lost my job. I don't got no money. I don't got nowhere to go. I'm so ashamed of myself." Big tears rolled down his cheeks. A spasm of pure despair rippled through his body.

Now it was my turn. Standing there in my well-scrubbed youthful pride, with my make-this-world-safe-for-democracy righteousness, I suddenly felt dirtier and more ashamed than he was.

Just then, the train arrived at my stop. Maneuvering my way toward the door, I heard the old man speak sympathetically. "My, my," he said with heartfelt care, yet undiminished delight. "That is a very difficult predicament, indeed. Sit down here and tell me about it."

I turned my head for one last look before leaving the now-crowded train. The laborer was sprawled like a sack on the seat, his head in the old man's lap.

The old man was looking down at him with smiling compassion, his hand stroking the filthy, matted head of his confused soul.

As the train pulled away, I sat down on a bench dazed with all that had just happened. What I had wanted to do with muscle and meanness had been deftly accomplished with but a few kind words.[1]

Emotional Change

In the story, the drunk man, having gone through the loneliness and loss of his family had, in essence, lost his sense of belonging, and life no longer had meaning. He let his emotions control the situation to the point that he didn't care what he looked like, how he behaved, or who saw him. He didn't care about his life or anyone else's. He was alive on the outside but everything good inside him felt like it had died. His violent behavior intensified his feelings of abandonment and validated his belief that no one really cared about him.

Not understanding or knowing how to handle his emotions, he covered them with alcohol, allowing pain to rule his behaviors as he lost his ability to function.

Not understanding or knowing how to handle his emotions, he covered them with alcohol, allowing pain to rule his behaviors as he surrendered his ability to function.

---

[1] Dobson, Terry. "Aikido In Action: Doing Combat with the Essence of Love." Context Institute. The Foundations Of Peace (IC#4), 16 Sept. 2011. Web. 23 Apr. 2015. <http://www.context.org/iclib/ic04/dobson/>.

The Aikido master thought he could rely on his training and abilities to handle the situation. Yet, just like the drunk man, his emotions were governing his conclusions and intended behavior. His conscious thoughts supported the idea of becoming a hero but the underlying force fueling his attitudes was that of arrogance and judgment.

Although the young man was training in the art of Aikido, he had not yet mastered his thoughts or emotions. In the moment, he unconsciously allowed his pride to override the lessons of the Aikido truth he was devoting his life to.

Blind to his actions and what was driving them, he took on an air of superiority and, in spite of his training, even justified his anger and his decision to resort to violence. It's interesting to note that he called the drunk man "mean" and "violent", yet he was considering employing meanness and violence himself—a sure sign that he wasn't using rational thought but was being directed by his emotions.

In contrast, the tiny gentleman took a much different stance. In the midst of a crisis situation, he demonstrated the real fruits of his emotional progression. In a highly emotional situation, facing two very strong and angry men, this tiny gentleman had the ability to see the drunk man as a lost soul full of pain. He was able to direct his energy into calming *the emotional storm* that was going on within the lost laborer.

In this unexpected and intense environment, the tiny man was able to separate himself from the emotional reactions and fear that were present on the bus. He had become the master of his emotions and was able to use the peace in his own life to bring peace to others.

You have the power to create these same types of emotional shifts, shifts that will remove the angst, transform your emotions, and create inner peace. The only thing that could get in your way is the structures that were formed before your logical mind was fully developed, much of which is based on fear. Pain does not define you and only has power to defeat or destroy you if you allow it to. Consciously facing the pain of your past will guide you to a path where greater power and self-mastery can occur.

Facing the Pain

I recognize that consciously choosing the direction of your emotional life is not a popular principle. In fact, the instant gratification society we live in would suggest you do the opposite and simply "go with the flow" of your feelings. The common perception is "if it feels real" you should just go for feelings of instant gratification, even if it is contrary to what you know will bring you happiness.

When we go with the flow of our emotions, we not only misunderstand our own pain, we misinterpret the actions of those that are in pain around us.

Most people in society would look at the drunk man in the story above as the young Aikido master did, and say, "This cruel animal is drunk, and I must use muscle and meanness to stop him," believing it is the behavior that is his problem, without noticing the pain.

However, when we take care of our own pain, we have the wisdom to take a different view of unruly behavior. When we are no longer ruled by our emotional reactions, we can be in such situations and ask ourselves, "Why all the pain?" and, "How can I help?"

Resolving our pain can also liberate us from the selfish habits that deprive us from the love and acceptance we desire.

The poor drunk man was so far gone he had given up all hope. The kindness of this tiny gentle man gave him the space to calm his fears and acknowledge his pain.

Unfortunately, pain is a natural part of the human experience, and every one of us will feel the uncomfortable effects that emotional pain can cause. Emotional strength comes as we move through our pain and create the resolve needed to heal.

Many years ago, I had a dear friend who was suffering from cancer. He shared how, even though he was in tremendous pain, his sickness had softened him and changed him for the good. The man he used to be had a lot of secrets. He had been mean, had no time for anyone but himself, and was completely caught up in the instant gratification that came from "vain things of the world."

His illness gave him the opportunity to stop and look at the destructive patterns caused by his selfish attitudes and behaviors. As he examined his actions and became accountable for the pain he had caused others, he recognized the changes he could make. With this change he began to truly cherish those things that were most important to him. How grateful he was for the opportunity to ask for forgiveness and to serve the ones who had been patient and loving with him as he grew. As he changed, he was committed to showing the people in his life how much he loved them. In return, his love and appreciation grew in every area of his life. His life was extended three years longer than expected and his emotional change became a blessing to all who knew him.

Fortunately, we don't need to wait until the end of our lives to change. Resolving our pain can liberate us from the selfish habits we have formed that deprive us from the love and acceptance we desire.

In order to create an emotional change that will promote a sense of wellbeing, we must face the reality of who we really are. An honest look will help us notice how our emotional pain is not only the cause of other's pain, it is cutting us off from those things that matter most.

Looking at the results that we have created can be uncomfortable, but we must face the pain enough to establish a trusting environment where emotional safety can occur.

Think about it like this; if your appendix burst and the doctor told you emergency surgery was the only way to preserve your life, would you refuse the surgery due to the pain involved just to avoid feeling uncomfortable? You may refuse the surgery, but would that eliminate the pain? Whether we face our emotional pain or avoid our emotional pain, there is still pain. The only difference is, facing the pain is the only way to eliminate it.

Face the Pain To Stop the Pain

In the '60s, Gale Sayers was a great football running back for the Chicago Bears. In 1968, he suffered a severe knee injury and was out for the rest of the season. In 1970, he ruptured his other knee but, ignoring the pain, Sayers continued to play two additional games.

Disregarding the pain and not allowing his body proper time to heal shortened his amazing running back career.

In the '80s, a young basketball player broke his foot and was very frustrated when the Chicago Bulls refused to let him play until the bone was completely healed.

He missed 68 games, but when he came back, he showed the world how basketball was supposed to be played.

After taking time to heal, Michael Jordan went on to become one of the greatest basketball stars in NBA history.

Even though it took time and caused frustration, Jordan had to acknowledge the pain and respond appropriately in order to properly heal, and we must do the same.

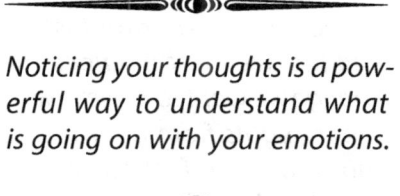

Noticing your thoughts is a powerful way to understand what is going on with your emotions.

An important concept to remember is this: A detrimental emotional anchor will only be established if we have felt uncomfortable or experienced pain. This detrimental anchor will cause *more* uncomfortable feelings each time it is triggered by something in our current environment that is even vaguely similar to the pain we have felt before.

We must FACE THE PAIN TO STOP THE PAIN. When we consciously notice our triggers and acknowledge our pain we begin to realize that the path to healing is through processing our emotional anchors and the fear-based beliefs that are attached to them.

Mastering your emotions is a process that takes time and can feel uncomfortable, so be gentle with yourself.

Hidden Messages

In several places throughout this book, you may have noticed a phrase similar to this, "Look at the thoughts, feelings, attitudes and beliefs that are perpetuating your pain."

Noticing your thoughts is a powerful way to understand what is going on with your emotions. Here's an example: I was invited to speak at a youth treatment center in Spokane, Washington. Travel and hotel accommodations were confirmed and I spent several days preparing for the opportunity. When I arrived at the airport, a friendly escort met me, took me to the hotel, and then spent some time showing me some of the beautiful sites. The next morning, I looked forward to a day of doing what I love —facilitating "The Power to Change" workshop. My escort texted me and said that there were some things going on at the facility and I would not be able to work with the youth. I couldn't believe they would make accommodations for me to be there and, as I was waiting for my ride, tell me my services were no longer needed. I was really confused because I had never had this kind of thing happen before. I went back in the hotel and worked on a project for the rest of the day. The next morning, there was no escort to take me to the airport so I took the hotel shuttle the 30-minute ride back to the airport. I continued to feel sad and, over the next couple days, noticed random memories of past events coming to my mind; but I shook them off.

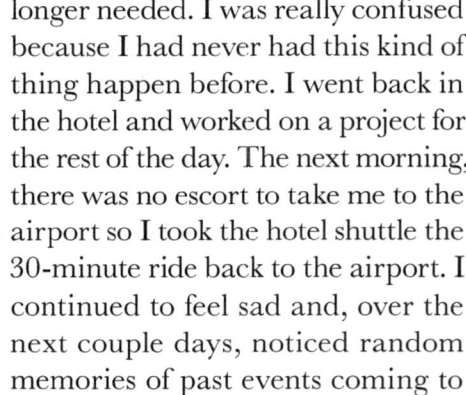

However, to generate lasting change, we must interlock the change we want to achieve with the thoughts from our rational mind and the feelings of our emotional mind.

About three days later, I was talking to a friend about what had happened in Spokane, and it hit me that my experience had left me feeling rejected and, to some degree, even abandoned. What I thought were random memories were not random at all; they were reminders of other times I had felt rejected and abandoned. My memories were trying to help me resolve the angst I felt by showing me other times I had felt the same way. This was a valuable insight as I also realized how feelings of abandonment were preventing me from moving on from other experiences I had recently had. Discovering the hidden message of my "so called" random memories gave me the final piece I needed to acknowledge the underlying pain, let go of the emotions and experience peace.

Change Your Life

You have most likely heard the saying, "Change your thoughts, change your life." Sometimes, just noticing our thoughts can give us the understanding we need to change. Our thoughts are very powerful and have tremendous influence over the way we perceive the world. However, to generate lasting change, we must interlock the change we want to achieve with the thoughts from our rational mind and the feelings of our emotional mind.

When working together, our thoughts and emotions can be a very powerful. Our conscious mind will help us decipher connections of emotional patterns that get in the way of our happiness and growth, and our emotional mind will give us the motivation to master our emotions and create what we want.

The opposite is true as well. When we suppress our pain and shut off our emotions, we lose other connections that are essential in our continued happiness and growth. Those who truly don't know how to manage, control or change their uncomfortable emotions will dismiss them. The sad thing is they never seem fully present, engaged or connected to the people around them. They keep themselves busy with mindless tasks that inadvertently prevent them from establishing the deep and fulfilling connections that they truly desire.

I have met many people who are confused by their emotions and will only deal with an emotional circumstance *if* they feel they can confidently control the situation, otherwise they will do whatever it takes to avoid it. Because they truly don't know how to process their own emotions, they simply don't have the capacity to deal with an emotional challenge and will push their feelings aside, or suppress and forget about them. People who don't know how to handle *their* own emotions, are very intolerant when people around them express or show emotions. They will often say things like, "Snap out of it;" "Handle it and move on;" or, "I don't know what you are getting so upset about!" They may also believe: "Having an anxiety attack is an attention tactic."

Shutting off our uncomfortable emotions will prevent us from accessing and ultimately mastering the reoccurring, emotional patterns that perpetuate our misery and pain.

Engaging the power of the emotional mind and utilizing the skills of the rational mind will ultimately be a key element in mastering our emotions. When both minds are unified in a powerful purpose, we experience loving relationships that are fully present, engaged and connected.

One of the most effective ways we can master our emotions will occur when we understand the power, strength and productive nature of the neural pathways that form the structures of our mind.

Chapter 19

Establishing New Neural Pathways

"Letting go helps restore our balance. It allows others to be responsible for themselves and for us to take our hands off situations that do not belong to us. This frees us from unnecessary stress."

~ Melody Beattie

Throughout this book we have addressed how the structures we have formed have helped construct our thoughts, feelings, attitudes and beliefs. The scientific term for these structures is called neural pathways. The neural pathways in our brains map out our perceptions. The exciting thing about this map is it is ours to design and maneuver any way we choose. The power of the human mind is amazing and the possibilities that can be created are endless. Yet, we see over and over how those in society seek to limit our potential. Society is especially limiting to those born with cognitive challenges.

Kristine Barnett saw that play out in her life when her son Jacob was born with autism. Kristine was told that Jacob would never speak. She started her son in programs and therapies aimed at addressing his limitations. At age three, Jake was enrolled in life skills classes so he might learn, as Kristine says, to "tie his own shoes by age sixteen." Often though, Jake was so absorbed by other things: shadows on the floor,

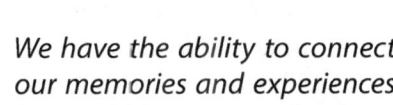

We have the ability to connect our memories and experiences in astonishing ways; we just have to realize that we have the power to do so.

plaid patterns on clothing and, especially, alphabet flashcards, that he couldn't be persuaded to attend to the lessons.

Kristine describes a chilling comment made by Jake's special ed teacher on a home visit. The teacher insisted that the boy stop bringing his beloved alphabet cards to school: "We don't think you're going to need to worry about the alphabet with Jacob."

Kristine decided right then and there that she would stop focusing on Jacob's limitations and resolved to follow his spark and passionate interests. She stopped concentrating on what he couldn't do and began to focus on what he could.

"Jacob liked repetitive behaviors. He would play with a glass and look at the light, twisting it for hours on end. Instead of taking it away, I would give him fifty glasses, fill them with water at different levels and let him explore," she says. "I surrounded him with whatever he loved."

The more she did that, the more it worked. Then one night, as she was tucking him into bed, Jacob spoke. "It was like music, because everyone said it was an impossible thing," Kristine recalls. "I would tuck him in every night and say, 'Good night baby Jacob. You're my baby angel, and I love you very much.' One night he looked straight at me and said, 'Night, night, baby bagel.'"

At age three, Jake was arranging hundreds of crayons in the order of the color spectrum; a few years later, he memorized pi to the 200th digit and could recite it forward and backward. At 9, he began working on a theory in astrophysics that, according to those who can understand it, may put him in line for the Nobel Peace Prize; at 11, he started college. At age 12, he became a paid university researcher in quantum physics.

The key, according to his mother, was letting Jacob be himself by helping him study the world with wide-eyed wonder instead of focusing on a list of things he would never have the ability to do.[1]

Kristine Barnett created an environment that allowed Jacob to explore the wonders of his world in a miraculous way. Jacob was given the freedom to learn from the things that fascinated him, and the neural pathways in his brain connected that information in astonishing ways.

Recently, I listened to 13-year-old Jacob speak on TEDxTeen. In his talk he said that, "In order to succeed you have to look at things with your own unique perspective."

---

[1] Barnett, Kristine. *The Spark: A Mother's Story of Nurturing, Genius, and Autism.* New York: Random House Group, 2014. Print.

Our unique perspectives are formed by the neural pathways that connect the thoughts, feelings and memories of our experiences to various regions of our brains.

Like Jacob, we have the ability to connect our memories and experiences in astonishing ways; we just have to realize that we have the power to do so.

We are born with billions of neurons, which are specifically designed to communicate with one another. As we learn and grow, these neurons branch out and form neural pathways that construct our visual and sensory memories. The connections between the neural pathways are called neural networks. These neural networks can be attach to more than 50,000 different experiences at a time.

The job of a neural pathway is to transport information activating electrochemical surges that will stimulate action throughout the neural networks.

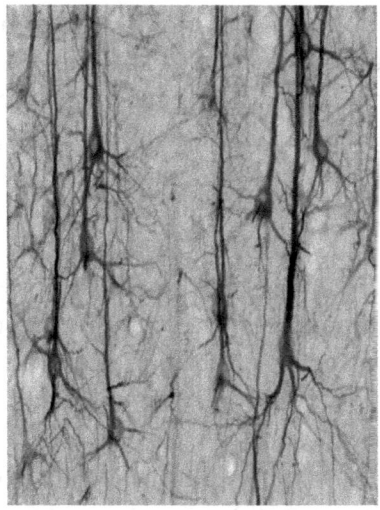

When an electrochemical surge is activated, it releases chemicals into our system that will encourage action. It occurs like this: When we have an experience, our brain will take in the new information and link it to our existing knowledge. Linking occurs as neurons branch out and form new neural pathways that connect our current experiences, such as the things we see, hear, feel, touch and taste, to other networks that contain similar logical and emotional components.

Scientists tell us that the neural networks do not actually touch each other; the networks are able to communicate across small, synaptic gaps that are between the networks.

Because the neural networks have no concept between what we see and what we remember, it can attach recent events to networks that are irrelevant to our current reality. The problem is that even these misdirected neural pathways will send electrochemical surges and anchor thoughts, feelings, attitudes and beliefs that control our habits and behaviors.

> *Because the neural networks have no concept between what we see and what we remember, it can attach current events to networks that are irrelevant to our current reality.*

Our anchored events can trigger both painful and pleasant memories of the past. It just depends on the emotional components, such as the feelings and physiological reactions, that were present when the initial event was anchored. An example you may relate to is music. We all have songs that bring back fond memories and those that bring back memories involving pain. Have you ever been somewhere and the smell of something takes your mind back to a wonderful memory of your childhood?

I have a friend who loves the smell of peppermint and shares a sweet memory of her grandmother every time she smells that wonderful scent. She also has a very fun tradition of having her grandchildren over for movie night. On one of these fun nights together, she played the animated musical fantasy, "Anastasia." The movie is about how Anastasia, the Grand Duchess of Russia and only survivor of Tsar Nicholas II, finds her grandmother, who has also been searching many years for her. When meeting Anastasia the empress is skeptical of her granddaughter's true identity, because she has been tricked so many times before. Then one evening Anastasia smells peppermint and shares with her grandmother a memory of how she had spilled a bottle of peppermint all over the carpet. While watching this scene, my friend's grandchildren began to giggle and said, "Her grandmother loves peppermint just like you, Grannie." The smell that triggered memories of her own childhood was now instilled in the minds of her own sweet grandchildren.

All of our memories and familiar experiences have the ability to influence and direct the way we think, feel, and behave.

When we have an experience that is familiar to something we have felt before (like the smell of peppermint), our mind will send out an electrical zap that will release small sacks of chemical molecules into the neurological system. This electrochemical serge immediately initiates a mental and physical response. In this case, it sends out warm feelings of a loving grandmother.

The Super Highway of our Mind

Neural pathways are like the super highway of the mind and are connected to billions of thoughts, feelings and experiences. These pathways have tremendous power and when we connect into the pathways that ignite our passions we can create anything we desire.

An important thing to remember is, when we become conscious of the painful events we have encountered, we gain the conscious ability to disconnect ineffective pathways and create something new.

This advantage comes from the fact that the emotional mind has a reality based on the way we feel. We can create anything we want by creating stronger emotional associations with what we see, hear, feel, touch and taste.

That is why motivational speakers encourage us to create mind maps or vision boards so we can physically see the changes we would like to create. These motivators also encourage us to repeat positive affirmations, connecting our vision to what we hear. In addition, talking to people who already have what we seek can spark new and innovative ideas for the rational mind to put into action.

Remember, the more emotional circuits we connect to uplifting sights, sounds, smells, emotions, and physiological sensations, the stronger our motivation becomes to accomplish what we want. Every time we take action to achieve our vision, what we see, hear, and do, will send electrochemical surges through the new neural pathways. This energy will not only release feelings of excitement and strengthen the pathway, it will also increase our confidence, giving us the drive and determination we need to succeed.

Changing Ineffective Habits

Strong emotional circuits can be beneficial in changing ineffective habits. In order to create effective change we must interrupt the pathway's ability to send information. Every time we interrupt a trigger, we break a connection of a neural pathway and weaken its ability to send electrochemical surges. Now, it would be pretty easy to break a well-established habit if we were only dealing with one neural pathway connection, but our memories and experiences are connected to thousands of neural networks that require conscious rigor to release.

A habit I have anchored well throughout the years is my love for dark chocolate. Chocolate is one of my greatest companions, and it has comforted me through many trials. The problem is, there are times in my life when I rely on these sweet treats a little too often for comfort. I hate to admit it, but, in times of struggle, these delicious little friends even call to me. They say, "Tori, come eat me," and I willingly obey.

After a few weeks of this wonderful indulgence, I step on the scale and am irritated that I have gained some weight. I decided many years ago that feeling healthy is important to me, and I determined that I would never let my weight get above a certain number. Dedication to this decision has served me well over the years. When I notice I am getting too close to the highest weight I allow, I know I must trade my devoted little friends in for a while.

> *Now it would be easy to break a habit if we were just dealing with one pathway, but our neural pathways are connected to thousands of networks.*

At first, it is hard to turn my back and walk away because their sad little voices are still calling my name, but, as each day passes, the road gets easier. For me, I have already established neural pathways that will support my success, and it just takes some committed devotion to get back in a routine that supports my goal.

There are, however, emotional times when my drive and determination to resist my little friends are waning. Because I am consciously aware of the effects weight gain has on my mental and physical wellbeing, I know drastic measures must be taken. I know this is a silly example and you are probably thinking, "Just throw the temptation away!" That seems so easy, but that is so hard for me. I would rather eat the lovely little morsels and start my healthy routine another day. But if I place strong smelling coffee beans next to my little treats, I have no desire whatsoever to eat the chocolate. In fact, when the coffee smell is around, the thought of eating anything makes me nauseous. This may occur because the smell of coffee is associated with my unpleasant childhood.

One of the quickest ways to break a connection to an ineffective habit is to begin associating that habit to something you really don't like. Remember the statement that says, "Change occurs when the pain of remaining the same outweighs the pain of change"? The emotional mind has no concept of what is real and will create emotional shifts based on the way what we are associating with makes us feel.

Rerouting Neural Pathways

Every time we break a connection of an ineffective habit, it weakens the ability of the neural pathways to send electrochemical surges. Again, it would be easy to break a habit if we were just dealing with one pathway, but our neural pathways are connected to thousands of networks. That is why researchers say it can take up to 45 days to break an old habit and establish a new one.

So what goes on in the brain that continues our unproductive choices and compulsions?

Let's take a look at my chocolate cravings. When chocolate hits my tongue a chemical called beta-endorphin is released. Beta-endorphins create that endorphin rush that will give me a surge of instant energy. Beta-endorphins also create a sense of wellbeing and will reduce physical and emotional pain. Then the feel-good chemical, dopamine, is released to help me focus, and a serotonin release calms my fears or anxieties, and the world feels better.

Understanding why I feel so attached to chocolate has given me a new way to look at dieting. So now when I am successfully losing weight, I do things that promote those same kinds of feel-good chemicals.

For instance, exercise will release beta-endorphins. Working on goals that will give me more opportunities to interact with others increases my dopamine levels. Positive interactions with others also increase the much needed serotonin levels in my brain. I also get outside more, I listen to uplifting, happy music, and I dance. I consciously choose to get out of my cave more and enjoy things that increase my energy and create happiness.

Consistently dedicating myself to these types of habits has created the productive neural pathways needed to enjoy my life to the fullest. When I am on vacation, I give myself a break and enjoy all kinds of eating experiences.

I trust myself enough to know, when it is time to take extra weight off I will do it, and I have already developed the habits and strengthened the neural pathways that will support my success.

The Power of the Human Mind

What is so exciting about the incredible function of the human mind is that you can accomplish anything that you are willing to dedicate your energy to, or, as some would say it, you can accomplish anything you "put your mind to." You just have to remember that new neural pathways grow stronger the more you use them.

It is also helpful to understand that the brain will connect new learning experiences to habits and patterns that have already been established. The power of the human mind is really quite amazing!

Recently I was reading an article about Pat Ireland. He was the student who was labeled "the boy in the window" after the Columbine shooting in 1999. Ireland was shot in the foot and then was shot twice in the head as he quietly reached out to help another. It took three hours for him to have the conscious ability and strength to get to and then thrust himself up and out of the library window. The initial prognosis for Ireland was grim. He was unable to speak and doctors didn't hold out much hope for his survival. Against all odds and with one of the bullets still lodged in his brain he has made a full recovery and has gone on to become a successful businessman.

Stories of survival like these are nothing short of a miracle and we hear these types of medical marvels all the time. The power of the human spirit to survive is incredible and, due to the human brain's ability to adapt, we have the power to learn, grow, and develop in amazing ways.

It seems miraculous that, after severe brain injuries like the one Ireland suffered, many people overcome enormous obstacles as they relearn the ability to walk, talk and speak. They do this by connecting to the neural pathways formed when they initially learned these skills.

For some, the neural pathways that create change are strong and easy to access. Yet, for others it is a much more daunting task. Like anything new, beginning the process is the most uncomfortable part.

In some cases, the mind will conceal important facts from the conscious mind. The emotional mind does this in order to shield us from the intense pain or frustration that the physical memory has caused. At times, this shield can make it extra challenging to remember some of the details of anchored events and the associated beliefs that get in the way of our happiness and growth.

Networks work in layers to protect us from experiencing more pain.

If you are trying to process an event and are having a difficult time, don't let discouragement deter your progress. Take time to notice the thoughts and feelings that are affecting your emotional wellbeing, and start from there. Get clear on how your current thoughts and feelings are keeping you in an unproductive place. Once you have determined this, decide how you want to think and feel and consciously devise a plan to direct your emotional responses the way you want.

Here are a few things to ponder when approaching change.
- To reroute ineffective neural pathways, we must consciously direct the process. We do this by noticing our triggers, identifying the associated emotions and beliefs, then logically understanding the anchored event.
- Because lasting change occurs on an emotional level, we can't just think it is a good idea to change, we have to have an

emotional desire to change. The process to begin the change you seek will begin as you consciously get in touch with how you currently feel and then truly acknowledge how those feelings are keeping you stuck. Like the saying goes, "You can't change what you do not see." If there are things you are not willing to look at, then you will not have the mental capacity to manage, control or change your situation.

- Dedicate yourself to applying the types of thoughts, feelings, attitudes and beliefs that will strengthen neural pathways that will support your happiness and growth.

- Remember, when you consciously interrupt ineffective habits and begin to reroute pathways, the old patterns eventually lose the automatic ability to control you. The more rigorous you become with yourself to consciously reinforce new neural pathways, the more success you will experience.

- One way to successfully reroute neural pathways is to interrupt the electrochemical flow by creating statements to consciously disrupt the chemical surge from occurring. I have done this in my life by acknowledging my experiences and thinking statements such as, "Those were difficult times," or, "My life was very hard." Statements like these put the emotional mind at ease, by reinforcing feelings that the old pathway has done the job it was set up to do. After the validation process is complete I can follow up with statements such as, "Those were difficult times, and I am glad I had the strength I needed to get through them as well as I did;" or, "My life was very hard. I am glad I have given myself permission to create something new." By doing this, I validate the need for the original pathway while creating the perception that the current structure is no longer relevant, giving me the energy and the motivation to move on. Thoughts like these will give me the

The power of the human spirit to survive is incredible and due to the human brain's ability to adapt, we have the power to learn, grow, and develop in amazing ways.

Establishing New Neural Pathways

freedom to consciously let go of the past and create something new.

- We can also use gratitude to reroute neural pathways, by using statements such as: "I am grateful I don't live like that anymore," "I am so glad that all of that is behind me," "I am ready to learn from these experiences," "That was then, this is now," or "I love my life and I am grateful for new growth opportunities."

This is just an interesting fact: I know this was briefly mentioned, but did you know that the amygdala or emotional mind, is fully formed at birth, whereas the conscious more rational mind is not fully developed until we are in our mid- to late-twenties? That explains why we may take some crazy risks in our twenties that we laugh about in our thirties.

In the next section, we can apply the principles that were just learned as we identify ways to clean the closet by eliminating habits and behaviors that have created detrimental feelings and results.

Tier IV

The Power of Transcending Perceptions

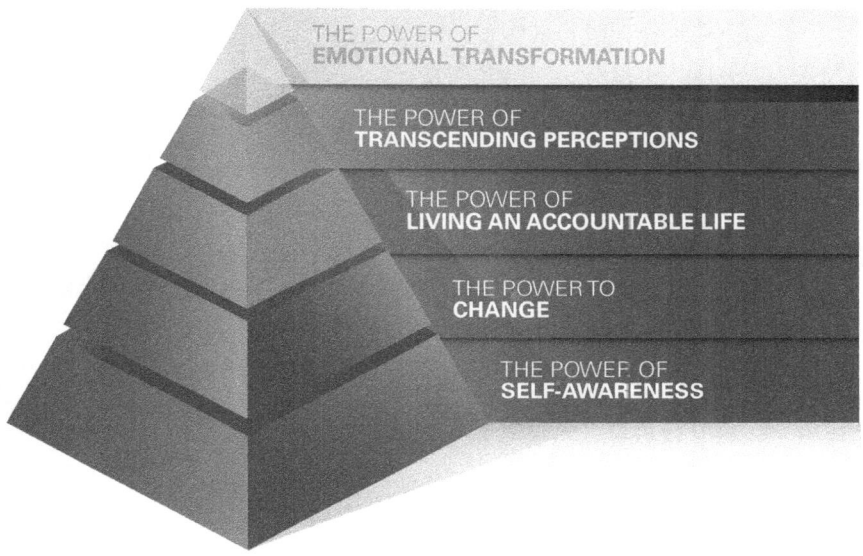

"I will act as though what I do makes a difference."

~ Benjamin Franklin

In Tier IV, the Power of Transcending Perceptions, we explore the importance of self-trust and the significance of implementing forgiveness in our lives.

We will also look at the unconscious belief systems that shape our thoughts, feelings, and attitudes and that ultimately direct our behaviors. We then discover ways to consciously override fear-based beliefs and establish new, empowering patterns, which will encourage happiness and growth.

Chapter 20

Letting Go of Painful Memories

Do not brood over your past mistakes and failures as this will only fill your mind with grief, regret and depression. Do not repeat them in the future.

~ Swami Sivananda

In order to master our emotions, we must first look at our perceptions, or the way we view the world, and examine how those perceptions get in the way of our happiness and growth. Our perceptions are formed based on the way we view our experiences. We can see the world as a happy place that is full of wonder or as a miserable place full of sadness; the choice is up to us, as demonstrated in this little story.

Long ago in a small, faraway village, there was a place known as the House of 1000 Mirrors. A small, happy little dog learned of this place and decided to visit. When he arrived, he bounced happily up the stairs to the doorway of the house. He looked through the doorway with his ears lifted high and his tail wagging as fast as it could.

To his great surprise, he found himself staring at 1000 other happy little dogs with their tails wagging just as fast as his. He smiled a great smile and was answered with 1000 great smiles just as warm and friendly. As he left the house, he thought to himself, "This is a wonderful place. I will come back and visit it often."

In this same village, another little dog, who was not quite as happy as the first, decided to visit the house. He slowly climbed the stairs and hung his head low as he looked into the door. When he saw the 1000 unfriendly looking dogs staring back at him, he growled at them and was horrified to see 1000 little dogs growling back at him. As he left, he thought to himself, "That is a horrible place, and I will never go back there again."[1]

Just like the 1000 mirrors, people view others through their own perceptions. Those perceptions reflect back their view of themselves and the world as they see it. If I love myself, it is easy for me to love you, even if you don't love me in return. But if I don't even like myself, it will be very hard for me to like you, even when you are kind to me. My perceptions will prevent me from seeing who you really are.

With this in mind, it is important to remember why we don't need to take things personally.

Thankfully, when we are conscious we understand that each of us has the ability to generate circumstances in our lives any way we choose, we can construct a life that is a wonderful place to live, or let our unconscious mind rule and live a life that is an unhappy place to exist; the choice is up to us.

An unhappy life occurs when we are blindly caught in The Victim Addiction, and the results in our lives seem outside of our ability to manage, control or change. We give our power away to blame, denial and justifications and try to hide from the emotional consequences that weigh us down and limit the peace and happiness we could otherwise enjoy.

In order to master our emotions and create an effective emotional change, we must let go of painful experiences that interfere with our ability to create inner peace and happiness.

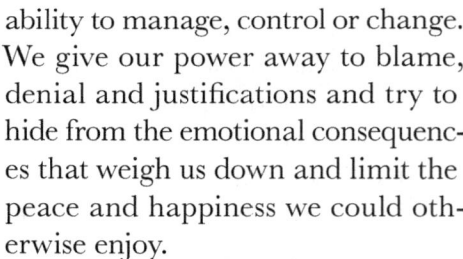

There are times when we make emotional decisions that destroy our peace and stifle our relationships. Because we don't want to face the pain or deal with the consequences we try to hide from the emotional ramifications by suppressing, withholding or ignoring them, which will create even more sorrow and regret in our lives.

---

[1] "*The House of 1000 Mirrors* (Japanese Folktale)." Inspirational Christian Stories and Poems. N.p., n.d. Web. 23 Apr. 2015. <http://www.inspirationalarchive.com/3131/the-house-of-1000-mirrors-japanese-folktale/>.

Mastering Our Emotions

In order to master our emotions and create an effective emotional change, we must let go of shameful experiences that interfere with our ability to create emotional stability and inner peace.

The next few subjects are difficult to address but in order to release from destructive emotional patterns these areas must be looked at with honesty. The intention of addressing these specific habits isn't to make anyone bad or wrong, it is to release the binding hold these experiences have had over your emotional life, so be objective, patient and kind. Many of the scenarios may not apply to you but, even if they don't, understanding these important concepts will give you the understanding needed to help someone in your life who may be caught in this type of pain.

Grief, Loss and Regrets

Have you ever wished you could rewind the clock just enough to make a different choice? Those moments have happened to all of us in one form or another. Yet, in some instances, the way an individual has reacted to an event leaves them with a deep sense of regret that can be completely consuming.

I have worked especially hard in my personal growth and very rarely do I put myself in a position where I let my emotions get the best of me. While writing the section on amygdala hijacking, I had a devastating experience that filled my life with pain, overwhelming sorrow and deep regret.

The Gift of an Amygdala Hijacking

I guess to some degree I felt I had understood the source of my emotional reactions well enough that I was confident I would be able to manage any childhood emotions that would happen to surface. Then one day, I was completely ambushed by my emotions and felt helplessly confused.

When I was writing the chapter on amygdala hijacking, I included an experience I had in my 20's that gives a good description of what happens when an amygdala hijacking occurs. It was a good example and I was glad that I had a personal experience I could reference. I was fairly certain the more "evolved" me would never have to face something like that again. Then months later, as I was editing that section, I actually had another hijacking that triggered a series of extremely painful events from my childhood.

The trigger instantly created overwhelming feelings of insecurity, and with it came all the shame, guilt and fears attached to a long term, childhood trauma. The most unfortunate part of this emotional ambush for me was that it occurred when I was in a new friendship with an amazing guy.

Through my hysterical sobs, I began illogically rambling details of the events and asking irrational questions. My poor friend was loving and kind and talked with me for a long time until I calmed down.

After my friend and I said goodbye, and I had time to calm down, I wanted to understand what triggered the extremely painful memories I had just encountered and did my best to consciously sort through the pain and confusion of the previous hijacking.

I was almost afraid to rethink what had happened, as I didn't want the excruciating emotions to take over again. After the experience had passed, feelings of embarrassment and regret began to torment me. However, I was surprised and grateful that I was able to keep the traumatic emotions from returning as I began to sort through the details of the emotional breakdown. It took about 10 days before I was logically able to put enough of the sensory pieces together to figure out the environmental elements that had triggered me.

Processing My Experience

My experience: It had been a wonderful night. I was in the company of a man I admired and really enjoyed. We had a nice dinner and I felt comfortable in his presence. It had been a long time since I had allowed myself to appreciate this kind of relationship, and new feelings of how nice this friendship could be were beginning to rise. After dinner we went to a movie. The movie brought back feelings of fear from my violent childhood as the movie depicted the anger of an alcoholic father towards his daughter.

What triggered my emotional reaction: At first my heart was racing and I felt a rush of tears threatening to flow, but even in this heightened condition of fear I was still consciously aware of what I was feeling, and was reasonably sure I knew why I was feeling it.

Then, sensing that I was feeling uncomfortable, my friend reached down and took my hand to comfort me. In that moment, the physiological sensations of his gentle touch tapped into feelings of a childhood crush with a brother-in-law, who later became very abusive. The physiological sensations intensified my fears and triggered an outright emergency. In a flash, the increased fear, the abuse on the big screen, and the warm feeling I felt as my friend reached out and touched my hand, triggered enough sensory factors to energize a memory that had been long forgotten, and the dormant circuits came alive.

Even though my date was wonderful with me and I got to experience his gentle and amazingly compassionate side, when I began to panic, all I wanted to do was get away as fast as I could. Even days later, the panic was still overwhelming. I was so lost and confused by my emotions it was hard for me to consciously connect what had triggered the irrational fear I was experiencing.

I went over the details of the triggered environment again and again to determine the link. It took almost 10 days of processing to know with a surety I had all the right pieces.

I initially considered the trigger to be the scenario of the father who, because he had a drinking problem, was treating his daughter poorly. It was true that the sadness the young girl demonstrated broke my heart and connected me to my own childhood sadness involving my alcoholic father.

The only problem was, the traumatic event that surfaced did not involve my father.

Frustrated, I continued to search for the connection. I went over everything in my mind; what I saw, what I heard, how I felt. It wasn't until I acknowledged the feelings I had unconsciously eliminated after the hijacking occurred, that the pieces fell into place.

The connection was illogical and I realized that the hijacking would never have occurred if I was with someone other than the friend I was beginning to have feelings for.

Here, the missing piece was the physiological sensations of his gentle touch.

Continued Growth

I knew it was important to put all the pieces together in a way that would help me let go of the past, and I felt reasonably sure I had done that.

There was still one problem. Every time I thought about how I had behaved with my friend, I felt a burden of regret. I hadn't had any contact with my sweet friend after that night, so about a week later I reached out to thank him for his kindness.

I didn't ask for or expect a response, I simply wanted to acknowledge him, but when he didn't respond, I felt all the pain and sorrow of the past week return. Time went by and I reached out, in a similar way, again without requesting a response, and, again, none was given.

The regret and pain continued to grow and I felt like it was suffocating me. I knew I had acted like an emotional freak, and even though I hadn't asked for a reply, I really wanted one. Still, at some level, I felt like I didn't deserve anything from him.

I had reoccurring thoughts that validated everything I was feeling like: "There's not a man on this earth who would want to be in a relationship with someone who appeared to have the extreme emotional problems as I had." I was so sad. Through my insecure perspective, I could see how completely pathetic I must have appeared, which was not at all a true representation of how I felt about myself. The angst became overwhelming and I reached out to a good friend for comfort. I began telling her how embarrassed and ashamed I felt. I said to her, "You know, it's funny, but I behaved so poorly that I feel like I'm bad or I have done something wrong and I don't deserve to be forgiven." I was beating myself up with statements like "How could I have been so stupid?" and "I have completely humiliated myself." Then, she said, "I have known you a long time and I have never known you to feel this way or even hold on to something like this. You should talk to him."

Even though I was consciously aware of the fears and beliefs that were present, I was feeling extremely insecure and vulnerable. I knew

Letting Go of Painful Memories

another rejection from him would just add more pain and confusion, but I also knew she was right. I needed closure and felt, in order to let this go, I had to talk to him again.

Not wanting to burden him any more than I already felt I had, I sent him a text, this time with a request to talk. Again, I received no response. It had been over a month since we had any communication so the next day I decided to call. I tried hard to contain my emotions, but the second I heard his voice and I opened my mouth to leave a message, the tears began to flow.

After waiting several hours for him to respond, and feeling stupid for not containing my emotions, I sent him a text wishing him well, with a promise I would not reach out again. At some level, I was still feeling that I had behaved so badly, I really didn't deserve a response.

The impact of how my emotional behavior had terminated this relationship, and my impression of what he must have thought about me came crashing down. The burden I felt was almost too painful to bear.

With all this "evidence," my detrimental beliefs began to scream even louder than before, and I felt lost in my pain, with nowhere to turn for comfort.

I mourned over the things I had told him and the questions I had asked. In the middle of beating myself up, I got a text from him saying, "Please don't be so sad. I have been thinking about you. Thank you for the kind emails you have sent; I will call you later tonight."

Panic set in. Even though talking with him is what I thought I needed, I felt so insecure about the entire interaction involving him, I didn't trust myself, and I was afraid to talk to him.

Besides, I had just resigned myself to the fact that I would need to process this on my own, but something deep inside felt I needed to apologize and say goodbye. I knew if we talked, I didn't want to validate the emotional freak theory again by crying! I had to figure this out before he called.

I began to think about the all-encompassing sadness I felt over our disastrous date. This was the conversation I had with myself.

Question: "What do I need to hear from him?"

Answer: "I need him to reassure me that he forgives me."

Question: "Why do I need him to say he forgives me?"
Answer: "Because I acted like an emotional freak."
Question: "He has already said everything was okay and you know he really means it, so why is it so important to hear him say that he forgives you again?"
Answer: "I'm not sure."
Question: "What else do you need to hear?"
Answer: "I would like him to say goodbye."
Question: "Why do you want this from him? He owes you nothing."

As I pondered this question, it hit me! All of the overwhelming angst and sorrow I had associated with the emotional breakdown with my friend were actually unresolved feelings that had been dormant since the traumatic events of my childhood.

It was finally starting to make sense.

Because the childhood events were so painful, I not only suppressed the memory but also separated from the emotions caused by my thoughts, feelings and beliefs. When I was triggered, the feelings I had experienced were overwhelming, and in the moment I couldn't handle them, so I transferred the surfacing emotions onto the breakdown.

Yet, by having the courage to move through the pain, and giving myself time to heal, many other painful experiences have surfaced and healed as well.

The voices in my head were saying, "How could I have been so stupid?" "I have completely humiliated myself," "I feel so ashamed," "I am so embarrassed," and "I feel like I have done something bad." I realized that many of these statements and the heightened emotions I had been experiencing were not relevant to the interaction I had just faced. Nothing about the date or even about my breakdown should have provoked such intense feelings; in fact, to the contrary, as when I needed him this man was genuinely loving and kind.

Even the need I felt to ask for his forgiveness was not about him. I realized that what I really needed was for my sister to forgive me for pain I blamed myself for. My sister and I were never very close. I felt guilty for the abusive relationship that took place and for abandoning her. I also felt hurt that she had abandoned me as well. She died before we could talk about the impact these experiences had in our lives.

The reason I wanted my friend to say goodbye was because I hadn't talked to him in a while, which triggered reoccurring feelings of abandonment.

Our emotional mind continually tries to heal unresolved emotional issues. This is why we are triggered. Dealing with the details of an emotional hijacking can help us heal.

I felt truly blessed that I had this breakdown with a genuinely good man, and if I had let him know I was still struggling he would have gladly responded sooner.

This experience has been very interesting to process. I have known my whole life that this abuse had happened; what I didn't realize was how I had completely separated all emotional attachments from the abuse in order to survive. By doing this, any time a thought of this event would come up I would feel nothing—no shame, no guilt, no regrets. Because I had no feelings attached to the traumatic events it was almost like it had happened to someone else, so I never felt the need to look at or resolve it.

Looking back on this experience, I can see how the safety I felt with this man opened the door to release the suppressed emotions from this painful event.

Gratefully, I now understand the power this emotional anchor has had over my life. I've also come to realize that healing is an ongoing process. It has taken time to comprehend all the effects these childhood experiences have had on my life. Yet by having the courage to move through the pain, and giving myself time to heal, many other painful experiences have surfaced and healed as well.

This experience has been one of many that have been quite challenging for me to share, but it has caused me to ponder how many others hold themselves back or transfer emotions from grief, loss or regret because they don't know how to handle the trauma that has occurred in their lives.

If you have experienced a painful event, or you personally understand how an amygdala hijacking can affect your emotional stability, this process can help you.

THE PROCESS OF LETTING GO OF GRIEF, LOSS, AND REGRETS

The purpose of this process is to assist you in deciphering illogical facts from an amygdala hijacking so you can let go of past pain and confidently move forward.

Identify the grief, loss, or regret you would like to release.
Ask yourself the following questions:
- Due to grief, loss, or regret, what part of my life feels like it will never be the same?
- What do I wish I could do over?
- What would I do differently?
- What insights have I gained and how have those insights increased my understanding and compassion for others?
- Are there ways in which I am unwilling to forgive myself or others?
- Do I need to apologize? If so, what is preventing me from doing so?
- Is there any guilt or shame that needs to be addressed?
- If so, what will it take to release the guilt or shame and forgive?
- How has this situation blocked me from moving forward?
- What have I compromised to hold on to my pain? Laughing, socializing, taking time to enjoy the things I like?
- What will I have to accept, to let go of the grief, loss, or regret that holds me down?
- It's time to let go of the past and process your grief, loss, or regret. Give yourself permission and the proper amount of time to heal from the sadness. Then, move forward and find happiness.

Journal any thoughts or ideas that will encourage growth and promote change.

Secrets and Lies

Those who get caught in the unfortunate habit of holding secrets and telling lies deprive themselves of the peace and happiness they could otherwise enjoy. Usually these types of patterns are developed out of guilt and carry substantial consequences. The pain of regret and guilt that seems too shameful to admit usually carries a heavy burden that can destroy even the most precious of relationships. I previously shared with you how a person close to me used to say, "You think I'm a monster." They were living in a world of secrets and lies and felt guilty for their actions. They did not want to admit how the choices they were making had created their internal angst and suffering. It was easier for them to blame others for the angst than to go inside and do the real work.

The real work is admitting you are human and acknowledging, as humans, we make mistakes; sometimes we are disappointed in ourselves and occasionally those disappointments hurt others.

Some people are unwilling to admit to their mistakes because they do not know how to process their guilt and shame; or, they minimize the choices they have made or hide their mistakes and pretend the experience never happened. The problem with them hiding from mistakes is that the angst causes burdens that will impact the way they feel about themselves, and have a major impact on their relationships.

Because they feel badly about themselves and are unwilling to do what is needed to release their pain, they often blame others to justify the choices that they have made. Justifications like these open the door for more mistakes that generate more secrets, lies and anguish.

The secrets and lies we hide, and the things we tell ourselves to justify our deceptions, contain a lot of emotional energy that will hold us down and deprive us from the ability to feel at peace or create true happiness. Whether it's the lies we tell ourselves or secrets of guilt from actions we are unwilling to admit, the internal torment can be hard to bear.

The real work is admitting you are human and acknowledging, as humans, we make mistakes; sometimes we are disappointed in ourselves and occasionally those disappointments hurt others.

Shame is an emotion that can destroy our peace and consume our self-worth. Shame is much harder to cope with than guilt, because shame integrates into our identity and affects the way we view ourselves, whereas guilt is about the things that we do, which can be much easier to manage, control and resolve.

For some, the shame of the burdens they carry is not caused by the choices that they have made, but instead, the pain they bear has been caused by the abusive actions of others. Their secrets and lies are a coping mechanism to hide from the pain they don't feel they can handle. Shame enhances their feelings of insignificance and will cause them deep despair.

Whether the burdens you carry are from choices that you have made or they are from choices that have been forced upon you, the need to release the pain is the same. Choosing to hold on to burdens like these will weigh us down, zap our energy and destroy our self-worth. Holding secrets and telling lies is an uncomfortable game that we play with ourselves to avoid the consequences of our actions. Yet, as uncomfortable as it may feel you cannot pick and choose the things you are willing to let go of and the things you won't. This is an all or nothing exchange; holding back will only keep you in this vicious cycle. There may be aspects of this cycle that may seem too painful to admit, but the only way out is to take an honest look at any self-deception that you hold. Take some time to evaluate your judgments, perceptions, triggers and any automatic defense mechanisms you have been using. Admit your mistakes and acknowledge how the choices you have made have impacted your relationships. Give yourself time to grieve and then forgive yourself. To complete this process and truly let go, you must admit your mistakes and ask for forgiveness from those who have been hurt. Understanding the choices that you have made, and having the courage to take an honest stand for yourself, will release the hold these painful habits once held.

THE PROCESS OF RELEASING THE EFFECTS OF SECRETS AND LIES

The purpose of this process is to get to a place where you can look at the thoughts, feelings, attitudes and beliefs that have prolonged guilt or shame. You will also address the burdens you have placed upon yourself by holding secrets and telling lies.

Do you have secrets that compromise your relationships and zap your emotional resources?

If so, get a journal and, in a private place, write down all that comes to your mind. Getting your secrets out will give you the ability to look at the choices you have made. Acknowledging any burdens these choices have placed on you and on others will help you face things as they really are. Write without thinking, self judgment and without concern that it might sound illogical.

Letting go of mistakes can be uncomfortable, so be gentle on yourself. Keep asking questions and writing until your knowledge increases and you can truly forgive yourself for all the pain your choices have caused.

The first part of this process is best done in private, but, if it becomes too painful and you have a trusted friend in your life, don't hesitate to reach out for support. Strive to raise all of your thoughts, feelings and beliefs to a conscious level where you can analyze them. Remember, feelings of hate, anger, guilt or shame WILL sabotage the process. Don't stop just because you feel uncomfortable. Push past the pain and keep writing. The more illogical, the better understanding you will have about your thoughts, actions, and feelings. Again, be gentle, but don't justify your actions. Be completely honest with yourself. Honesty will help you get to a place where you can let go and truly forgive yourself.

Once you have truly forgiven yourself you can go on to forgive others and, when necessary, ask others to forgive you in return. If you are burdened by multiple mistakes, start with the ones you can handle and then move on to the ones that cause you the most pain. You deserve to let these painful memories go and move on to live a peaceful, happy life. The choice is up to you. You can choose the burden that comes with the fear you have created or the freedom that comes from facing the pain and releasing the weight.

As you begin listening to your thoughts around the events, you will know the questions to ask. If you get stuck, here are some questions that may help.
- What am I hiding?
- Why have I held on to this secret for so long?
- What fears hold me back from revealing these secrets?
- What has holding secrets cost me?
- How have I justified withholding my secrets?
- In what ways have I concealed my secrets?
- Who do I most fear to tell? Why?
- What am I protecting?
- What do I think I have to gain?
- What am I afraid people will think?
- How have secrets affected the way I trust myself and others?
- Where have I pushed others away?
- Who do I blame for my mistakes (self or others)?
- How has holding on to my secret affected my life?
- What am I afraid of losing?

Journal any thoughts or ideas that will encourage growth and promote change.

Remember, journaling can be very liberating because feelings buried alive are more intense in an unconscious form than they are after we consciously understand them.

Be gentle with yourself, accept wherever you are in the process and acknowledge the choices you are currently making to create the inner peace you deserve.

Keep writing your thoughts, feelings, attitudes and any beliefs you have formed until you have a clear understanding of the price you have paid for your deception. You may find it is as simple as, "I withhold because I am too discouraged to ask for what I want," or "I have been rejected so many times, I'm afraid to ask again. I don't think I can handle more rejection." You may find it is something deeper, such as the belief that "It is better to conceal, so I don't have to feel."

Be gentle with yourself, accept wherever you are in the process and acknowledge the choices you are currently making to create the inner peace you deserve.

As we shift out of making excuses for our actions and release the guilt, regrets and secrets, we can open the door for the peace that comes to us through forgiveness.

Chapter 21

Learning to Forgive

"We must develop and maintain the capacity to forgive. He who is devoid of the power to forgive is devoid of the power to love. There is some good in the worst of us and some evil in the best of us. When we discover this, we are less prone to hate our enemies."

~ Martin Luther King, Jr.

Forgiveness is an amazing way to let go of the past, which will renew our energy to create a bright new future. But sometimes it is hard to forgive when someone has hurt us. In fact, the deeper the pain, the harder it is to forgive.

As hard as it is to forgive others, the bigger trial many of us face is the ability to forgive ourselves. We live in silent misery as we beat ourselves up over and over again for the mistakes we have made. Some of us beat ourselves up even when our pain was caused by a defenseless act of violence.

Like accountability, forgiveness requires consciously evaluating our emotional reactions and looking at the choices we have made that add to our inner conflict. Again, when you choose to forgive someone who has hurt you, you take back any power they might have had over you. Even though it is hard and, at times, even painful, forgiveness is the only way we will ever attain lasting peace. Understanding why we hold on to emotional events will make forgiveness much easier.

It seems that most of the conflict we experience and have a hard time getting over occurs with those closest to us who have broken our trust and left us hurting. What can be even more painful is when they walk away without even acknowledging the pain that they have caused.

Yet, we are the only ones who can manage, control, or release our emotional pain. The easiest way to do this is to analyze the ways we give our power away by holding on to blame and refusing to forgive. When we focus our energy on ways we can forgive and let go of the burdens we carry, we have more energy to create the kind of life we want.

Reconciliation

Forgiveness does not always mean reconciliation. There are times, after taking measures to forgive, we realize our trust has been gravely violated. After evaluating the relationship, we can clearly see that there is no way a safe, trusting or productive relationship can be re-established.

Productive relationships should be based on common values of mutual respect. In situations where values and respect are ignored or have been violated multiple times, it is best to re-evaluate the relationship.

> *Like accountability, forgiveness requires consciously evaluating our emotional reactions and looking at the choices we have made that add to our inner conflict.*

When possible, determine what can be done to set new boundaries and reestablish a trusting relationship. If reconciliation is impossible, take accountability, make sure you clear up any miscommunications that have occurred and, if you feel you have hurt or offended someone, apologize, ask for forgiveness, then do what you can to make restitution. Forgive yourself for any mistakes you have made. Readjust the relationship in a way that will create positive growth for all parties, say goodbye and move on.

The moment you forgive someone is the moment you release the power and control they once had over your emotional life. When you forgive yourself, you give yourself permission to live in your own power.

Taking Back What Once Was Lost

Throughout my life, I have worked hard to resolve the pain and sorrow caused by my childhood events. I have been truly humbled at the compassion, insights and strength that I have gained. With all my heart, I know that I could not have accomplished the progress and growth I have without the gift of forgiveness. Let me share the strength that came from processing one of my more painful experiences.

Learning to Forgive

When I was 11, my 18-year-old brother committed suicide. I was devastated because he was my hero, my protector and my friend. Shortly after his funeral, I was walking in my neighborhood, when two of his friends drove up in a car next to me and rolled down their window. They told me what a good guy my brother was and how sorry they were about his death. I loved that somebody would talk to me about my brother. I was in so much pain and missed him so much.

The moment you forgive someone is the moment you release the power and control they once had over your emotional life. When you forgive yourself, you give yourself permission to step back into your own power.

In the midst of the conversation, one said to the other, "Hey, we should kidnap her," and they both began to laugh. Being neglected and feeling abandoned and alone in my pain, I was grateful for the attention, and I let them reach out and pull me through the car window.

I don't remember much of their conversation. What I do remember is that both boys were drinking a lot. We ended up in the mountains and, one at a time, they began to use me to satisfy their desires. When I tried to resist, one said to the other, "Get the gun, and we'll just shoot her and leave her here." I stopped fighting. When they were done with me, they gave me a very strong warning. They said if I told anyone what had happened they would not only kill me, they would kill my family, too.

In an attempt to make some sense out of what had occurred, I blamed myself. For the longest time, I went over and over the things I did to cause this horrible event. It wasn't until later in life I realized that this was typical in someone who had been victimized. Those who have been victimized feel completely powerless and, even after a traumatic event is over, they often find reasons to blame themselves for the crime.

We all have painful events in our lives that we must let go of. For some, it may be the loss of someone they loved; for others, it may be the pain and sorrow they carry from being mistreated.

Forgiveness is not about blaming yourself for the pain you have felt or the bad things that have happened to you. Forgiveness is about taking your power back. I was already immersed in shame before this incident with my brothers' friends occurred, and this experience just amplified my feelings of unworthiness and self-blame. It took me more than three decades before I finally realized I would never heal by blaming myself or resenting others.

As I began to process this experience, I realized it would help to consider my physical and emotional state when I was 11. At that time, I had already suffered a lot of negligence and abuse; I felt abandoned in my pain. The boys were saying kind things about my brother whom I loved, so I innocently trusted them. I was completely oblivious of what was about to occur.

While evaluating my 11-year-old life, I realized the only mistake I made was in not stepping away from the car window. I did not initiate, ask for, want or deserve the violence and abuse that occurred that night.

With that understanding, I actually began to have compassion for myself, and for the first time was able to face the pain and separate myself from the trauma of their abuse. I realized my one innocent mistake and could completely understand why I made it. I now had the power to take accountability for my naive mistake and release myself from the shame, blame and guilt I had harbored as a result of their actions. When I acknowledged the one thing I could have done differently, I could give back what did not belong to me and forgive myself for all the ways I had thought what happened to me was my fault. Because I was ready to put my past behind me, I was able to truly forgive the boys for their actions, and, as I did, I was able to release the pain and heal.

This formula has given me a realistic perspective of why I structured certain events the way I did. By accurately examining my choices, and considering the age at which the choices were made, I have been able to forgive and release events that otherwise would have had the power to destroy my life.

From Bad to Worse

Although this event in my life was traumatic in and of itself, what hurt even more was the way my father handled the situation. His reactions only served to reinforce my pain and all the detrimental beliefs that came along with the reality of my life.

I don't really remember how long it was before I talked to my mother about my painful experience, but, when I did, she told me, whatever I did, I shouldn't tell my father, and then she left to meet him at the bar.

I was terrified of my father and relieved when my mother had assured me she wouldn't tell him, and that she and I would talk about this experience later.

When my parents returned home from the bar, my father was in a rage.

He grabbed his belt, yanked me by the hair and began beating me, and thrashing me around the living room, calling me terrible names. My father screamed at me and said, "If this really happened, we will go to the police right now!" I was confused and frightened and was still afraid for my family's safety, because of what the boys had said.

It was not until I took control, faced the pain of my emotional anchors, forgave a lot of people, but, most importantly, forgave and learned to trust myself, that I was able to find lasting peace.

I ran away from home shortly after this incident occurred, and never returned. After living in various places for about a year, I was picked up by the police and placed with my sister and her husband, which only increased my shame and sorrow. When that ended, I was placed in the California foster care system.

I grew up as an unprotected child in a cruel world. My core structures were based on feeling worthless and unimportant, and the belief that I was unlovable. I had a lot of evidence validating those feelings, and for many years those feelings haunted me.

It was not until I took control, faced the pain of my emotional experiences, forgave a lot of people, but most importantly forgave and learned to trust myself, that I was able to find lasting peace.

In the story of the two wolves from earlier in the book, it says, "Holding on to anger is like drinking poison and expecting your enemy to die." I think, when we refuse to forgive, we slowly poison ourselves with all the resentment, pain, and sorrow we accumulate. This kind of poison can block us from feeling wanted, accepted or even loved.

I have shed many tears writing this book, and this section has been particularly uncomfortable for me. When my father was alive, I was too afraid of him to establish a relationship, and I really regret that. Instead of fearing him my whole life, I wish I would have realized the strength the challenges in my life had created before he had died. I may have been able to make a difference in his life.

"Holding on to anger is like drinking poison and expecting your enemy to die."

The greatest gift I now possess is that I have the conscious ability to separate myself from others' actions, by acknowledging that their reactions stem from the way they have filtered their experiences and structured their own emotional patterns. I now realize that pain and fear cause illogical decisions and irrational behaviors. When I am in pain and you come to me with your pain, I can't hear you. It's not that I don't want to have compassion, it's that my own pain is screaming so loudly I can hear nothing else.

Most of my memories of my father included anger, but his violence was totally out of control the night he learned of my abuse at the hands of my brother's friends.

I believe my father was probably devastated and, at some level, he might have felt responsible for the abuse I had incurred and for my brother's recent death. My father was an angry man who used drugs and alcohol to cover his pain. Anger was how he handled everything in his life. Looking at this from that perspective, I'm sure he was angry with himself and he had plenty of evidence to feel like he was a complete failure as a father or maybe even as a human being, by having his oldest son commit suicide and his youngest daughter violated.

Evaluating my father's feelings of inadequacy and the lack of love he felt in his own childhood has helped me separate from my feelings of powerlessness created by his anger and abuse. This understanding has also given me the ability to feel empathy for the fact that he did not know how to give love and was probably never able to feel loved either.

Forgiveness helps us process emotional pain and grief in our lives and progress from feeling captive and powerless to feeling powerful and free!

Freedom in Forgiveness

Forgiveness does not justify, excuse or deny any pain the offense has caused.

Our forgiveness practices have nothing to do with others acknowledging our pain or accepting an apology. The act of true forgiveness will set us free from the self-imposed burden the offense has had over our emotional life.

When we choose not to forgive others, we remain in bondage to the person who has hurt or offended us. This bondage can dominate our thoughts and emotional energy and change the way we look at life.

When we don't forgive, we cannot be fully present or positively engaged in relationships with others, because the pain or resentment is unconsciously occupying our emotional resources.

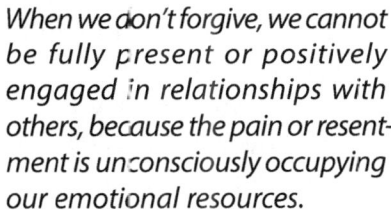

When we don't forgive, we cannot be fully present or positively engaged in relationships with others, because the pain or resentment is unconsciously occupying our emotional resources.

Some people hold themselves back from forgiveness because, unconsciously, they carry a great deal of blame and guilt for the way they have been treated or for the way they have mistreated others. Instead of resolving the pain, they believe that forgiveness is not available to them or that they don't deserve to be forgiven, so they cut themselves off from peace and perpetuate their misery.

There are others who don't forgive because they are caught up in perfectionism. The unconscious belief that fuels perfectionism is, "I am not good enough." Perfectionists set high standards and unattainable goals to validate their unconscious belief of not measuring up. They often pay a high price, as they deprive themselves of the personal satisfaction that comes from completion. This perception also affects their ability to be in close relationships, as they push people away with their "Nothing is good enough" attitude.

To these perfectionists, and to anyone who is struggling to reach a goal but continually raising the bar and falling short, I would say: Perfection is an illusion that will only create a life full of sorrow and pain. Yet when used in the right way these strengths will set you on a path to success. Set attainable goals that will validate your hard work. Forgive yourself. Value progression, not perfection; and use gratitude as your guide. Look for the greatness within and celebrate the strong, wonderful person you have become. Learn to value the gifts that others have to offer as well.

The unconscious belief that fuels perfectionism is, "I am not good enough."

"Easier said than done," you may think. Yes, but as you make a conscious effort to acknowledge your accomplishment and exercise patience for human frailties through forgiveness, you will find it becomes doable.

Researchers say that holding on to pain and resentment can have adverse effects on our health. High blood pressure, headaches, stomach problems and back pains are just a few symptoms that may affect those who hold on to pain and resentment.

Forgiveness helps us learn from our emotional experiences and will get us out of living in them.

True forgiveness does not include forgetting, because if we completely forget the offences against us, we set ourselves up for reoccurring mistreatment, wondering why we keep experiencing the same type of pain over and over.

When we truly forgive ourselves, it will be much easier to seek for others' forgiveness.

The forgiveness process has healing powers that will boost your self-worth and lift you to greater heights. Remember, you do not have the capacity to forgive another until you forgive yourself first.

THE PROCESS OF FORGIVENESS

The purpose of this process is to gain a deeper understanding of why you protect yourself by holding on to pain and sorrow. This awareness will increase your ability to let go of the past and truly forgive.

When we choose to forgive, we release the emotional hold others have had on our lives. Look at any thoughts, feelings, attitudes, and beliefs that prevent you from forgiving yourself and others. Then ask:

- Is there pain in my life that requires forgiveness?
- Of what do I need to forgive myself?
- Who in my life is the hardest to forgive? Why?
- What price have I paid for hanging on to pain, sorrow, hate, or resentment?
- How would letting go of the burden I carry benefit my life? How would it benefit others?

Journal any thoughts or ideas that will encourage growth and promote change.

Chapter 22

Empowering Beliefs

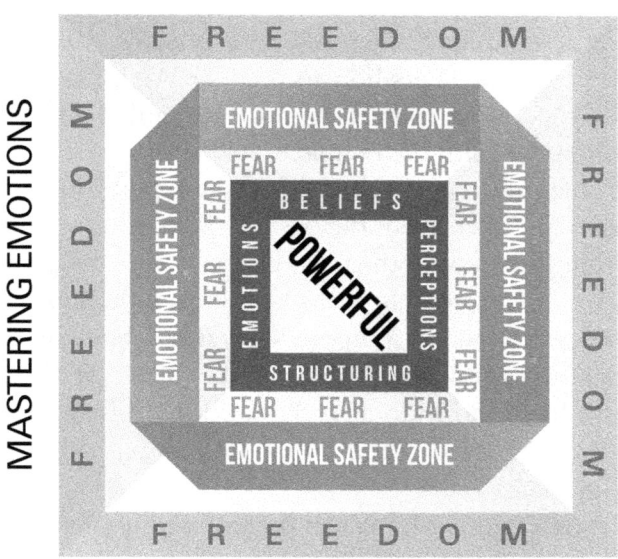

"Change the way you look at things and the things you look at change."

~ Dr. Wayne W. Dyer

Transcending our reality will start when we learn to change our beliefs.

A number of years ago, a seminary professor was vacationing with his wife in Tennessee. One morning they stopped to eat breakfast at a small restaurant, hoping to enjoy a quiet family meal.

While waiting for their food, they noticed a distinguished-looking, white-haired man moving from table to table visiting with the guests.

The professor leaned over and whispered to his wife, "I hope he doesn't come over here;" but, sure enough, the man did approach their table.

"Where are you folks from?" he asked in a friendly voice.

"Oklahoma," they answered.

"Great to have you here in Tennessee," the stranger said. "What do you do for a living?"

"I teach at a seminary," the professor replied.

"Oh, you teach preachers how to preach? Well, I've got a really great story for you." With that, the gentleman pulled up a chair and sat down at the table with the couple.

"See that mountain over there?" he asked, pointing out the restaurant window. "Not far from the base of that mountain, there was a boy born to an unwed mother. He had a hard time growing up, because every place he went, he was always asked the same question: 'Hey boy, who's your daddy?' Whether he was at school, on the street, or in the grocery store, people would ask the same question, 'Who's your daddy?' He would hide at recess and lunchtime from other students. He would avoid going into stores because that question hurt him so bad."

The old man continued, "When the boy was about 12 years old, a new preacher came to his church. To avoid hearing the question, 'Who's your daddy?' from the new preacher, the boy made it a habit to go to church late and slip out early. But, one day, the new preacher said the benediction so fast the young man got caught and had to walk out with the crowd."

"Just about the time he got to the back door, the new preacher, not knowing anything about him, put his hand on his shoulder and asked him, 'Son, who's your daddy?'"

"All the members of the congregation got deathly quiet. The boy could feel the eyes of everyone in the church looking at him. By now, everyone knew the answer to the question, 'Who's your daddy?' This new preacher, though, sensed the situation around him, and using discernment that only the Holy Spirit could give, said the following to that scared little boy.

'Wait a minute! I know who you are. I see the family resemblance now. You are a child of God.'

"With that, he patted the boy on his shoulder and said: 'Boy, you've got a great inheritance. Go and claim it."

The old man paused briefly, and then went on with his story. "The boy smiled for the first time in a long time and walked out the door, a changed person. He was never the same. Whenever anyone asked him, 'Who's your Daddy?' he'd just tell them, 'I'm a child of God.'"

The distinguished gentleman got up from the table and said, "Isn't that a great story?" The professor responded that it really was a great story! As the man turned to leave, he said, "You know if that new preacher hadn't told me that I was one of God's children, I probably never would have amounted to anything!" And he walked away.

The seminary professor and his wife were stunned. He called the waitress over and asked her, "Do you know that man who was sitting at our table and just left?"

The waitress grinned and said, "Of course. Everybody here knows him. That's Ben Hooper. He's the former governor of Tennessee!"[1]

Creating Powerful Beliefs

In the story above, the Governor was able to restructure his identity by consciously choosing a new belief and reinforcing that belief every time someone asked him, "Who's your daddy?"

By consciously restructuring the way he viewed himself, he was able to replace the pain that came from not knowing his father with a sense of satisfaction for who he truly was and what he could become. As we develop more awareness of the unconscious structures that dictate our belief system like Ben Hooper did, we can reframe our beliefs and create a sense of satisfaction.

We can look at the composite of our belief system like the pieces to a very complex puzzle. Trying to put the pieces together in the unconscious mind is like putting together a three-dimensional puzzle with layers of pieces and no image to look at or follow. The problem

---

[1] Related by Dr. Fred Craddock, seminary professor of homiletics at Emory University in Atlanta, Georgia.

with the unconscious pieces of this puzzle is, we feel like our future happiness depends on solving it.

Then, in the midst of our confusion, we discover the solution was within our grasp all along. The image of the complete puzzle we seek can be easily accessed in the chambers of our conscious mind.

Our belief system is part of an intricate puzzle that interlocks the structures that connect incoming information, opinions, interactions and even opportunities.

Our Beliefs Define How We Feel

Our beliefs define how we feel about ourselves, which determines how we fit in and interact with the world around us.

Here's an example:

When I was in the fourth grade, I was invited to an end-of-the-year party. Because I believed that nobody liked me, even though I was personally invited to the party, I didn't want to go, but was worried about offending the one who invited me; so I went. When I got to the party, I quietly slipped in the back gate and watched everyone from a distance.

Because unconscious beliefs have a lot of influence they will affect every decision we make.

If I saw someone walking toward me, or if anyone looked like they wanted to talk to me, I would feel anxious and would act busy or walk away. I only stayed a short time and then cried all the way home because nobody talked to me, which reinforced my belief that nobody liked me.

I was completely blind to the fact that I didn't give anyone a chance to get anywhere near me, let alone talk to me. Even into adulthood, these same types of insecurities held me back from making new friends.

We generate a lot of fears based on what we believe others may think of us. These fears can hold us back from gaining a sense of safety and belonging necessary to achieve the acceptance and balance we seek in life.

Because unconscious beliefs have a lot of influence, they will influence every decision we make.

Empowering Beliefs

We have all kinds of beliefs that can affect our responses and prompt our reactions. Two types of beliefs that are important to note are beneficial beliefs, which will assist us in responding to life in a way that encourages confidence and empowers success, and fear-based beliefs, which will discourage and bring us down. Thoughts like: "How could I be that stupid?" "I knew I shouldn't have come," and "Why does this always happen to me?" are some examples of detrimental beliefs.

When it comes to detrimental beliefs, it does not matter how much evidence we have that the belief is not true, the only thing that matters is what we feel or believe to be true. We will filter everything based on our feelings and beliefs. This filter can affect the way we perceive others as well.

If I have a low self-esteem and someone tells me that I am pretty, and I don't believe I am pretty, I won't trust what he or she says to be true. I may even withdraw and become suspicious of their motives.

When it comes to our perceptions, *what is really being said* in a conversation isn't what is heard. What we hear is filtered through the feelings and beliefs we have inadvertently attached to the current interaction or event.

The challenge is, unless we consciously identify the illogical beliefs influencing our feelings and perceptions, nothing will change.

I know many successful people who are not very happy. It doesn't matter how much money they make or how much respect they earn, they have so many detrimental beliefs that they don't enjoy the inner peace and personal satisfaction they have worked so hard to gain.

Unless we are consciously aware of our detrimental beliefs, they will continue to disrupt our thoughts and limit our happiness. Unfortunately, detrimental beliefs will be the most prevalent when we are out of our comfort zone and feeling vulnerable. When we are already feeling vulnerable, these beliefs have the ability to create some illogical outcomes.

Sometimes its hard to separate familiar emotions from reality. After my husband of 28 years left, it took me a while to gain enough courage to date again.

When I did, I met a wonderful British man on a Christian dating site. After talking for several months we agreed to meet. The day before our date, I was overcome with fear and didn't want to go. I had no idea what I was afraid of. What I did know was that my fear was not about him.

I called a friend to talk about the situation. After I finished telling her about my dilemma, she began pushing me so I could get to the bottom of my fears. I kept giving her all the logical reasons I did not want to go; and she kept telling me, "Stop thinking and get out of your head!"

I was getting frustrated. I was trying as hard as I could to get out of my logical mind to find the emotional reason for my fears. I only succeeded in becoming more irritated. My friend kept pushing me, until we were both aggravated. She raised her voice and said, "Why are you so afraid to let someone love you?" Those words sent my mind into a frenzy of confusion, I began to panic. I lost all sense of reason. Then I screamed, "Because Love is Violence!"

She softened her voice and said, "And who told you that?"

I broke down and cried! This wonderful man I was about to go out with had pushed me into all my fears, because what he had to offer was unfamiliar and not like anything I had ever experienced before. In that moment, I discovered how easy it was to to let my unconscious fears and beliefs sabotage a relationship.

When I hung up the phone, I began to think about what I had said, "Love is Violence!" Who in their right mind would think such an illogical statement? Yet, when it came out, it was my shocking but sad truth. The very thought of love being violent is kind of crazy, but, in my life, love had felt violent.

Have you ever had thoughts that didn't make sense and wondered, "Where the heck did that come from?" I have met people who thought they were a bit loco because of some of the thoughts that go through their minds, when in reality, what they are experiencing are expressions from past events that have been illogically inserted in the present moment.

Becoming the master of our emotions requires us to notice when illogical emotional patterns are influencing our decisions.

When we get out of these beliefs and fears, we can take charge of our actions and make decisions that will support us in creating the kind of life we want.

If we want a raise, we take the action to make it happen. If our boss is a busy man who appreciates hard work, we give him a summary of our accomplishments at the end of every month. We can also acknowledge him for his accomplishments and offer our time for extra work as needed. Then, when it comes time for a raise or a promotion, the boss will remember the consistent hard work we have displayed and will feel good about encouraging our contributions by giving us the promotion or raise we desire.

However, what typically happens when we let detrimental beliefs, such as, "I am not good enough," silently run in the background of our minds, is that we begin to worry excessively about what others will think if we acknowledge our accomplishments to the boss.

So we work hard then sit by, hoping the boss will notice what a great job we are doing and give us the promotion or raise we believe we deserve. Then we are hurt, angry or frustrated when we are passed by for that raise or promotion we wanted, and we blame others for our lack of success.

While some bosses may notice all of our hard work, most bosses have pressures of their own. They appreciate people who take the quiet initiative to let them know that things are getting done and they don't have to worry.

So, how do you rise above your detrimental beliefs and implement empowering beliefs that will encourage growth?

The first step is to get intensely curious about your emotional reactions. Curiosity and consciousness will increase your ability to successfully restructure your detrimental beliefs. The best time to discover most detrimental beliefs is when you are feeling insecure or vulnerable. As discussed earlier, most people feel vulnerable anytime they face change.

Some detrimental beliefs will take more effort to restructure because they have been reinforced many times throughout our lives. With these more powerful beliefs, it is particularly important to understand the habitual patterns that sabotage our wellbeing because they tend to be the familiar automatic ones that take control when life throws us in a different direction.

Habitual patterns include any detrimental thoughts, feelings and perceptions that disrupt our balance and leave us with a sense of despair.

Let's consider the "I'm not good enough" belief. This is a common belief structured in our childhood and is often triggered when we are offended or get our feelings hurt.

In times of despair, acknowledging the habitual patterns of our underlying beliefs will help us accept where we are and consciously reestablish safety, which will allow us to get back on track more quickly.

Because our fear-based beliefs have so much power, I thought it would be good to introduce restructuring fear-based beliefs in this chapter. In Tier V, you will expand upon this process, which will give you more power to overcome your limiting beliefs and create empowering beliefs that will increase your ability to enjoy a rich and fulfilling life.

THE PROCESS OF RESTRUCTURING FEAR-BASED BELIEFS

This is the first stage of processing fear-based beliefs. The purpose of this stage is to begin acknowledging the detrimental beliefs that sabotage your success.

Here is a basic list of detrimental beliefs that can help you identify the self-defeating beliefs that silently sabotages your success.

I am not good enough	I am unloved	I am weak
I am not important	I am a failure	I am unhappy
I am not social	I am undeserving	I am unlovable
I am not wanted	I am uncomfortable	I am unhealthy
I am not accepted	I am uneasy	I am unprotected
I am not appreciated	I am emotional	I am unsafe
I am not approachable	I am unstable	I am unpopular
I am not attractive	I am unfairly treated	I am unstable
I am not heard	I am unworthy	I am unproductive
I am unprepared	I am undesirable	I am unsatisfied
I am not worthy	I am uneducated	I am unsupported
I am not valued	I am unfocussed	I am unwanted
I am not cared about	I am unfulfilled	I am untrusting

As you can see detrimental beliefs have a variety of different meanings. The meanings we have attached to different situations in life will only show themselves when we are looking through different eyes. If you read through this list and a belief jumps out at you, you may want to specifically identify when you have felt that way. Detrimental beliefs are challenging to locate on a conscious level, so you may find it helpful to process using the childhood beliefs of the governor of Tennessee.

- What beliefs limited the boy in his early childhood?
- How did his beliefs affect the way he viewed himself in relation to others?
- How did his beliefs affect his relationships with children his own age?

- How did his beliefs affect the way he interacted with those in his community?
- How did his past beliefs influence thoughts, feelings, and attitudes in his life?
- How did those beliefs limit the way he saw his potential?
- Name some of the ways his beliefs were triggered.
- How did the well intentioned people in his environment attempt to protect him from pain?
- How did this attempted protection allow the belief to grow?
- What insecurities did this attempted protection perpetuate?
- The people in the town felt sorry for the boy. How did their pity add to and validate his false beliefs?
- What did this validation give him permission to avoid?
- What new perspective instantly transformed his belief system and his perception of himself?
- What was his new belief?
- How did his new belief change his life forever?

Now see if you can take an event from your own childhood and personalize the process you just practiced.

To begin the process it is important to identify where you are. You can utilize this process with areas in your life where you feel unable to progress:

- I am curious why _____ happens.
- When _____ happens, my thoughts are _____
and I feel _____ .
- The automatic assumptions that occur from my thoughts and feelings include the following: _____
- In retrospect, these assumptions were based on these facts: _____
and these feelings: _____
_____ .

- Some of the beliefs I am conscious of include the following: _____.
- This belief extends _____ reoccurring results in my life in the following ways: _____.

There is no right or wrong way to complete this process. If you are not consciously aware of the beliefs that distort your perceptions, use a common belief such as "I'm not good enough." Label fears attached to your emotional events with a belief. "I'm afraid that my boss gave my co-worker the raise because I'm not good enough."

Make sure you pay attention to any ineffective self-talk. When you listen carefully, your self-talk will give you clues to the attitudes and beliefs that cause your discomfort. Your judgments will help reveal some of your beliefs as does any habits of procrastination or reluctance to take action.

Once you have uncovered the belief, answer the following questions:

- What belief did I discover?
- What reoccurring fears fuel my beliefs?
- In what ways has this belief compromised my happiness?
- How has the protection of this belief served me?

Journal any thoughts or ideas that will encourage growth and promote change.

We will continue this process in Tier IV; for now, acknowledging the benefits you have received from your beliefs will help you move on to create something new. Restructuring the unconscious patterns that get in the way of our happiness and growth can be a very uncomfortable process, but when we don't do the work and let deep-rooted beliefs go unnoticed, it can have devastating results.

Unnoticed Deep-Rooted Detrimental Beliefs

I have a friend who, for years, would drink to avoid his feelings. He has had a hard time separating the guilt he feels from the results he has created. He's been very distraught over the many losses his drinking problem has caused, including his failed marriage and strained relationships with his kids.

He felt like the only thing he could do was to drink more to escape the pain, or die.

Sometimes it takes living through a lot of destructive experiences to take an honest look at the emotional choices we make and the pain they have caused.

Sometimes it takes living through a lot of destructive experiences in order to take an honest look at the choices we make and the destruction they cause. When my friend finally began to look at the results he had caused, he was so discouraged he felt all hope for happiness in the future was gone.

We should acknowledge here that deep rooted beliefs can cause overwhelming havoc and pain, and the results can become so devastating we don't know what to do.

My friend in the above story was stuck in a destructive cycle. He justified his drinking by believing that it was genetics that caused his weakness to alcohol and created his problem.

Now he understands that the beliefs that have caused him the most pain existed long before his drinking or his marriage had ever begun. As a child, he really struggled in school. The more he struggled, the more discouraged he became. His siblings did fairly well in school and his mother always seemed proud of their accomplishments. He, on the other hand, was always getting bad grades. He grew up hearing things like "If you weren't so lazy" or "You don't even try." Even when he did try, he would be put down. His ineffective beliefs were, "I am not good enough," "I am a failure," and, "Nobody loves me."

These deeply rooted beliefs generated the actions that led to his lost job, lost home, broken relationships and failed marriage.

Our detrimental beliefs will skew our view by adding fuel to our already uncomfortable anchors every time we are triggered. Therefore, it is important to be rigorous in identifying the beliefs driving our discouragements.

Remember, predominant beliefs are the result of countless numbers of emotional experiences, so their influence will be strong.

It is essential to identify how some of the detrimental beliefs that influence our feelings may be directing our perceptions and influencing our behaviors. It is only through restructuring our belief system that we will gain the ability to create the life we want.

By understanding habitual patterns like fighting to be right, getting angry, withdrawing or going silent, we recognize the ways that we give our power away to The Victim Addiction. Understanding how to restructure our fear-based beliefs will be one of the most powerful tools we can use in changing our lives and owning our personal power.

Our beliefs are most observable when our defense mechanisms are in a state of protection, so we are more likely to discover a detrimental belief shortly after a triggered event has occurred.

Some of our detrimental beliefs have formed unconscious habits and behaviors that have produced damaging consequences. Consciously acknowledging the consequences of our beliefs and behaviors will give us the ability to restructure our focus and create something new. Lets complete this section by identifying how your beliefs and feelings affect your behavior and produce your results. Start with:

The belief or beliefs directing my feelings and perceptions are ____ _____.

Ways these feelings and beliefs have caused me to feel powerless and unable to change are_____.

Ways my feelings and beliefs have contributed to the loneliness I have felt in my life are _____.

How these beliefs have affected relationships in my life are_____ .

Up until now, the unproductive results I have produced have been_ _____.

The results I would like to create are _____ .

Like the boy who became the Governor of Tennessee, when new beliefs are chosen and solidly anchored, astounding results are not only possible, they are inevitable! Processing and restructuring our detrimental beliefs will give us the power to succeed! The key is to restructure old beliefs with empowering beliefs that will help you create amazing shifts. Below is a list of Empowering beliefs. Use this list to identify new beliefs that will support the kind of life you want to live.

Empowering Beliefs List

I am good enough	I am worthy	I am trusted
I am beautiful	I am important	I am wanted
I am accepted	I am appreciated	I am approachable
I am attractive	I am cared about	I am comfortable
I am valued	I am deserving	I am free
I am desirable	I belong	I am supported
I am educated	I am treated fairly	I am focused
I am fulfilled	I am happy	I am healthy
I am heard	I am lovable	I am loved
I am popular	I am prepared	I am stable
I am productive	I am protected	I am safe
I am satisfied	I am sociable	I am deserving
I am creative	I am capable	I am worthwhile
I am forgiving	I am smart	Life is easy
I am heard	I am fun	I am successful
I can succeed	I love my life	My life is full of love

Above is a list of beliefs that can assist you in restructuring a new, more empowering belief. By looking at all the aspects of your life, consciously construct a new belief that will support you in creating the life you want.

A belief that would better support my happiness and growth is ___ _____ .

The evidence I can create that this belief is true is _____ .

I can implement this evidence into my life by_____ .

Journal any thoughts or ideas that will encourage growth and promote change.

In Tier V, we will take this process and expound upon it as we anchor beneficial emotions that will energize your success. In that process, you will specifically decide where you've been and how you want your life to look, feel and sound.

For example, the young boy who changed his belief around his identity went from feeling worthless to feeling valuable. Although nothing in his physical environment had actually changed, this new belief changed everything.

What he saw in himself invited people to reach out and encourage his success. He felt love and acceptance, where he had once felt rejected. Before his shift he thought people were talking about him. After his beliefs shifted he heard people talking to him, welcoming him into their lives. Everything in his environment changed because his new belief changed the way he felt about himself, which changed the way he perceived everything in the world around him.

Because our emotional structures are established in layers, keeping a journal gives us the ability to remember what we are working on and assist us in noticing the emotional patterns that reinforce beliefs.

To put the puzzle of our minds together, we must "face our fears" and challenge our detrimental beliefs. Once we do this, we can step outside our Emotional Safety Zone, identify inaccurate beliefs and implement a powerful belief system that will propel us to greater heights.

Chapter 23

Trusting Yourself

"Trust yourself, you know more than you think you do."

~ Benjamin Spock

Trust is an essential element in successful relationships. One of the unfortunate things about relationships is that at some time in our lives we will be subjected to the pain and sorrow that comes when someone we care about violates a trusting relationship. In many cases, accountability softens the blow and gives us the strength to get back up and try again; but, when deep bonds of trust have been broken, we may find it temporarily difficult to move on.

The end of my second marriage was a good example of this. When I married, I knew I was willing to do whatever it took to create a lasting relationship. Tristan and I both understood his anxieties and struggles around having my children in his environment, but we both felt if we worked together we could overcome any obstacles.

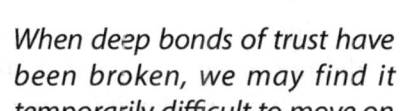

When deep bonds of trust have been broken, we may find it temporarily difficult to move on.

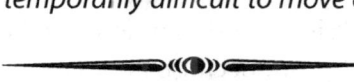

I knew living in Tristan's world would not be too challenging for me because having a clean, well-organized home had always been a priority for me.

My children and I worked very hard to keep things the way he liked them. With Tristan, everything in his home environment had to be perfect for him to feel calm, but the slightest scratch on a cabinet or a scuffmark on a door or baseboard would throw him into anxiety.

It wasn't long before Tristan began to resent the changes in his world, and it became harder and harder for him to tolerate the environmental intrusion and he ultimately removed himself from my life.

I couldn't believe I was alone again. I had been very careful in my decision to marry him and I thought I had chosen a partner I could spend the rest of my life with, and now he was gone.

There I was, abandoned again. I had such a hard time moving on.

Tristan had many of the qualities I truly wanted in a partner and I deeply mourned the loss of the relationship. I convinced myself I was strong enough to handle life on my own, and I would never look for love again.

Yet, the thought of living life without someone to share my life with broke my heart and left me feeling hopeless. I slipped into a mild depression and pulled away from everything and everyone, which enhanced my loneliness and created more pain.

Trying to pull myself together, I realistically pondered the relationship between Tristan and me. We had only lived together for a few months. I looked at all the ways I compromised things that were important to me to live in his world.

I knew his decision to move on was best for both of us, but I was deeply hurt and felt very discouraged.

I kept reminding myself of the concerns I had before we were married, hoping that would bring a semblance of peace. However, looking at what I was accountable for in the ending of the relationship did not bring me peace at all.

Then one day it hit me; I hadn't just fallen head over heels with Tristan and married him because of infatuation. I decided to marry Tristan because he was a good man and I believed that his deep love for me was real and would last. I realized that the failure of this second marriage tapped into deep insecurities and I didn't trust myself.

Ralph Waldo Emerson, once said, "Self-trust is the first secret of success."

Self-Trust

What is trust and why is it so important for us to trust ourselves?

The Merriam Webster Dictionary defines trust as an "assured reliance on the character, ability, strength or truth of someone or something" and "one in which confidence is placed." How is self-trust different than trust in others?

As seen in the definition above, trust is focused on something outside ourselves whereas with self-trust we look inside. Self-trust is not based on the reliance or strength of others. It is an inner knowledge, a feeling of security in one's personal ability to perform and achieve.

We develop self-trust as we overcome our weaknesses. Each time we exercise restraint or discipline, we create evidence that strengthens our ability to progress. The by-products of self-trust include self-confidence, self-reliance and self-respect.

It was important for me to notice a significant aspect of the story regarding my second divorce: I had made a mistake. I had misjudged the potential of a very substantial relationship, and when that relationship failed I not only questioned my decision-making skills, but I temporarily lost trust and confidence in my ability to love or be loved.

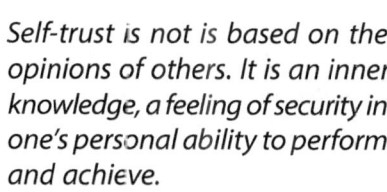

Self-trust is not is based on the opinions of others. It is an inner knowledge, a feeling of security in one's personal ability to perform and achieve.

When we don't trust ourselves, those closest to us pay the price, even if they had nothing to do with the original offence. Because we don't trust ourselves, we protect ourselves from further pain by pushing away those who could bring us the most comfort.

Our Emotional Safety Zone takes over to protect us from more pain. We close ourselves off by becoming guarded or suspicious, thus further limiting our ability to love or to be loved. Then we feel lonely and blame others for the way we feel.

Yet, trust is the foundation for all working relationships. Trust builds respect, creates safety and leads to deeper, more loving relationships.

When you trust yourself, you live in the *present* moment, and face challenges in a way that allows you to confidently move into the *future*.

You have more power than you realize to direct your own life. Self-trust allows you to listen to and follow the inner sense that guides your path. This sense prompts you to do things that will make your life easier.

Many years ago, I read a book called *The Gift of Fear* by Gavin De Becker. The book taught me a lot about recognizing, trusting and responding to my own intuition. A few years later, I improved those skills when I learned a technique that helped me clarify my internal instincts.

THE PROCESS OF ENHANCING INTERNAL INSTINCTS

The purpose of this process is to help you understand your feelings and use that understanding to create self trust.

The technique goes like this:

Close your eyes and relax. Think of something you really enjoy. Stay relaxed until you are aware of how good you feel just thinking about what you enjoy.

Open your eyes and process what you felt and where you felt it. For example, "I thought of someone I love and:

- I had a warm feeling in my heart."
- There was a rush of joy that filled my chest."
- I had butterflies in my stomach."

Understanding this feeling will help you recognize where your empowering intuition dwells and how you will feel when you know something is right.

Now let's look at fear. When you have had an event where you felt fear, process what you felt and where you felt it. For example, "I saw a snake on the trail and:

- I felt sick to my stomach."
- I felt anxiety in my chest, upper arms or the back of my neck."
- I felt panic. My chest became tight and my heart began to race."
- I was afraid and the hair on my arms stood up and I felt 'the chills.'"

You can also use this same process to identify happiness, sadness and other types of feelings.

Remember, the mind does not know the difference between what you see and what you remember so you can simulate such an experience by simply closing your eyes and thinking of something you fear, such as disappointment, heights, or snakes. What is important is that your thoughts produce an emotional fear response.

Journal any thoughts or ideas that will encourage growth and promote change.

It's important you have an awareness of the physiological and emotional responses you have to your natural emotions. This understanding can help you make important decisions by giving you a good indication as to how it feels when you make choices that will bring satisfaction or choices that bring despair. Understanding your intuition will also help you maintain personal safety.

The more you rely and act on your own intuition, the easier it becomes to trust yourself in all areas of life.

THE PROCESS OF SELF-TRUST

The purpose of this process is to look at the areas in your life where you trust yourself and define areas that you would like to improve.

- Define areas of your life where you know you trust yourself. Describe how that trust looks, feels, and sounds. Similar to this: How it looks is I am open and honest. How it sounds is people come to me for advice. How it feels is I have the confidence to try new things.
- Define areas of your life where you would like to increase your ability to trust.
- Now take the distinct habits of trust that you already posses and apply them in a way that will encourage growth in the areas of your life in which you would like to progress. Remember that trust begins with you. If there are areas of your life where you are out of integrity with someone or something clear it up so you are at peace with yourself. Once you are at peace with

yourself you can enjoy the benefits that come from trusting relationships.

Journal any thoughts or ideas that will encourage growth and promote change.

Whether you never learned to trust, or your trust has been broken and must be reestablished, following your own intuition will be an important key in generating a trust and living a fulfilling life.

Once you begin to truly trust yourself, your confidence goes up and your whole attitude about life begins to change.

Chapter 24

Attitude

"Worrying is like a rocking chair: it gives you something to do, but doesn't get you anywhere."

~ Erma Bombeck

The attitudes we produce in life affect the direction our thoughts, feelings, attitudes and beliefs go. Our attitudes also have the power to influence others. Some unconscious attitudes can really skew our perspective and weigh us down, making it hard to be motivated or happy.

Take this story for example:

> I had not really planned on taking a trip this time of year, and yet I found myself packing rather hurriedly. This trip was going to be unpleasant and I knew in advance that no real good would come of it. This was my annual "Guilt Trip."
>
> I got tickets to fly there on "WISH-I-HAD" airlines. It was an extremely short flight. I got my "baggage," which I could not check. I chose to carry it myself all the way. It was loaded down with a thousand memories of "what might have been." No one greeted me as I entered the terminal to the Regret City International Airport. I say international because people from all over the world come to this dismal town.
>
> As I checked into the "Last Resort Hotel," I noticed that they would be hosting the year's most important event — the annual "Pity Party." I wasn't going to miss that great social occasion. Many of the town's leading citizens would be there.

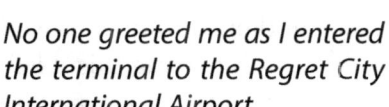

No one greeted me as I entered the terminal to the Regret City International Airport.

First, there would be the "Done" family; you know, "Should Have," "Would Have" and "Could Have." Then there would be the "I Had" family. You probably know old "Wish" and his clan. Of course, the "Opportunities" family; "Missed" and "Lost" would be present. The biggest family there would be the "Yesterdays."

There are far too many of them to count, but each one would have a very sad story to share. Of course, "Shattered Dreams" would surely make an appearance. "It's Their Fault" family would regale us with stories (excuses) about how things had failed in their life. The "Don't Blame Me" and "I Couldn't Help It" committee would loudly applaud each story.

To make a long story short, I went to this depressing party, knowing full well there would be no real benefit in doing so. And, as usual, I became very depressed. But as I thought about all of the stories of failures brought back from the past, it occurred to me that this trip and subsequent "pity parties" COULD be cancelled by ME!

I started to realize that I did not have to be there. And I didn't have to be depressed. One thing kept going through my mind: I can't change yesterday, but I do have the power to make today a wonderful day. I can be happy, joyous, fulfilled and encouraged, as well as being encouraging.

Knowing this, I left Regret City immediately, and didn't leave a forwarding address. Am I sorry for mistakes I've made in the past? YES! But there is no way to undo them.

So, if you're planning a trip to Regret City, please cancel all reservations now. Instead, take a trip to a nice place called: "Starting Again." I like it so much that I've made it my permanent residence. My neighbors, the "Been Forgiven" and the "We're Saved" are so very helpful. By the way, you don't have to carry around the heavy baggage anymore either. That load is lifted from your shoulders upon arrival at "Starting Again." But don't take my word for it, find out for yourself.[1]

---

[1] Inspirational and Christian STORIES -- *Regret City*. N.p., n.d. Web. 23 Apr. 2015. <http://www.skywriting.net/inspirational/stories/regret_city.html>.

Unfortunately, many think this type of attitude is normal, but there is a different way to experience life. The following is a great example of the far-reaching effects and influence an encouraging attitude can have.

Michael is the kind of guy you love to hate. He is always in a good mood and always has something positive to say.

When someone asks him how he was doing, he replies, "If I were any better, I would be twins!" He is a natural motivator.

If an employee is having a bad day in the office, Michael is right there telling the employee how to look on the positive side of the situation.

Seeing his style really made me curious, so one day I went up to Michael and said, "I don't get it! You can't be a positive person all of the time. How do you do it?"

Michael replied, "Each morning I wake up and say to myself, you have two choices today.

You can choose to be in a good mood or ... you can choose to be in a bad mood. I choose to be in a good mood."

He continued, "Each time something bad happens, I can choose to be a victim or... I can choose to learn from it. I choose to learn from it. And every time someone comes to me complaining, I can choose to accept their complaining or... I can point out the positive side of life. I choose the positive side of life."

"Yeah, right, it's not that easy," I protested.

"Yes, it is," Michael said. "Life is all about choices. When you cut away all the junk, every situation is a choice. You choose how you react to situations. You choose how people affect your mood. You choose to be in a good mood or bad mood. The bottom line: It's your choice how you live your life."

I reflected on what Michael said. Soon thereafter, I left that company to start my own business. We lost touch, but I often thought about him when I had opportunities to make a choice about life instead of reacting to it.

Several years later, I heard that Michael was involved in a serious accident, falling some 60 feet from a communications tower.

After 18 hours of surgery and weeks of intensive care, Michael was released from the hospital with rods placed in his back. I saw Michael about six months after the accident. When I asked him how he was, he replied. "If I were any better, I'd be twins. Wanna see my scars?"

I declined to see his wounds, but I did ask him what had gone through his mind as the accident took place.

"The first thing that went through my mind was the well-being of my soon to be born daughter."

Michael replied. "Then, as I lay on the ground, I remembered I had two choices: I could choose to live or... I could choose to die. I chose to live."

"Weren't you scared? Did you lose consciousness?" I asked.

Michael continued, "...the paramedics were great. They kept telling me I was going to be fine. But when they wheeled me into the ER and I saw the expressions on the faces of the doctors and nurses, I got really scared. In their eyes, I read, 'He's a dead man.' I knew I needed to take action."

"What did you do?" I asked.

"Well, there was a big burly nurse shouting questions at me," said Michael. "She asked if I was allergic to anything. 'Yes,' I replied. The doctors and nurses stopped working as they waited for my reply. I took a deep breath and yelled, 'Gravity.'

Over their laughter, I told them, 'I am choosing to live. Operate on me as if I am alive, not dead."

Michael lived, thanks to the skill of his doctors, but also because of his amazing attitude. I learned from him that every day we have the choice to live fully.

Attitude, after all, is everything.[2]

---

[2] *Michael Is the Kind of Guy You Love to Hate.* N.p., n.d. Web. 23 Apr. 2015. <http://mrmom.amaonline.com/stories/michael.htm>.

Choosing our Attitude

It is remarkable how much control our attitudes can have on our health and wellbeing. There are many motivational stories that testify to the power of having a healthy, optimistic attitude.

Life is all about the attitude we choose. As humans, there are predominantly two types of attitudes we use to structure our perceptions.

The first is an *optimistic attitude*. An optimist's view of the world includes *the ability to create desirable outcomes*. Optimism gives a sense of confidence, and strength to rise above challenges and learn something new along the way.

Optimistic people trust in their intuition and influence others through their example, hard work and contribution.

A pessimistic view of the world perpetuates *undesired outcomes*. Pessimists believe that bad events happen *to them*, and believe that this is the way life has always been, and the way it is always going to be.

Optimists know good things will happen through them.

Pessimists believe bad things will happen to them.

An optimistic attitude will give you the momentum needed to get out of the Emotional Safety Zone and be accountable for your choices.

A pessimistic attitude will keep you stuck in the Emotional Safety Zone feeling sorry for yourself. Here, you give your power away to people and circumstances that are outside of your ability to manage, control or change.

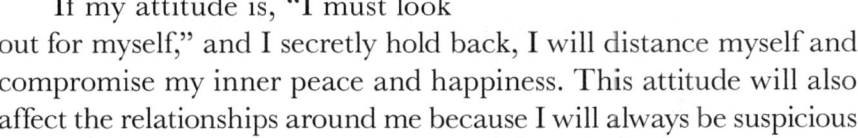

Optimism gives a sense of confidence and strength to rise above challenges and learn something new along the way.

If my attitude is, "I must look out for myself," and I secretly hold back, I will distance myself and compromise my inner peace and happiness. This attitude will also affect the relationships around me because I will always be suspicious and anxiously looking for errors in others.

If you look at the world we live in, it seems that many of the attitudes of society are based on competing, comparing and never measuring up. When we compare or try to measure up, we usually decide that we are better than or less than others.

Sometimes the way we are perceived, or how we think others perceive us, can seem more valid than the truth of who we really are.

No wonder creating attitudes that will encourage us to value ourselves can be such a difficult and confusing process.

Any time we choose attitudes that compromise our ability to love, honor and respect ourselves, we frustrate our peace and happiness.

The most damaging attitudes we can encounter are the self-judgments that come from our own mind. These judgments limit the way we perceive everything, and make it particularly challenging to create relationships where we feel loved, honored or respected.

Stephen Chbosky once said, "We accept the love we think we deserve." Have you ever thought about the type of love you think, or better yet, feel you deserve?

Remember you will only love, respect and honor others at the level you love, respect and honor yourself.

I really appreciate the quote: "If you settle for less than you deserve, you get less than you settled for."

People caught in The Victim Addiction often settle for less than they deserve and then they wonder why things in their lives never seem to work out. They get stuck in their Emotional Safety Zone and become complacent about their jobs, relationships and their limited potential as they feel that they can create nothing better.

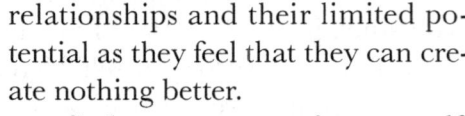

Did you know that laughter is one of the quickest ways to experience an optimistic attitude?

So how can you value yourself enough to create the type of love, honor and respect you desire?

The best way to find value and establish self-love, self-trust and self-respect is by choosing attitudes that will encourage, support and acknowledge those things that are unique to you.

Did you know that laughter is one of the quickest ways to experience an optimistic attitude?

Let me share an experience I recently had. One day, while feeling overwhelmed with deadlines and the demands of single mom-hood,

Attitude

I received this silly email from a friend who knew how stressed I was feeling.

> Hey Tori, thought you could use a smile.
>
> ---
>
> *A couple decided to go on a tropical vacation. The wife had a business trip right before they were to leave, so the husband went to the destination first, and his wife would meet up with him the next day. When he reached his hotel room, he decided to send his wife a quick email.*
>
> *Unfortunately, when typing her email address, he mistyped a letter, and his note was directed instead, to an elderly preacher's wife, whose husband had passed away only the day before.*
>
> *When the grieving widow checked her email, she took one look at the monitor, let out a piercing scream, suddenly fainted and fell to the floor.*
>
> *When they heard the sound, her family rushed into the room and saw this note on the screen:*
>
> Dearest Wife,
> Just got checked in. Everything's prepared for your arrival tomorrow.
> P.S. Sure is hot down here.
>
> ---
>
> Laughter makes even hard days feel better.

Points to Ponder

The emotional mind will influence our attitudes by releasing chemicals, which will emotionally strengthen our perceptions of the world.

It only takes 17 seconds of thinking happy thoughts to get the feel-good chemicals starting to flow. If you continue these happy habits, within 30 minutes your attitude will completely shift.

The rational mind can influence our attitudes through uplifting thoughts and empowering beliefs and can have an enormous influence in the attitudes we choose.

Tier V

The Power of Emotional Transformation

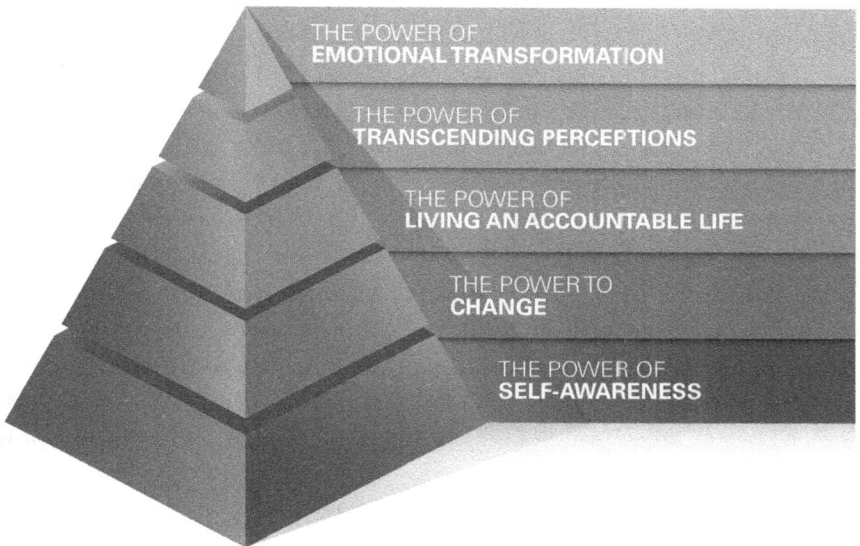

If you live a life of love, you will love the life you live.

In Tier V, we reach the pinnacle of the Personal Power Pyramid and enjoy the Power of Emotional Transformation. Here you will raise the bar on the many important concepts that you have acquired through out this book. You will also learn additional tools that will help you overcome obstacles, establish values, and set personal boundaries, giving you the ability to step into creatings the life that you have always wanted.

One of the most powerful ways to experience emotional transformation is through love. An extraordinary example of this type of transformation comes from a remarkable man by the name of Nicholas James Vujicic.

Nick's struggles began the moment he was born. At an early age he learned that when we feel like we are not accepted it's easy to lose hope; and when we lose hope, we start losing the strength to live.

Even Nick's parents struggled, knowing the kind of obstacles that he would have to face throughout his life. What makes Nick so remarkable is the way he took the obstacles of his birth and turned them into opportunities to show his compassion for human suffering.

You see, Nick was born without limbs. Growing up with no arms and legs made him a target for ruthless ridicule and harsh judgments.

As much as his parents tried to protect him from the cruelties of the world, they could not shield him from the destructive thoughts, beliefs, desperation, and deep loneliness his deformities caused him to feel. Some of these destructive thoughts and beliefs included, "You are not good enough," "Just give up," "You'll always be a burden," "You can never get a job," "You won't get married, you wouldn't even be able to hold your wife's hand," "What kind of father would you be if you couldn't even pick up your children when they're crying?" "Look at all the things you can't do?" Because there was no one who could relate to his struggles, he felt alone.

At age 8, discouragement over the bullying at school completely overwhelmed him.

He tells about a particularly hard day where he began to count all the mean things others had said to him. After counting twelve unkind comments, he decided if he heard one more person say something mean he was going to go home and end his life. Then, when he was going out to his parent's car after school, a girl yelled, "Hey Nick." He thought to himself, "Here it comes, I really can't take this anymore." But then the girl said, "You're looking good today!"

Nick's heart immediately brightened.

Those kind words brought much needed hope and gave him the courage to face another day. Yet, at age 10, the belittling from schoolmates was again unbearably painful, and brought on such despair, that Nick tried to drown himself.

As discouraged as he was, thinking about his family's love and realizing they had already endured considerable heartache and pain due to his deformities, stopped his suicide attempt.

Through his personal trials, Nick has gained compassion for the suffering felt in the hearts of many who struggle with everyday life.

Today, Nick runs an anti-bullying campaign and reaches out to people all over the world. The message he shares is a message of hope. Nick communicates the hope he has found in his love for Jesus Christ, explaining that it was only when he stopped the anger and surrendered his life to the Lord that his healing process began. Nick believes, "If God can use a man without arms and legs to be His hands and feet, then He will certainly use any willing heart!"

Nick understands how scary it is for those who live in violence and anger, and feels particularly sad when he sees those who have been treated badly give up the hope of a better life and become angry at everything and everyone. He knows the dangers that come when people become angry with others, but what is even more frightening is when that inward anger turns into a feeling of worthlessness.

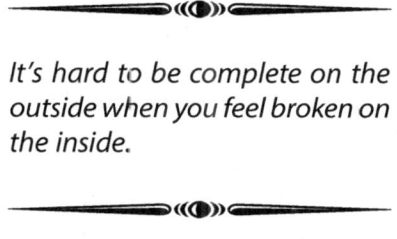

It's hard to be complete on the outside when you feel broken on the inside.

He truly relates to how hard it is to be complete on the outside when you feel broken on the inside. To those wounded souls he says, "I know how it feels to have a broken heart and feel alone. I started believing I was not good enough, I started believing I was a failure, and how I would never be someone people would like or accept."

He asks his audiences, "What are you going to believe? Are you going to believe in yourself? Or in other people's judgment of you? Are you going to believe it when others say that you are a failure and no one really likes you or cares about you?" He explains that when our mind starts growing with lies and we begin to believe those lies, it can be difficult to get beyond our discouragement. He shares: "There were many times in my life where I had nothing to look forward to. I had no value. My value has never been determined by how I look, where I am from, what job I have, or how much money I make. Why do we look at ourselves in the mirror and see ugly instead of valuable? What I have realized is that every single human being has value, and money cannot heal the soul. Love heals the soul. Even the worst parts of my life can be turned into good. I'm beautiful the way I am, and to me, it doesn't matter what you look like, you are beautiful too, and I love you just the way you are."

Nick says that for him, "Peace came when I stopped focusing on what I didn't have and what I couldn't do, and started putting my energy into what I did have and what I could do." "You are not forgotten. God knows your suffering, and if you turn to Him, He will give you the strength to get through the pain enough to know that life is worth living." He shares, "If God doesn't change my circumstances, he is going to use my life as a miracle for someone else! There is great power in loving yourself. When you love yourself you have a greater capacity to love others."[1]

Nicholas James "Nick" Vujicic was born with tetra-amelia syndrome, a rare disorder characterized by the absence of all four limbs. Beyond his physical limits is a life that transforms pain and suffering through Love. Nick Vujicic is a Christian evangelist and motivational speaker who shares his story of hope and love with thousands of people every month. He is also the author of several books and has a wonderful music video where he uses his beautiful voice to share his message of hope. He has also risen above his self-sabotaging beliefs and gone on to create a truly extra ordinary life, and shares that life with his lovely wife and amazingly beautiful little boy.

He is a true example of how powerful it can be when you rise above emotional challenges and consciously create the life you have always wanted to live!

The acronym I use to describe Emotional Transformation is L.O.V.E.

> L represents Learn
> O represents Overcome obstacles
> V represents Value self and define values
> E represents Engage in the life you love

---

[1] "Life Without Limbs // Nick Vujicic." Life Without Limbs, Inc., n.d. Web. 23 Apr. 2015. <http://www.lifewithoutlimbs.org/>.

Chapter 25

Learn

"If you live long enough, you'll make mistakes. But if you learn from them, you'll be a better person. It's how you handle adversity, not how it affects you. The main thing is never quit, never quit, never quit."

~ William J. Clinton

The L in L.O.V.E. represents Learn.

Learning how the mind functions can be very useful in owning our personal power and creating a life full of inner peace and personal satisfaction.

As we have previously discussed, much of our structuring occurs between zero and six years of age. In this stage of development, our mind has the capability of taking in massive amounts of information, without the limits of facts or reality.

Again, the amygdala, which houses our unconscious mind, is fully formed at birth. Yet, the rational mind is not fully developed until our mid-to-late twenties. This means that in our primitive years, our emotional mind is leading and guiding the rational mind.

Perhaps this explains why the rational mind is so dependent on the emotional mind for decisive action. Because these early years are so impressionable, more often than not, children believe everything they see, feel, hear, touch and taste is reality. They have no concept of the difference between fact and fantasy.

By the age of six we have structured approximately 22,000 hours of unfiltered experiences.

Primitive Structuring

I've heard it said that, by the age of six, we have structured approximately 22,000 hours of unfiltered experiences. In those 22,000 hours we have anchored too many emotional events to count, and have also associated some very powerful beliefs to those anchors.

Between the ages of six and eight we begin the cognitive stage and start to decipher the difference between what is fantasy and what is fact.

Most of our perceptions begin as interactions with the sensory organs, such as the eyes, ears and nose. What we sense then proceeds to the part of the brain called the thalamus. The thalamus is like the receptionist of the mind and carries messages to the cortex, or thinking part of the mind, for processing.

The thinking mind processes the information and determines the proper action. The cortex then signals the emotional mind, which is structured for stimulus and response, to launch a physiological stimulus to encourage a response. The stimulus includes the release of chemicals into the system to motivate action.

When we are in our rational thinking mind, our reality will be influenced by our thoughts.

However when we are emotionally triggered, the thalamus bypasses the rational mind and sends the stimulus directly to the emotional mind. The emotional mind quickly scans its past structuring for anchored experiences and floods the system with all kinds of chemicals, such as adrenalin, hormones and peptides to match the urgency felt in the events it has connected to.

When we are triggered into an emotional state of mind, our feelings become louder, stronger and much more demanding than our rational thinking mind. This triggered state makes it nearly impossible to control the emotional situations we encounter with our thoughts.

When we are in a heightened emotional state, our perceptions are influenced by our feelings.

Our mood is even influenced by the chemicals that are released in our brain. If we are in a good mood we will see the world as a wonderful place to live. If we are discouraged, not only will we notice things in our environment that validate and increase feelings of separation and sadness, we may do or say things that will discourage us even more.

When you notice that you are feeling down and want to consciously shift your mood, all you have to do is listen to upbeat music or focus on something positive. After about seventeen seconds the brain will start producing chemicals that will elevate your emotional state. It may take up to 45 minutes to produce a complete shift but knowing where to start is the first step.

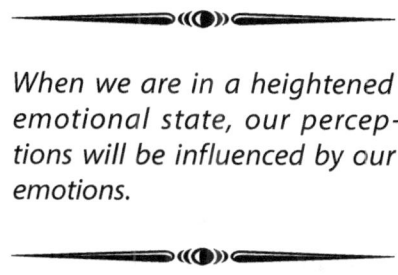

When we are in a heightened emotional state, our perceptions will be influenced by our emotions.

What are these brain chemicals and how do they affect us?

Brain Chemicals – Source of Emotional Transformation

Research has proven that brain chemicals have a great deal of influence over our mental and emotional feelings of wellbeing. When we have enough dopamine, for example, we are focused and motivated. Serotonin allows us to relax and feel supported. Endorphins energize us while minimizing pain.

These chemicals, also known as neurotransmitters, produce both pleasant and painful feelings. However there are times when these neurotransmitters don't produce the results we expect. For instance, "good feelings" can cause us to compromise or trade our values for the instant gratification of a "momentary high."

On the other hand, some of our painful feelings may generate productive results, as they elicit a sense of urgency for us to take action.

Studies indicate that genetics can also play a role in the way brain chemicals affect our brains. In fact, it is estimated that one out of every ten people suffer from some type of a chemical imbalance. These individuals do not produce the same amounts of feel good neurotransmitters as others around them.

When we have occasion to interact with others who are stressed out over something that may seem inconsequential, it is helpful for us to remember these statistics and understand that the person may be lacking some of the necessary chemicals produced by the brain to feel balanced.

As with our ability to handle stress, our ability to tolerate pain is also linked to the chemicals in the brain. Other documented studies indicate that those who have greater amounts of endorphins can handle pain from the same kind of injury far better than those who have lower levels of this energizing neurotransmitter.

It is now understood that stress is one of the biggest causes of chemical imbalance in the brain. Thankfully there are many ways to reduce stress and get the healthy boost we need. We can turn to adequate sleep, healthy food choices, spending time with friends and family, and scheduling moments outdoors to enjoy life's simple pleasures.

Tribal Rituals for Depression

In a TED talk, *Depression, the Secret We Share*, Andrew Solomon interviewed a man in Rwanda about their tribal rituals for depression. When Solomon described a ritual he had experienced in Senegal years earlier, the man agreed the rituals did have similarities, but there were some differences between those found in East and West Africa.

The man related that, after the genocide in their country, they had a lot of trouble with western mental health workers who came into the country to assist their people with depression. When Solomon asked why, the man responded that the mental health workers would do the most bizarre things.

He said, "They didn't take people out into the sunshine where they could begin to feel better! They didn't include drumming, or music, to get their blood going. They didn't involve the whole community! Or, externalize the depression as an invasive spirit! Instead… what they did was, they took people one at a time into dark, dingy little rooms and had them talk about their problems. We finally had to ask them to leave the country!"[1]

Understanding these brain chemicals and utilizing nature's gifts that help to balance them will influence our mood, affect our behavior, and assist us in creating emotional transformation.

---

[1] Solomon, Andrew. "Depression, the Secret We Share." TEDxMet, Oct. 2013. Web. 23 Apr. 2015. <http://www.ted.com/talks/andrew_solomon_depression_the_secret_we_share>.

Keeping a Mood Journal

You may also want to consider keeping a mood journal. There are many easy apps available for this type of tracking.

Using a mood journal can assist you in noticing your triggers and identifying the consistent emotional patterns that affect your thoughts, feelings, attitudes and beliefs. A mood journal can help you track your moods, anxiety levels and the elements in your life that you would like to change.

Notice, Identify and Express Emotions

One of the most challenging things we must develop as human beings is the ability to notice, identify, and express emotions in a way that allows us to feel understood. The ability to express ourselves accurately creates the opportunity to receive the love and support needed to live a rich and fulfilling life.

It becomes challenging to express ourselves when we haven't learned how to define our emotions. As children we may have even received mixed messages about the emotions we can freely express and the ones we are not allowed to have.

> *One of the most challenging things we must develop as human beings is the ability to notice, identify, and express emotions in a way that allows us to feel understood.*

Some children may have been asked not to talk about sad events in their lives, so they grew up feeling unsafe to express any emotions at all. For others, a painful event, such as their parent's separation or divorce, left them feeling lost and alone. Confused by all the emotions and not knowing how to talk about their feelings, they shut down and chose not to feel anything at all.

When we grow up feeling that it isn't safe to share our feelings, we create an emotional block that prevents us from understanding or expressing feelings.

When we shut off painful emotions, we also shut off productive emotions, which, in the long run, may affect all future relationships. People who hold all their emotions in, often feel like martyrs. Their belief is that they are unimportant and have no right to burden others with their problems. They may even rationalize their silent suffering by believing if they don't share how they are feeling, they are sparing others from experiencing emotional pain of their own.

By holding emotions in, people easily reach a breaking point. They may lash out, justifying their built up resentments and actions by saying things like, "It's about time someone put them in their place." Instead of noticing, identifying and expressing their own feelings in order to create understanding, they exhaust all their emotional energy being angry at the world, and blame others for the powerless way that they feel.

Sometimes emotional pain is carried when we feel that we have been wronged. When this pain burdens us, we seek validation. But seeking validation that we have been victimized, and doing so without knowing how to properly express our feelings, only perpetuates the problem.

Identifying Unnecessary Drama

Destructive emotional patterns, like getting angry every time things don't go your way, will reinforce the perception that the world is unsafe and unsupportive. Obviously, this is not a productive way to live life.

If we don't know how to handle emotional situations, it will create a lot of confusion and unnecessary drama in our lives and in the lives of those around us.

It is important to identify how we are feeling so we can respond appropriately.

Anytime we are hurt, irritated or sad, we must identify what it is that is bothering us.

To live a happy life, it is essential that we learn how to separate the facts, or what is really going on, from how we are feeling. Doing so will assist us in processing our present events, without the overwhelming emotional influence of our past events.

For example, if you get angry every time someone reminds you to do something you have put off, and you connect to childhood events where you heard the same impatient reminder over and over.

Now that you are older, you get easily offended anytime someone even suggests that you should do something, or asks you why you are putting things off. The unconscious feelings of "I'm not good enough" begin influencing your perception, and you lash out, blaming others for the way that you feel.

Each time the neural pathways are triggered, the connection will strengthen, making the reaction easier to access.

Then, we create a story to justify our position. A particular trigger (someone reminding you to do something) can be especially difficult where the personal stakes are higher, like in our family relationships.

This explains why creating new relationships can be so difficult. When we find a person we want to have a relationship with, we start out being very curious in the way we interact and converse, because we don't want to be hurt or rejected. Yet, unconsciously, we are looking for, and, at times, even formulating, flaws and traits that would have the potential of hurting or rejecting us. We also don't want the person we are in relationship with to be irritated, so we hide our true selves and carefully dance around anything we think might upset them.

When approached properly, triggers help us to release the past, which is the only way to live in the present and create something new. Yet unconsciously, most people don't want to feel uncomfortable so they blame their reactions on others or ignore their own reaction and transfer their attention somewhere else.

To process our feelings, we must take ownership for our results, push through the pain and uncomfortable feelings, and then produce enough evidence to create an emotional shift. Once a shift has occurred we have the ability to create something new.

This is what is so exciting! *You* get to choose the direction of your life by simply defining what that something new is going to be! As you define what it is you want, keep in mind that the emotional mind has no comprehension of reality, so there are no limitations. You can design your life any way that you want; you just have to keep trying new ways to approach change untill it happens. Don't be afraid to ask for what you want in a way that will support your new direction. It has been my experience that most people are looking for win/win relationships and enjoy assisting others in their success.

The Intensity of Emotional Patterns

Discerning the intensity of your emotions will assist you in understanding the hold particular patterns have over your emotional life. The more intense the trigger, the more power the anchored event has over your ability to think and act clearly.

On a scale of 0 to 10 (0 being less intense and 10 being extremely intense), examine your emotions surrounding triggered events by asking yourself a couple of questions.

- In the heat of a moment, do you have the conscious ability to know what you are feeling?
- In those instances, can you regulate your thoughts and emotions in a way that you feel you can express yourself clearly?

Because we have not been taught how to process our emotions, looking at the way we feel can be very uncomfortable. Here are some attitudes that could get in the way of expressing ourselves. See if you can identify with any of them.

- I don't know what to do with my emotions once I find them.
- I am afraid, embarrassed or ashamed of the way I feel.
- I think I shouldn't feel the way I do because it is wrong or bad.
- I don't even know how I really feel.
- No one can understand how I am really feeling.
- Expressing how I feel is too uncomfortable.
- I fear that if I open up I will be vulnerable and then get hurt.
- It's better to disregard uncomfortable feelings rather than express them.
- I shouldn't share my feelings because I am strong and should be able to handle things on my own.
- I can't share my feelings because I don't want to hurt others.
- I really worry about the consequences if I am honest about my feelings.
- I believe that showing or talking about my feelings is a sign of weakness.

- I'm afraid if I open up things will get out of control and I won't be able to turn my emotions off.

The above are all fears that will inhibit our ability for inner peace.

Expressing Feelings

Most people live a life of quiet desperation because they have never learned to or don't feel comfortable with expressing their true feelings. Learning to identify our feelings and then having the ability to express ourselves is an essential key needed to interrupt the emotional patterns that we give our personal power to.

There are times in life when our emotions can be confusing and we have a hard time deciphering our feelings. Below is a list of words that can assist you in identifying the different ways that you feel when you are triggered.

You may find it beneficial to practice identifying your emotions by thinking of something you are currently struggling with. Then go to the list below, read the words out loud and choose words that resonate with the emotions you feel.

You will find it helpful to keep a journal, as this will support you in noticing the intensity and repetitious nature of the emotional patterns that you have formed. Below you will find a list of painful words. The purpose of this list is to help you identify feelings you tend to overlook, ignore or avoid.

Painful Feelings

Abandoned	Abused	Addicted
Alone	Angry	Anxious
Ashamed	Attacked	Bad
Badgered	Belittled	Betrayed
Blackmailed	Blamed	Broken
Bullied	Burdensome	Chaotic
Cheated	Conflicted	Confused
Controlled	Criticized	Damaged
Deceived	Defective	Demeaned
Demoralized	Dependent	Depressed
Desperate	Deprived	Detached
Devalued	Discouraged	Disposable
Embarrassed	Emasculated	Enraged
Excluded	Exhausted	Exposed
Falsely accused	Fearful	Forgotten
Frightened	Frustrated	Furious
Grief stricken	Guilt-tripped	Guilty
Hassled	Heartbroken	Haunted
Helpless	Hindered	Hurt
Ignored	Impulsive	In the way
Inadequate	Incompetent	Indifferent
Ineffective	Inferior	Infuriated
Insecure	Intimidated	Irrational
Jealous	Judged	Jerked around
Labeled	Lectured to	Left out
Lied to	Lonely	Lost
Mad	Manipulated	Miserable
Misplaced	Mistaken	Misjudged
Mistreated	Mocked	Misunderstood
Nagged	Nervous	Numb
Obsessed	Offended	Overwhelmed
Pain	Panic	Pathetic
Picked on	Pissed off	Powerless
Provoked	Punished	Put down

Rage	Rebellious	Regret
Rejected	Resented	Resentful
Responsible	Ridiculed	Robbed
Sad	Scared	Self-conscious
Self-destructive	Sensitive	Sensitive
Stereotyped	Stressed	Stuck
Stupid	Suffocated	Suspicious
Terrified	Threatened	Tired
Tormented	Traumatized	Troubled
Unaccepted	Unappreciated	Uncomfortable
Undervalued	Undeserving	Uneducated
Unfulfilled	Unhappy	Unimportant
Unloved	Unsafe	Unwanted
Unworthy	Used	Useless
Victimized	Vindictive	Violated
Vulnerable	Worthless	Wounded

Again, this list is a tool for those who have a hard time identifying and expressing their emotions.

By recognizing how we feel, we can learn to express ourselves and acknowledge all aspects of our emotional life. This will give us the ability to direct our feelings the way that we want.

For those who are diligently seeking understanding of their emotional life, this next exercise will be very useful. It will also be helpful for those who want to gain more clarification around troubling events. It is always best to process your emotional experiences after a triggered event has passed. You can begin by completing the following statements:

I feel or I am feeling: (identify a feeling) _____

Times I have felt this way before include: _____

Reactive behaviors attached to these emotions are: _____

The thoughts and attitudes I have used to avoid, blame or justify my emotions are:_____

Now that you have identified your feelings and, to the best of your ability, have connected each feeling to its emotional pattern, it is time to replace your painful feelings with beneficial feelings that will align with the thoughts, feelings and desires you wish to create.

Beneficial Feelings

Able	Abundance	Accepting
Accepted	Accomplished	Active
Adaptable	Admired	Adventurous
Agreeable	Alert	Alive
Amazed	Amazing	Ambitious
Appreciated	Appreciation	Astonished
Attractive	Awesome	Balanced
Beautiful	Beneficial	Bold
Brave	Brilliant	Calm
Comfortable	Compassionate	Complete
Confident	Connected	Content
Courageous	Crazy about	Creative
Curious	Daring	Desirable
Decisive	Determined	Dynamic
Eager	Ecstatic	Effective
Efficient	Enlightened	Empathy
Empathic	Encouraged	Energized
Engaged	Enthusiastic	Excellent
Excited	Fabulous	Fantastic
Fascinated	Free and Easy	Friendly
Fun	Generous	Genuine
Good	Graceful	Gratified
Great	Grounded	Happy
Healthy	Helpful	Honest
Honorable	Honored	Hopeful
Humble	Important	Independent
Innovative	Inspired	Intellectual
Incredible	Invigorated	Lovable
Loved	Lovely	Loving

Lucky	Marvelous	Motivated
Motivating	Open	Outstanding
Open-Minded	Optimistic	Overjoyed
Passionate	Peaceful	Playful
Perceptive	Pleased	Popular
Positive	Powerful	Priceless
Productive	Proud	Purposeful
Radiant	Ready	Refined
Reliable	Realistic	Reassured
Relaxed	Remarkable	Respected
Restored	Safe	Satisfied
Secure	Sensational	Serene
Skilled	Special	Spectacular
Spontaneous	Strong	Successful
Sure	Tenacious	Terrific
Thankful	Thoughtful	Touched
Thrilled	Thriving	Tranquil
Trusted	Upbeat	Understanding
Unique	Useful	Understood
Valued	Valuable	Visionary
Wealthy	Whole	Willing
Wise	Wonderful	Worthy

Now that you understand that lasting change can only occur when you change the way you feel, decide the kind of feelings you want to have and create scenarios in your life to support that change.

The change I want to create is: _____
_____

Powerful feelings I want to incorporate into this change are: _____
_____

Outcomes these beneficial feelings will create are: _____
_____

Contributions this change will have in the lives of others are: _____
_____

In chapter 22, Empowering Beliefs, we began the process restructuring our beliefs to accomplish lasting change. Now, let's take that process further by incorporating empowering beliefs with the emotions you have chosen to create.

I am good enough	I am worthy	I am trusted
I am beautiful	I am important	I am wanted
I am accepted	I am appreciated	I am approachable
I am attractive	I am cared about	I am comfortable
I am valued	I am deserving	I am free
I am desirable	I belong	I am supported
I am educated	I am treated fairly	I am focused
I am fulfilled	I am happy	I am healthy
I am heard	I am lovable	I am loved
I am popular	I am prepared	I am stable
I am productive	I am protected	I am safe
I am satisfied	I am sociable	I am deserving
I am creative	I am capable	I am worthwhile
I am forgiving	I am smart	Life is easy
I am heard	I am fun	I am successful
I can succeed	I love my life	My life is full of love

The following are questions you can use to generate new beliefs that will align with the feelings that you want to create.

- Do you have any detrimental beliefs around money, success, love, trust or forgiveness? If so what new beliefs could you incorporate that will put you on the path to success? What current actions already support the beliefs you want to incorporate?

Now complete the following:

The new belief I choose to live is _____

I now feel _____

_____

The thoughts and behaviors I will incorporate to energize my new beliefs are _____

Which motivates me to take the following actions of _____

Which will create _____ results in my life.

After you have created a new belief and chosen empowering feelings to go with it, it's time to anchor your new belief with your new feelings.

You can do this by closing your eyes and connecting to a time when you have felt these types of feelings before. Let's say one of the feelings you chose was confidence, and the new belief is, "I am successful."

Now think of a time when you felt really confident. This may be as simple as remembering when you got an "A" on a school report you had worked hard on, or when you gave a successful presentation at work.

While thinking of a time you felt confident, take a breath and connect to the way it felt to have that much confidence. As you inhale, feel the power of the confidence that you experienced and that already exists. Slowly exhale and, while breathing in again, tighten your fists to enhance your confident feelings and anchor these feelings even deeper. Continue this process until you fully connect to the confidence you desire.

Now think of a time when you felt very successful. This may be a time when you were chosen to be on a team or received a promotion.

While thinking of a time you felt successful take a deep breath and connect to the way it felt to have that much success. As you inhale, feel the power of the success that already exists.

While breathing in, tighten your fists to enhance your feelings of success even more and anchor them deeper. Continue this until you feel fully connected to the success you desire.

Now let's bring the feeling of confidence and the belief of "I am successful" together.

Think of a time when you felt confident and successful. Again, it may be as simple as the way you felt when you learned how to ride a bike. Connect to the confidence and success you felt as you took off for the first time.

While thinking of a time you felt confident and successful take a deep breath and connect to the way it felt to have that much confidence and success. As you inhale, feel the power of the confidence and success that already exists. While breathing in, tighten your fists to enhance your feelings of confidence and success and anchor these feelings even deeper. Do this until you feel fully connected to the confidence and success you desire.

Now that you have anchored confidence and success together, choose a scenario where having confidence and success will create the kind of results that you want.

Now, close your eyes and imagine yourself in the scenario that you have chosen. Notice the confident way you communicate to those around you. Experience all the support you are getting from others. Hear the excitement in their voices as they respond to your confidence and success. Relax and enjoy how easy it feels to be totally and completely confident and successful.

Now take a deep breath, to complete the anchor, and when you are ready, open your eyes and clarify what you have just created.

I am now creating the life I deserve. My new belief is _____

The way my new belief is observable in my life is_____

What I now hear is _____

The feelings I have are _____

New habits that will support my new belief are _____

Now that you have created a new, more powerful, neural pathway, continue to connect yourself to the confidence and success you now possess.

Journal what you have just created as though you are living it now. Pay particular attention to the action steps you have committed to, that will reinforce this new belief in your life.

Use this exercise often to reinforce and strengthen the neural pathways that you have generated.

These principles are life changing and, when applied, the results are incredible!

By taking conscious committed action over our emotional life, we will have the ability to create the self-love, self-respect and self-trust required to establish a balanced, happy and healthy life.

Supporting Others

In addition to changing our own lives, the more we restructure our beliefs and transform our emotional patterns, the greater our capacity becomes to support others.

Just like you want to feel validated and safe when you are unhappy or upset, others yearn for that same comfort.

If you encounter a person in a heightened emotional state, do not give them advice or try to convince them to take action. Just listen to them until they get out of the protection zone and can think clearly.

You can support them by using small gestures of support, such as "aha," "Yeah," "I agree," "That must be hard," "I would feel the same way," "That's a lot to deal with," "I can see why you are struggling," and "That would hurt my feelings, too."

You can also rephrase what they say, so they know you are listening. It is helpful when you say things like, "Wow, it sounds like this is really bothering you."

In order to create balance in life, it's important not only to feel supported in times of struggle, but also have the capacity to provide emotional support to those in need. Supporting others becomes much easier when we realize that most people don't know how to deal with their emotional pain and have gotten very good at hiding their true feelings.

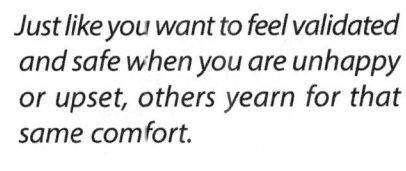

Just like you want to feel validated and safe when you are unhappy or upset, others yearn for that same comfort.

In my trainings, I have noticed a reoccurring struggle that limits individual's willingness or ability to communicate or ask for support. The common challenge seems to be that they don't feel safe when they want to discuss something they are upset about.

Some have said that they feel their partner seems to remember everything they have ever done wrong, and will bring it up in the heat of an argument. They often say things like, "It's not worth the fight, so I just agree to keep peace," or "How can I ever resolve things if I get yelled at any time I try to express how I am feeling?"

It is helpful to remember that the longer you discuss an emotional issue, the more likely it will be that you will trigger past events, which will intensify the discussion.

It is important to establish agreements of respect to effectively address reoccurring issues that arise in your relationships. But keep in mind that most people will only have reoccurring discussions with issues they feel uncomfortable with.

If a person doesn't feel emotionally safe enough to be heard, or they sense that the way they feel is not acknowledged, understood or important, it won't matter how many times you talk about an issue. It still feels unresolved and uncomfortable; so they may fight or withdraw, without reaching any resolution.

In order to produce the resolution you want, make sure to create clear agreements that will support a rational conversation. Because the emotional mind can take control of the dialogue and stop any possibility of having a rational conversation, mutual agreements are necessary to keep the conversation productively moving forward.

Here is how this can be done. In the beginning of your conversation, agree to communicate by taking turns and speaking, in short intervals. Continue the discussion until both parties agree that they have been heard and the other person has a good understanding of how they are feeling.

Make an agreement that, if emotions escalate, you will change the subject by going for a walk, listening to uplifting music, or changing up the conversation by talking about something funny, like sharing your most embarrassing moments.

One way to allow a logical conversation to take place and keep the emotional responses at bay is to obtain a three-minute timer and a small item you designate as your "conversation enhancer." Set the timer, then the person with the enhancer must speak for the full three minutes. The first speaker passes the enhancer to the other person, sets the timer and the second person speaks for their three minutes.

You can keep the rotation going until each person feels understood. Once each party agrees that they have been heard, you can move on to create agreements, and resolution will occur. Remember, do not continue to talk if emotional safety is compromised or emotions begin to escalate. If emotions rise, show compassion to the one who has been triggered and take a long enough break to reestablish safety and trust, then begin again. Do not continue prematurely. It is better to change your focus, reestablish the relationship and reschedule your discussion for another time than damage your relationship by arguing.

Stephen M.R. Covey has said, "Trust is both the foundation and the test of a relationship." If you are aware of vulnerabilities that could trigger contention with your partner, be respectful in the way you address those issues.

Another way we can support relationships and maintain trust is by being thoughtful of others when we are struggling.

There will be times when events occur and life changes so suddenly that it leaves our head spinning, and we are momentarily unsure how to reestablish a sense of safety.

In times like these, some people find it valuable to talk about their situation in order to put things into proper perspective. Yet others have to wrap their brain around their own situation before they have the ability to really talk about their circumstances.

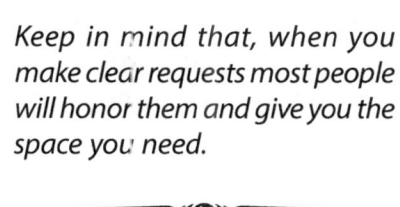

Keep in mind that, when you make clear requests most people will honor them and give you the space you need.

For those who process their thoughts and feelings by talking to others, the calls and visits of concerned friends and family are most welcomed.

But, for those who must process before being around others, calls and visits may increase their struggle. Here are a few suggestions that can help if you are the type of person who must process before you can talk.

First, it is helpful to understand that the people in our lives who love and care for us want to help, because when we hurt, they are hurting too.

Second, with this in mind, develop strategies that will not only support you, but will support those who love you as well.

Third, let those who will be concerned about your welfare know that you are okay.

Fourth, create certain phrases you can say to comfort those around you, such as: "Thank you for your concern, but I'm not sure how I feel right now. Do you mind if we discuss this when I can think more clearly?" or "I'm not really sure what I need right now, but when I figure it out I promise I will let you know," or "I appreciate your concern. What would help me is a little time on my own to process my situation. Can I reach out to you later?"

Fifth, acknowledge those who reach out and return calls or send short text messages that will let them know you are okay and will talk to them later.

Sixth, once you have processed your struggle, reach out and let others support you. It is amazing how much healing can occur when you allow others to love and support you in your time of need.

Keep in mind that, when you make clear requests, most people will honor them and give you the space you need. When you ignore the people who care about you and are trying to support you through your trials, it may increase their concern and their need to contact you.

It is important to develop the ability to ask for what you want, even if it is that you need some time on your own. Allowing others to support you in your times of struggle will comfort them, give you the space that you need and strengthen the relationships around you.

Chapter 26

Overcoming Obstacles

*"There are plenty of difficult obstacles in your path.
Don't allow yourself to become one of them."*

~ Ralph Marston

The O in the acronym L.O.V.E. represents Overcoming Obstacles.

Overcoming obstacles can be even more difficult when we are faced with an experience that is different than anything we have ever faced before.

In such moments, we instinctively understand that life is changing and, to some degree, we know that it will never be the same.

I wrote *The Victim Addiction* to help you not only notice, but also overcome, the emotional obstacles that hold you back from experiencing your full potential. My hope is that, through this journey, you have become aware of the unconscious ways you have held yourself back; but even more, I hope you understand that you have the power to actually design the life you have always wanted to live.

When we are connected to the inner peace that comes through consciously directing our own lives, we have the strength and courage to stand as a contribution in the world.

Change is a natural occurrence that comes with the happiness and growth we all must experience in order to progress. Some of those changes will be full of excitement and others may include obstacles we have never faced before.

In emotional times, is best to feel the sorrow so we can let go of the past, giving us the energy to create something new. However there are times when our mind will bring up past, painful events in our lives so we can resolve them. In times like these, it is best to remember that it doesn't make sense to let our unconscious mind throw us back into the past to re-experience the pain and suffering over and over again, so we should do what it takes to release the pain and move on. As long as we allow triggers to direct our emotional life, we remain a prisoner of the past.

Disarming Triggers

Disarming our triggers is an essential part of the Emotional Transformation that makes up the capstone of the Personal Power Pyramid.

It is only when we have the courage to face the pain associated with the challenges we have faced and the mistakes we have made, that we can overcome our obstacles and connect to the inner peace and strength we need to overcome life's circumstances.

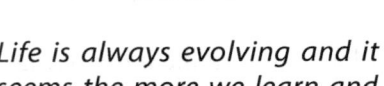

Life is always evolving and it seems the more we learn and grow, the more adversity we face, especially if we want to make changes that will make a difference.

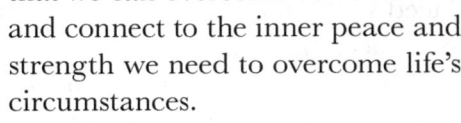

Life is always evolving and it seems the more we learn and grow, the more adversity we face. Especially when we choose to make changes that will enhance our lives and make a difference in the lives of others.

Standing in the world as a contribution is a lofty goal that takes consistent rigor. Part of the conscious rigor will come as we truly understand the automatic place we are thrown into when life temporarily overwhelms us and we struggle.

Strength from Struggle

Struggling is a natural part of the growth process and seems constant in the world we live in. Even nature provides examples of strength that comes from the struggles of life.

For a baby giraffe, the struggle of life will begin the moment he is delivered. When a baby giraffe is born, it usually falls 10 feet from the womb, usually landing on their back. The first thing the baby will do is tuck its awkward legs under its body. As the baby is adjusting to their new environment, their mother bends down to make sure everything is okay, and instead of welcoming her new baby with nurturing love, the mother does the most outrageous thing. She stretches her long leg out and kicks her little one, sending it tumbling head over heels. When the baby doesn't get up, the mother sends it flying again. This violent process continues until the baby stands for the first time. The struggle to rise for the first time is momentous and you would think that the mother would be satisfied when her baby is able to stand. Yet, the moment the baby gets on their feet the mother sweeps their legs out from underneath them and the violent process begins all over

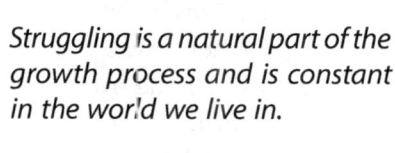

Struggling is a natural part of the growth process and is constant in the world we live in.

again. From the outside looking in, this could seem like an unfair and even cruel way to enter the world. You may be asking yourself why a mother giraffe would create such struggle for her new little one. As illogical as it may seem, she does this out of love. The reality is that, because of their long awkward legs, a baby giraffe can be an easy prey for predators. The mother giraffe knows that one of the most important lifesaving lessons she can teach her baby is how to get on their feet quickly.[1]

Nature is full of all kinds of examples. Have you ever seen a caterpillar slowly form a tight chrysalis and then, later, watched as the butterfly struggles with all its might to break free? Without that adversity to push fluid into the butterfly's wings, it would never have the strength to fly and become the beautiful and truly extraordinary creature it was meant to be.

Like the butterfly, adversity is necessary in order for us to break free of the protective chrysalis we have tightly formed around ourselves. The struggle to break free is the only way we can step into the beauty of our true potential which, for each individual, is something truly extraordinary.

Yet, sometimes we are confronted with times when breaking free from an obstacle we face seems so painful that the thought of struggling through it feels impossible.

---

[1] Giraffe storybook, "A View from the Zoo," by Gary Richmond.

Overcoming Loss

Anyone who has lost someone close to them through death knows the unquenchable anguish of the desperate pain caused by an abrupt, unsolicited, yet irrevocable separation.

My dear friend Sherrie has faced many devastating losses in her life. The following story is in her words.

When I was told that my brother, David, had acute lymphocytic leukemia, I would not consider the inevitability of his death. As close as we were, I wouldn't listen to him talk of dying. I felt that it would be a sign of weakness in me, or lack of faith. I believed that he was becoming too ill to have the energy needed to stay positive, so I had to be his unconditionally optimistic source of strength. Looking back I can see that all the while, without me knowing, he was coming to terms – knowing his time was getting close; and he was trying his best to help me prepare.

Sometimes we don't know why we don't get our way or we must face opposition or discouragement. However, it is only through overcoming each particular struggle that we are strengthened and refined.

What I would give to turn back the hands of time and spend one more precious moment with him. We could have reminisced about our pet monkey Jako, about mud cities made under the cottonwood trees, playing Swiss Family Robinson and 'trapping elephants,' making hay forts and the time we went flying as we ran into the wind, holding onto each other – and a huge piece of cardboard!

At the time of his death I felt that I was dying too... there wasn't anyone, or anything, that could 'make it all better.' Nothing made sense – especially not any plans for the future! How could life possibly go on? What would any of it matter anyway, without my brother to share it with? There was a hole in the fabric of my life and I didn't want to patch it, or replace it, with something or someone else – I wanted him to come back and fill it...to fix it. Yet with all of my wanting and wishing, it could not be; in that moment, it felt like I was all alone in my loss.

There is something my brother said one day that has stayed with me through the years. After losing his hair, all bruised from needles and in pain, he said, 'Remember, life is always worth living!'

Losing David was followed by losing four dear grandparents, two important mentors, some close friends, and my infant son, Nathaniel Scott. Later I would also lose two aunts and my former husband, the father of our seven children, followed by the death of my own father.

Even though it didn't feel like it at the time, the loss of my brother helped to prepare me for the many losses I would face, including the indescribable pain of losing my son. Because I was in the habit of loving God, and trusting Him, I was able to recognize an anticipative premonition that came about two weeks before my son's death. It felt like something painful was about to happen, but, I felt like I was being told that if I could 'endure it well', that one day I would realize how every painful challenge is part of a bigger plan.

Early, on the morning of April 6, 1985, when I found the lifeless little form of my infant son, my world shattered. He was the youngest of the five children I had at that time. Our oldest had just turned seven. I had no idea how on earth I was supposed to continue breathing, let alone function well enough to care for my other young children. And then I was reminded of the experience I had two weeks before, which brought some comfort.

In retrospect, I can see that this extremely painful experience has given me greater strength and empathy for those who suffer the loss of a dear loved one. It is also interesting to note that discovering the cause of my son's death has saved the lives of three of my grandsons.

Another time that I experienced loss, destroyed my plans for the future, and sent me spiraling downward, as though there was nothing to hold on to, was when my current husband, Frank, was diagnosed with Alzheimer's disease.

When something like terminal illness strikes unexpectedly, it can shake your foundation to the core. It isn't easy to cope with a loss that doesn't end. You still love the person so much! You don't want the problem to get worse, or to lose them.

While all of the emotions of impending and certain separation tears at you, there is a constant feeling of mourning the loss of your dreams and plans for the future.

Sometimes we don't know why we don't get our way or we must face opposition or discouragement. However, it is only through overcoming each particular struggle that we are strengthened and refined.

Overcoming Grief

Grieving the loss of someone close to you, whether it was expected or a complete surprise, and dealing with the aftermath of emotions can be one of the most difficult obstacles you may face. Whether the loss is from a death or the end of a significant relationship, giving yourself permission to grieve is the only way true healing can occur.

The grieving process will look different for each person. The important thing is that you don't suppress how you are feeling. Don't be afraid to scream, laugh, run, cry or even punch something if you feel like it.

But remember, you will not be able to escape painful feelings by avoiding them. Feelings buried alive never die, they grow, and if they are not processed and released, eventually they will overwhelm you. Some may fall into something destructive in order to mask their discomfort. This is a temporary fix and will not change the past or erase the pain.

It is natural to seclude yourself so others won't see your pain. Yet, the more you reach out and productively work through your pain, the easier it will be to move on. Socialize with the people you feel comfortable with. Don't be afraid to talk about any feelings that seem overwhelming or hard to bear. Talking about your loving memories can help to replace the pain of your loss. The more you talk about your loss the easier it will be to accept the past and establish a bright new future.

Don't speed the grieving process. Psychologists say that there are five stages of grief that we must experience to heal from the pain of a significant loss. The first is denial/isolation. In this stage we block out the facts to rationalize the intense emotions we feel. The second stage is anger. In this stage, we resent what has occurred and lash out. In the third stage, bargaining, we try to somehow rationalize the pain we feel. The fourth stage is the sadness/depression that occurs because we don't know how to separate ourselves from the pain of our loss. And finally, the fifth stage is acceptance, which comes after we have given ourselves time to process our pain, accept our loss and move on. The stages don't always occur in the order listed and the length of time required for each stage varies, but, to fully heal, most people will experience each stage of the process.

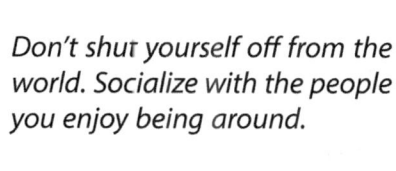

Don't shut yourself off from the world. Socialize with the people you enjoy being around.

Remember it takes time to heal from a significant loss. At first, your feelings may seem overwhelming, but by taking one step at a time and giving yourself permission to properly grieve, you will slowly start to feel better. Reach out and get the support you need and you will be okay.

Unexpected Change

Another obstacle that is hard to overcome is when we experience unexpected change. Unexpected change comes in many ways, and can be an excruciating form of loss. This was the obstacle that faced a young man named Charley, when he was in the prime of his life. He had been a hardworking, ambitious young man who excelled in school, and in the summer, he sold magazines and worked hard at the local steel mill.

Charley also excelled as an athlete, lettering in high school football, baseball and track, and then went on to play football for the

University of Alabama, helping them to win the first ever Southeastern Conference.

The year after college graduation, he had his sights set on a career in professional baseball with the New York Yankees. In 1941, before finalizing the contract, he felt the overwhelming desire to defend our country and enlisted in the army to serve in World War II.

He married his sweetheart, Kathleen, who was known as "Kitty," on April 5, 1942, just before starting Officer Candidate School.

Although he did not care for Army life, his passion caused him to excel and he was quickly assigned to a leadership position. Before going into the war zone, he became a company commander.

Charley loved his men and valiantly fought beside them as they encountered their many battles. One mission, delivering a load of much needed supplies, took Charley and his men into the thick of enemy fire. After rescuing what he thought was all of his men, Charley reached safety.

Just as he did however, he noticed a young gunman who had been shot and was falling back into the tank and unable to escape. Charley went back through the crossfire and jumped into the tank to rescue him. He quickly pushed the wounded soldier through the top of the tank, and just as he was about to jump, the tank exploded, sending him flying.

He was pierced with a smattering of steel splinters and was so badly burned that he could not even open his eyes.

His healing and rehabilitation started badly, as it was difficult to even cleanse his eyes properly because of the severity of his burns and wounds on his face. After many surgeries, he finally came to terms with the fact that he would live the rest of his life without the gift of sight.

All of his plans and dreams for the future were gone. He remembered the blind people on the corner selling pencils and couldn't bear the thought of becoming like them. His greatest fear was that he would be a burden to his family, friends and community.

While recovering in the Valley Forge Hospital, a young corporal and friend named Kenny Gleason invited Charley to join him for a game of golf. At first, Charley thought that Kenny was just kidding, but eventually went with him.

Charley had never played golf before. After Kenny explained the game and set up a practice tee, Charley felt his club connect with the ball.

Then he heard Kenny say, "The ball's about 200 yards down the fairway, smack in the middle. It was a beautiful shot."

"Gleason, don't you dare lie to me," Charley said through clenched teeth. "It's right where I said, Captain," he answered. "We can walk out there, if you want to."

"Something new was brewing in me – confidence. The good Lord must have been out there with us on that golf course, for only He could have known how desperately I needed something – anything – to turn me around."

Charley remembers that moment well. "Something new was brewing in me – confidence. The good Lord must have been with us on that golf course, for only He could have known how desperately I needed something – anything – to turn me around.

"A man never knows exactly when he's going to find the single vital force that he must have in order to keep on keeping on, and it is certain that I never expected that kind of miracle when I started that all important backswing. Maybe, just maybe, I'd finally reached my turn-around point."

Because Charley was a natural athlete, his golf skill progressed rapidly and he took second place in the National Blind Championship in 1946. The following year he won the title. Eventually he won 17 National and 11 International Championship. It is said by many that Charley Boswell was the greatest golfer that ever lived.

He also ran a successful insurance agency and served both locally and nationally, with fundraising organizations raising $1.7 million to advance medical treatment for the blind, with celebrities like Bob Hope and Arnold Palmer.

A favorite story is one in which he challenged Arnold Palmer to a game of golf – for money. Arnold felt sorry for him and said that he couldn't think of taking advantage of a blind man. After deliberation, Arnold finally agreed, but warned him that he would play to win. He said that Charley could name the place and time. Charley lit up and told him that they would meet on the green and tee off at midnight!

Those who knew Charley Boswell agreed that it was the way he faced his challenges that caused them to believe that nothing was impossible.

When life offers challenges that test us to our core, we can remember that nothing is impossible. We must not allow fear to hold us back. The unexpected changes we face are opportunities to grow and develop in incomprehensible ways.

Tools to Overcome Obstacles

It seems that the signs of The Victim Addiction are strongest in times when we feel frustrated or discouraged with the obstacles in our path. Defining where our thoughts, feelings and attitudes automatically go when we are frustrated or discouraged, can give us great insights in overcoming our obstacles.

One of the greatest tools we can use in overcoming obstacles is to consciously understand the automatic beliefs that hold us back. One of the automatic places I go when I am struggling is loneliness or feeling abandoned. Up until now these feelings have dominated my reality and I have created many situations validating more loneliness or feeling abandoned by secluding myself when I am struggling. Evaluating my automatic reactions caused by the fear of getting hurt or being abandoned again, helps me to filter insecure situations in a realistic way. The more I logically process the insecurities structured in my childhood, the stronger my ability to overcome my feelings of loneliness have become.

Overcoming Fear

According to Zig Ziglar, "Failure is a detour, not a dead-end street."
In order to succeed we must find the will to push past the obstacles we face, get out of our Emotional Safety Zone and overcome our fears.
One of the biggest fears that most people face is the fear of failure.

Overcoming Obstacles

Did you know even the great basketball player Michael Jordan has experienced failure? Michael once said in a TV ad: "I've missed more than 9,000 shots in my career. I've lost almost 300 games. Twenty-six times I've been trusted to take the game winning shot and missed. I've failed over and over and over again in my life. *And that is why, I succeed.*"

Success consists of pushing past failure, over and over and over again!

Another example is Thomas Edison who tried more than 1,000 ways to create the results he wanted before discovering the light bulb. Most people try one way, and when that way does not produce the results they expect, they try the same way, only harder.

Eventually they get discouraged, believe they are a failure, and give up, before accomplishing their desired result.

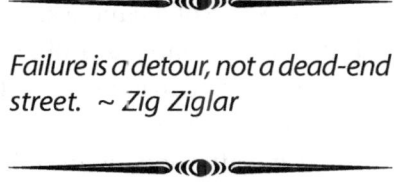

Failure is a detour, not a dead-end street. ~ Zig Ziglar

I have come to realize that the foolproof attitude to achieving success is never letting in-the-moment challenges get in the way of achieving what you truly want. Press forward. Even when you think you can't, keep looking for new ways until you succeed.

Michael Jordan and Thomas Edison had to get out of their fear of failure to rise to their greatness, and with some conscious effort, so can we!

The most important time to use the conscious tools we have accumulated is when we feel the gripping hold that fear has placed over our lives. Sometimes, not knowing how to proceed causes us to "play it safe" and remain in the familiarity of our Emotional Safety Zone, rather than take the risks associated with the unknown. Other times, ready or not, life forces us to make decisions no matter how terrified we might feel.

Can you imagine the fear that came over Boswell as he learned that he would remain in darkness for the rest of his life? It was only when he got out of his fear and connected to a completely new purpose that he could reignite the passion and strength that had always guided his life. This connection opened up the possibility of creating something completely new.

For Boswell, it took grasping the difficult news that his vision could not be restored. After the reality of that news sank in, he began rehabilitation at the Old Farmhouse, near West Hartford, Connecticut.

The Old Farmhouse Convalescent Hospital offered Braille lessons and other various studies for the blind. They even offered music, which Charley felt sounded awful.

Whenever Charley had the time, he would walk down a gravel road to visit a "congenial old fellow," who acted as watchman and gatekeeper.

The use of a cane was not particularly encouraged at Old Farms, but Charley had no problem getting down to the gate and back to the house because he would walk with one foot on the gravel, and one foot on the grass.

One afternoon while Charley was visiting with the old man, snow began to fall. Neither of them paid attention to it, and when they had finished talking, Charley started back up the hill toward the school, just as he always did.

After he had gone quite a ways, he realized he couldn't tell where the road was any more. It had been covered under the thick blanket of snow.

A terrible panic set in. Suddenly, he remembered hearing that to one side of the lawn, there was a sheer cliff that dropped off a couple of hundred feet into the Farmington River.

He had no earthly idea where he was in relation to the dormitory, the cliff, or the road. He yelled for help, thinking that the gatekeeper would be able to hear him. But the wind was louder than his voice was. Charley was pretty sure it was getting dark and he began to doubt that his chances for being found were very good. He said, "Standing there in the snow, feeling the bite of the cold air on my face's scar tissue, I realized what it really means to be absolutely helpless. Now I knew, as never before, what I had lost. Blindness became total frustration. Before, it had been a vexing, nagging, awkward, and often depressing fact, which had been bad enough. But now I was in the kind of situation where my inability to see could cost me my life."

He continued, "The snow, I guessed, was about six or eight inches deep. It was coming down at such a rapid clip, I was certain my tracks would be covered within a minute or two. A cane, or even a stick, might have helped—but I didn't have a cane, and the snow had covered any branches that might have been lying on the ground. I knew I would have to move. I was freezing, and I must have looked like the abominable snowman out there in that blizzard."

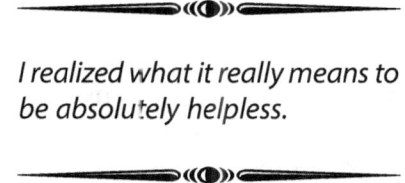

I realized what it really means to be absolutely helpless.

He said that, through the piercing cold wind, he heard a very faint sound of music. Hoping that the sounds were not welcoming him into heaven, he decided to try to get an accurate fix on the direction and source.

He took one step, then another, and another—and then listened. He knew that the storm would be playing tricks on him. The sounds could be coming from the other side of the river gorge. But he decided he would have to take the chance. The only option that seemed possible was to walk, stiff legged, with arms extended, homing in on the source of that music.

After what seemed like forever, he slammed into the side of a building and felt his way along the wall. It ended up being his dormitory and he stumbled inside. When he got to his room and climbed into bed, he thanked the good Lord for letting him hear that music. From that time on, he never made fun of the hideous noises from his fellow students in the band, they had saved him from a fate that could have easily had a tragic ending.

This story correlates so well with the fear we all experience and must overcome when facing the unknown. Like Charley, when our lives make unexpected changes and we are no longer able to decipher our way, we feel lost, and sometimes we freeze, feeling completely helpless, and are not able to see our next step. But we have all the power we need to overcome the blindness we face and create the change that we desire.

Overcoming Emotional Blindness of Blame

Charley Boswell was physically blind, and no matter how badly he desired it, there was truly nothing he could do to change his blindness.

There are many in this world that, although they have the ability to see with their eyes, are completely blind to the ways they are sabotaging their own happiness.

They fight to be right while blaming others to justify their reactions. They are completely oblivious to the ways their actions and behaviors create conflict. They are totally convinced that others are the cause of their frustration and pain.

It is helpful to understand that a majority of the way people view the world comes from the way they feel about themselves. The same perceptions that influence their perspective generate their bad behavior.

Overcoming the obstacle of our own blindness is a choice that will require uncomfortable change. Yet it is only when we release the blame and take accountability for our emotions that change can occur.

As talked about in the beginning of the book, the blame game is a self-destructive emotional pattern that will keep us completely blind to the ways we are generating our own obstacles. The blame game is where I don't want to deal with what is going on inside, so I am going to transfer all the detrimental ways that I am feeling to you. The blame game is one of those self-defeating emotional patterns that will keep you from attaining the emotional transformation essential to step into your own personal power.

Even if you have been victimized by the hands of another, you are not hurting those who have hurt you with your blame; you are only causing more pain and sorrow for yourself. There is no way to change the past, but the changes you make today can change the future. Do not give another minute of your precious resources to an experience where you will gain nothing productive in return.

THE PROCESS OF RELEASING BLAME

The purpose of this process is to notice the ways you transfer your feelings to others through blame.

- Is blame one of your self-destructive emotional patterns? If so, who or what do you blame?
- What are you avoiding with your blame?
- How long have you been giving your emotional energy to this person or event?
- What do you believe is outside your ability to manage or control?
- How does blaming this event on others make you feel?
- Does the person you blame know the reason for your blame?
- Do they even know you blame them?
- Who is suffering more, you or the person you blame?
- Is fear or pride or pain getting in the way of letting go of your blame?

Fear and pride stem from unmet needs and self-defeating beliefs. Take time to journal any fear you experience and the origin of any pride.

- Where do you use blame as an avoidance pattern?
- Are you transferring your internal angst on another so you don't have to acknowledge or process your own guilt?
- How is blame affecting your self-worth, relationship with others, your behavior, or energy in other areas of your life?
- In what situations has blaming others cut you off from the love and understanding you desire?

Blame Toward You:

- Is the cause of their blame targeted at you specifically?
- Was this personal or did you make this personal?

- How have you observed them using the same type of communication style or behavioral patterns with others?
- Try to understand the true source of their blame. Are they unconsciously trying to protect themselves?
- What kind of pain are they carrying?
- What detrimental beliefs could they be validating?
- How do their actions reflect in the way they feel about themselves?
- Why are you taking their emotional reactions personally?
- Is there something you need to do or express? If not, separate yourself from their blame and move on.

Journal any thoughts or ideas that will encourage growth and promote change.

When I let go of blame that comes from others, everything shifts. I am no longer perpetuating the blame cycle because I do not blame myself or accept the blame of others towards me.

When I use my power to separate myself from others' blame I no longer feel powerless.

If the obstacle you are facing is due to a loss, it is very important that you do not jump into anything until you give yourself the proper time to heal.

Clarify the obstacle – It is important to acknowledge when the habits of your own mind are the cause of the obstacles you are facing.

Most therapists say to give yourself at least a year before making any major changes in your life. Moving forward in an effective way includes giving yourself time to mourn your loss.

THE PROCESS OF OVERCOMING OBSTACLES

The purpose of this process is to help you identify, detail and overcome obstacles in your life so you can move forward and create the happiness you deserve.

Below is a list of strategies you can use to make the changes necessary to overcome any obstacle.

Clarify the obstacle
- Specifically name the obstacle you are facing.
- What can you control?
- What is outside of your ability to control?
- What must you surrender?
- What fears influence your ability to move forward?
- What unconscious beliefs support your fears?
- Create a clear vision of how your life will look when you have overcome this obstacle.
- Break it down into easy steps and create a plan you can follow to overcome the obstacle.

It is important to acknowledge when your habits are part of the problem with the obstacles you face. Ponder these thoughts below as you build a new understanding.

Points to Ponder in Overcoming Obstacles
- Take care of your physical resources through proper amounts of rest, eating healthy food and exercising in a way that maintains a healthy weight. This will give you the energy and vitality needed to overcome obstacles and enjoy life to the fullest.
- Carefully choose how you are going to direct your emotional resources. Only say yes to the things you can and want to do; but when you can't or even if you don't want to do something, don't make excuses, or overcommit, just say no. Saying no maintains integrity and establishes trust. People learn to trust what you say and believe they can count on you to keep your word when you are honest with your commitments.

- When you experience moments of breakdown, it is important to handle your own emotional reactions you may be experiencing before entering challenging conversations. When you deal with yourself first, you will not fight to be right or to defend your position. You will be more open to listening and to resolving the issue.
- Don't ignore or pretend a conflict didn't happen or wait for the other person to come to you. Promptly handle uncomfortable conflicts or disagreements. The longer you wait to handle a problem, the more emotional energy will build up, making it more difficult to talk about or resolve.
- When differences occur, be open, honest and sincere in your communication. Don't tell others what you think they want to hear. Tell them where you really are. Holding back will only produce mistrust and resentment.
- Openly discuss any misunderstandings. Make a conscious effort to listen and understand the other person's point of view, even if it seems irrational. Honesty and understanding will create a safe environment to work out the issues and build great relationships.
- Always be honest with yourself and with others. Do not exaggerate your strengths, or lie about your accomplishments. This will only lessen your credibility and discredit others.
- If appropriate, sincerely apologize. If the other person feels you have made a mistake, the most important thing is to re-establish trust and safety. This will not be possible if emotional defenses get in the way. Remember, the emotional mind will not let its guard down until there is a sense of safety.
- Don't procrastinate. Whether it is fixing that noise in your car or getting your child a tutor, if you have things that weigh you down take care of them immediately. This will give you more energy for things you enjoy.
- Acknowledge and appreciate the unique gifts you bring to each interaction. If there are areas in your life you would like to

improve, gain the knowledge and skills needed to strengthen your abilities.

When you value yourself, you will automatically attract others who will value you as well. This happens because you feel secure in who you are and are not desperately vying for the attention or approval of others.

One of the best ways to overcome life's obstacles is to clarify the guiding principles that define who you are, and how you are going to live your life.

Chapter 27

Values

*"It is only when we truly live what we value that
we ignite the inner motivation to excel."*

~ Victoria Lee Carlyle

The V in the L.O.V.E. acronym represents Values.

Many people live their entire lives and never feel confident in the decisions they make because they didn't know how to clarify their values or set personal boundaries of safety. As a result, they experience stress and frustration when making important decisions.

Clarifying your values will have a positive impact on every choice you make throughout your life.

When we clarify which values are most important to us and make those values a priority in our lives we gain the ability to detail the actions needed to support a well-balanced, happy life.

Clarifying Values

A good place to begin clarifying your values is to define the things that are important to you.

To assist you in defining your values, let's imagine you had a rich uncle who absolutely adored you, and when he died, he left you two very important messages in two very special envelopes. On the outside of one envelope it said, "Open this first." Inside the first envelope was the following message:

> You are one of the most amazing people I have ever met and I love you dearly, Because I want you to be happy, I would like you to take some time and specify precisely what living a balanced, happy life means to you.

I would like you to create a distinct vision of how that life would look, how it would sound, and how you would feel, as if you were living that life today. We both know that money doesn't buy happiness, so focus a considerable amount of time on your mental, emotional, physical, spiritual, social, and intimate well-being. Also, define your ideal environment and the educational, financial and professional areas of your life you would like to develop as well.

After taking time to consider what your ideal life would include, you would open the second envelope and read:

I am so excited for the new life you are about to create! To assist you in creating the life you have just defined, I have left you an island, and access to all the money you will need, to create what you want; I want you to put your heart into this gift. Build an island that will represent all that you have just described.

As you ponder how to incorporate the things that matter most into your island, consider the rich blessings of the island that I created, and the many wonderful memories we have shared. Do you remember when you were a small child and how we played on the beach of the resort I built? We flew kites with the wind on our faces while enjoying the calming sounds of the ocean in the background. I created the beach to build precious memories that would last a lifetime with my family and friends.

One of my favorite and most relaxing areas on my island has been the spa. I love sharing my special formulas of energizing smoothies. Remember? The ones with the tiny umbrellas and a slice of pineapple on the rim of the glass, just for fun! I have enjoyed the value of health and wellbeing that it brought to my life and to the lives of others.

I want you to use your imagination and have fun creating an amazing island of your own with fun details that will enhance the lives of others as well!

This scenario is a fun way to clarify what is important to you and why you value it. You will also find innovative ways to implement these values into your everyday life. So what are you waiting for?

Obviously, no one is going to give either of us an island, or all the money we want to create the perfect life but the point is that we can create our own "island" that includes more of what we truly value.

As you decide on the things that are the most important for you to have on your island, be sure to contemplate all the rich details including colors, the things you hear, the things you smell, and the feelings that you want to accompany each element found on your island. The more neural pathways you connect to your vision the easier it will be to attain.

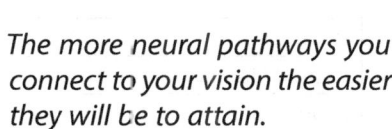

The more neural pathways you connect to your vision the easier they will be to attain.

Then clarify why these things are valuable to you.

The next consideration to add to "your island" would be the personal strengths, traits and characteristics that will define the person you have always wanted to become. You could consider qualities such as kindness, generosity, integrity, honesty, reliability and compassion.

Once you determine the strengths that are important to you specifically, define why they are significant to you and how these strengths are already in your life.

Record in your journal the values and personal strengths you have identified in the creation of your island.

The Values Clarification

Continue the exercise above by making a list of each item you have placed on your island. Then identify the value associated with that item, or in other words, why that particular item is important to you. Begin by identifying at least five items and the associated value.

Here's an example:

Item	Value
1. Good Mentors	Honesty
2. Orphanage	Service
3. Library	Education
4. Church	Spirituality
5. Fitness & Health	Well being

Now that you have carefully selected a few of the things that matter most to you and associated a specific value, the next step is to define your values.

Defining Values

Honesty is a value of mine. If I were to define that value and more fully clarify why that is important to me, I would say something like: Honesty provides the solid foundation that all my values are built upon. Honesty establishes trust within myself and forms trusting relationships with others.

Record in your journal the definition of the values you have identified.

THE PROCESSES OF DESIGNING MY LIFE

The purpose of this process is to specifically design the life that you want to live.

- How it would look, sound and feel to have emotional balance?
- How it would look, sound and feel to have physical balance?
- How it would look, sound and feel to have spiritual balance?
- How it would look, sound and feel to have social balance?
- How it would look, sound and feel to have intimate balance?

- My ideal environment looks, sounds and feels like _____
- My ideal education looks, sounds and feels like _____
- My ideal financial situation looks, sounds and feels like ____
- My ideal profession looks, sounds and feels like _____
- My ideal intimate relationships looks, sounds and feels like _____

- Qualities I admire in others and wish for myself are _____

THE PROCESS OF DEFINING VALUES

The purpose of this process is to clearly give definition to the values you have identified.

The values I have discovered are: _____

I define these values as _____

Living Our Values

With a clear and expanded definition of our values, we can begin incorporating those values into our lives. For example, as illustrated above, I have defined my value of honesty in the following way:

> "Honesty provides the solid foundation that all my values are built upon. Honesty establishes trust within, and forms trusting relationships with, others."

Next I want to record the ways in my life that I am already living that value and define ways that could expand this value as a more intricate part of my life. So, for the value of honesty, I have written this statement:

"I incorporate this value into my life by being honest with myself and others. Because I am honest, I communicate my thoughts and feelings with others, and have the courage to initiate difficult conversations when necessary. I do this even when it is uncomfortable."

This aligns with my value of integrity and creates productive relations and personal peace.

THE PROCESS OF LIVING OUR VALUES

The purpose of this process is to move your defined values into action by incorporating them into your daily lives.

The values I have discovered are: _____

I define these values as _____

Name the areas in your life that will change as you implement your new value.

Changes I will make to live the value of _____ are
_____

The process of defining values will continually improve over time. Identify where you are. As you implement each value into your life, be realistic of the changes you want to make. Then create a clear vision of what you want and look for new opportunities to apply your values into your everyday life. Be patient and consciously notice the habits that get in your way. Then give yourself time to change your old habits and implement new ones that will support your values.

Journal any thoughts or ideas that will encourage growth and promote change.

Once you have established personal values, you can define common values with those you have close relationships with. When working with someone else to establish common values, it is essential to align on specific definitions of shared values.

Miscommunication can easily occur in a relationship if my definition of integrity, for example, has not been made clear to my spouse, or looks different from my spouse's definition of integrity. A misinterpretation like this could inadvertently damage the trust that is essential in fulfilling relationships.

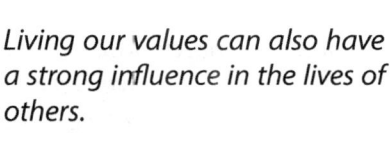

Living our values can also have a strong influence in the lives of others.

Aligning our values with another means that you know how I am going to live this value and I know how you are going to live this value and we are going to agree on a definition that will encompass both views. Again, this does not mean that our definitions will be exact, it does however mean that we will come to an agreement as to how that value will look in our relationship together.

Our values can also have a strong influence in the lives of others. If I value leadership, I will lead by example. As a team leader on a project, I will enter an assignment with a clear idea of the objectives and goals that we as a group want to accomplish. I will clearly communicate the objectives, timeline and milestones to my team. Because the project is not about me but about each person on the team doing their best, I will look for opportunities to uplift and encourage others' growth.

I will also look for those who can enhance the project with their natural talents and abilities. When delegating assignments, I will be specific in my requests and encourage others to do their best. Others will also learn that productive delegation helps create an effective, well-balanced, work environment.

Earlier, in Tier III, we addressed the fact that the world will love, honor and respect us at the level we love, honor and respect ourselves. Clarifying our values and aligning what is important to us will assist us in establishing personal boundaries that will let the world know how we want to be loved, honored and respected.

Establishing Personal Boundaries

Setting personal boundaries will give us the ability to live in a way that honors what we value.

Personal boundaries are the guidelines we set for ourselves that let those around us know how we want to be treated. These boundaries establish what we will and will not tolerate from others in our lives. Setting such boundaries is a matter of self-respect, and, in the process, we also gain the respect of others.

> *Setting personal boundaries will give us the ability to live in a way that shows others what we value.*

Part of the way I live the value of self-respect is to keep my body clean from any addictions that may take my personal power from me.

The personal boundaries I have established have created a sense of safety, as I maintain an environment free from these types of influences. I also trust that if I am in an environment where addictions are a challenge, I can stand as a sentinel and help others around me without judgment.

Again this does not mean I keep myself away from anyone who indulges in such behavior. It means, in my environment, my values and beliefs will not be compromised.

One of the greatest lessons I have learned is, in relationships, we get what we tolerate.

As a mother, I have had an adult child who has struggled with a drug addiction. The child knows I love them, but they also know that such behaviors are not tolerated in my home. When choices they make compromise the values of our home, they are asked to leave.

Now this does not mean that I turn my back and walk away. What this means is I model the importance of good values by establishing firm boundaries. When this child needs emotional support, I will take time to talk over the phone, and may even enjoy going out to a meal together. I also get to decide if I want to assist this child in other ways from time to time, but this is my choice. The most important thing for me to remember is that it will not assist my child to enable their destructive choices; but it is important to let them know that, no matter what they choose, I still love them, and to remind them I am here.

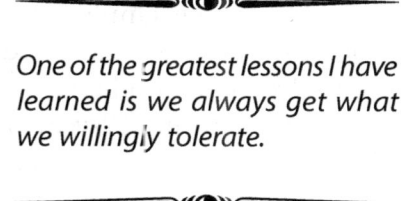

One of the greatest lessons I have learned is we always get what we willingly tolerate.

In this situation, it is important for me to remember that I am not the cause of their choices, and I should not take ownership or feel guilty for the choices they make. I also remind myself that I am not my child's Savior, and if I enable them, they will look to me for a temporary fix and not the healing solution that will come when they experience enough pain from the choices they have made and surrender their burdens to the true Savior.

My boundaries also show others how I want to be treated, based on the things I choose to tolerate.

While establishing the things that we will and will not tolerate, we must be diligent in communicating our needs. We cannot expect others to read our minds or know how we are feeling or what we want. In order to create the happiness we deserve, it is up to us to express ourselves in a way that teaches others how we want them to treat us and is in alignment with our values. We must teach them how we feel honored and respected.

The more grounded we are in our values, the easier it is to set clear boundaries with others and the more support we will receive to live them.

Here is a good example of how understanding and enforcing boundaries previously agreed upon, assisted me in creating a valuable learning opportunity with my daughter.

After I had identified values that were important to me, I encouraged my children to clarify their own values. Then, together, we sat down and defined family values that we all could live by. We listed our agreed values on a poster that we hung in our kitchen.

One of our family values was self-respect and in our definition of self-respect, we addressed wearing clothing that showed respect ourselves and for others.

One day, my 19-year-old daughter came over to my house to wash her car. She was wearing a skimpy bikini top and shorts that were so ripped you could see her underwear. I was furious!

I took a deep breath because I knew that if I had a conversation with her in that moment it would be about my anger. I took some time to get over my anger and clarified why I was angry. Besides the embarrassment I felt because she was so scantily dressed while washing her car at 5:30 in the evening when all my neighbors were coming home from work, I was also irritated that she had crossed family boundaries that she had helped to establish. After I worked through my own emotions, I was ready to have a conversation with her.

> *When you establish clear boundaries you show others how to love, honor and respect you.*

When I approached her, I began by asking how she felt about the family values we had established. I continued by asking her if she felt like there was still a need for these values in our home. She felt that there was good reason to keep the family values.

In our conversations, I was able to focus on our family values and standards and I reminded her that even though she no longer lived in our home, respecting the values was still important. I also reminded her that she was an example to the younger children.

Because I did not make her wrong or have a conversation while I was angry, she didn't feel attacked and was able to understand my concerns, and it was never an issue again.

When we have a clear understanding of our boundaries, we create better relationships because we communicate in a way that shows others how to love, honor and respect us, and in turn we love, honor and respect them as well.

SETTING BOUNDARIES PROCESS

The purpose of this process is to outline the steps needed to set and live within your personal boundaries.

Set boundaries by

- Identifying values
- Defining values
- Determining ways in which you feel loved, honored and respected
- Clarifying the action others could take to enhance these feelings in your life
- Deciding what you will and will not tolerate
- Defining what you will do when your boundaries are violated

Write down how your life will look with boundaries that create the love, honor and respect you desire.

Journal any thoughts or ideas that will encourage growth and promote change.

When Boundaries are Violated

When boundaries are violated, our trust is breached. Once that trust has been breached, it must be reestablished. The only way to reestablish trust is have enough reoccurring experiences involving trust to build up that emotional safety again. Trust is different than love. I can love someone, but if they continue to hurt me, I will not trust them.

When boundaries have been violated, it is important to clarify your expectations and make sure your expectations are in line with your values.

Setting well defined boundaries will give you the information you need to teach people how to be with you in a way where you feel honored and loved.

As you live the values that are important to you and establish personal boundaries, you will shape the foundation for the self-worth, self-reliance and self-confidence you need to live the life you have always wanted.

Chapter 28

Engage

"It Is Only When I Accept the Greatness of My Full Potential That I Give Myself Permission to Step Into It."

~ Victoria Lee Carlyle

When my sons were little they loved the adventures of King Arthur and the Knights of the Round Table. These men had a zest for life and the courage to stand for what was right. Many years ago I was in a neural linguistic programming training and the instructor, Nadine Cooper, told a rendition of the following story.

Arthur was ambushed and imprisoned by the monarch of a neighboring kingdom. The monarch could have killed him, but was moved by Arthur's youth and ideals. So, the monarch offered him his freedom, as long as he could answer a very difficult question. Arthur would have a year to figure out the answer. If, after a year, he still had no answer, he would be put to death.

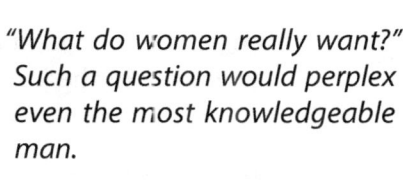

"What do women really want?" Such a question would perplex even the most knowledgeable man.

The question? "What do women really want?"

Such a question would perplex even the most knowledgeable man, and, to young Arthur, it seemed an impossible query. But, since it was better than death, he accepted the monarch's proposition to have an answer by year's end.

He returned to his kingdom and began to poll everyone: the princess, the priests, the wise men and even the court jester. He spoke with everyone, but no one could give him a satisfactory response.

Many people advised him to consult the old witch, for only she would have the answer. But, the price would be high, as the witch was famous throughout the kingdom for the outrageous prices she charged.

The last day of the year arrived and Arthur had no choice but to talk to the witch. She agreed to answer the question, but he would have to agree to her price first. The old witch wanted to marry Sir Lancelot, the most noble of the Knights of the Round Table and Arthur's closest friend! Young Arthur was horrified.

The witch was hunchbacked and hideous, had only one tooth and smelled like sewage. Arthur had never encountered such a repugnant creature in all his life. He refused to force his friend to marry her and endure such a terrible burden; but Lancelot, learning of the proposal, spoke with Arthur. He said nothing was too big of a sacrifice compared to Arthur's life and the preservation of the Round Table.

Hence, a wedding was proclaimed and the witch answered Arthur's question thus: "What a woman really wants," she answered, "is to be in charge of her own life."

Everyone in the kingdom instantly knew that the witch had uttered a great truth and that Arthur's life would be spared. And, so it was, the neighboring monarch granted Arthur his freedom and Lancelot and the witch had a beautiful wedding. The honeymoon hour approached and Lancelot, fortifying himself for the promises he made, entered the bedroom.

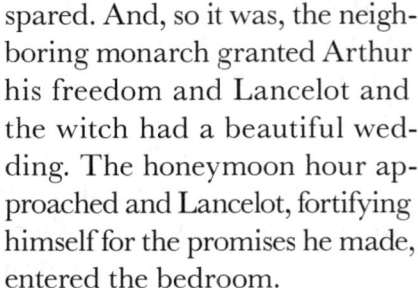

"What a woman really wants," she answered, "is to be in charge of her own life."

There, Lancelot gazed at the fire, pondering the pain his new bride must have endured throughout her courageous life. He was reluctant to approach her, until she requested a kiss. Bravely, he turned, only to find the most radiant woman he had ever seen. He stared at her in complete wonder and finally asked her how this could be.

She replied, "I have waited in that shape until I found a man gentle enough to marry me. Now I offer you a choice: I can be fair by night and foul by day; or foul by night and fair by day. Decide which you prefer."

Lancelot thought for a while, pondering the events that had led to this moment, and then dawned on him the answer he must give. "I cannot make such a choice; that is for you to decide."

She cried out in joy, "My lord, you are as wise as you are noble and true, for you have given me what every woman genuinely desires, sovereignty over herself. You will never see that hideous old hag again, for I choose to be fair from this time on."

Deep down inside, is self sovereignty not what each of us genuinely desires? The power to be wise, noble and true, and to direct our lives in a way that brings honor to all who know us!

The E in the acronym L.O.V.E. represents Engage.

Engage is about living a powerful life full of wisdom, honor and truth by holding yourself differently and taking your life on in a very different way. It's about inventing who you are and creating a life that creates value for you and for those around you.

One of the principles that have been consistent throughout this book is in order to fully engage in life you must take conscious control over the limiting, emotional patterns that have controlled your thoughts, feelings, attitudes, and beliefs.

Celebrating Transformation

The main focus of this book has been to help you to understand the many ways we as human beings give our personal power away to The Victim Addiction. One of the most important concepts we have focused on is the power of the emotional mind. We've shown how, when the emotional mind is triggered, it easily overrides the rational mind and inhibits our ability to think or act clearly. One of the first principles we addressed was the unconscious ways we get caught in our Emotional Safety Zone.

As you continue to understand the automatic habits that drive your thoughts, feelings, attitudes and beliefs, you gain the power to live outside of your Emotional Safety Zone and create something new.

To fully transform your life, it is important to realize and acknowledge the virtues that coincide with every vice you have discovered throughout this book. To encourage the transformation you desire, I have placed some typical emotional patterns that keep us in the Emotional Safety Zone alongside of the emotional habits that will empower you to live in your personal power. I encourage you to study the list below and really acknowledge the specific attitudes that get in the way of your happiness and growth. This list is just an example. You should customize your list to include the specific attitudes that not only get in your way, but also those that give you the power to engage your natural motivation to succeed.

THE PROCESS OF TRANSFORMATIONAL LEARNING

The purpose of this process is to release the limits that operate in your life and truly connect to the freedom, gifts and power within you.

Inside the Emotional Safety Zone	Outside the Emotional Safety Zone
Victim	Accountable
Guilt	Gratitude
Control	Freedom
Perfection	Progression
Fear	Confidence
Anger	Empowerment
Fighting	Accepting
Sadness	Joy
Depression	Vitality
Angst	Peace
Selfish Pride	Appreciation of Others
Anxiety	Exhilaration

Fighting to be right	Learning from mistakes
Judging	Accepting
Destructive	Productive
Taking	Receiving
Reasons	Results
Focus on cause	Focus on effect
Attacking others	Understand others

This list shows the automatic, impulsive reactions that occur when the emotional mind takes control. It also shows the power that comes when you consciously direct your emotional energy. The more clarity you have around the effective and ineffective ways you think, act and behave, the more power you will have to get out of the Emotional Safety Zone and create something new.

One of the biggest obstacles to living in your personal power will be the unconscious ways you live your life. Living unconsciously is easy and occurs automatically, which is why staying out of our Emotional Safety Zone can be so hard. Have you ever wondered why it is so easy to get out of the routine of habits that are good for you? Or why it is so hard to change bad habits that get in the way of your happiness and growth? It's because most bad habits require no conscious thought or effort on your part. In order to transform your life you must be rigorous with the mindless idleness that automatically takes control.

Let's continue the transformational learning by adding some more tools you can use to get out of your Emotional Safety Zone and into your personal power.

Take some time to review your journal. Acknowledge where you started, all the things you have learned and the conscious choices you have already made.

As you are going through your journal, pay special attention to the victim attitudes you have identified throughout your journey.

Most of the time, these victim patterns will show up in your behaviors, but now that you comprehend how much your behaviors are influenced by your thoughts, feelings, attitudes and fear-based beliefs, you can take the action necessary to change your life. Once you have specified your victim attitudes, get in touch with the language you use that keeps you in this victim mentality. You can do this by defining typical statements that justify your powerless situations. See if you can clarify any of these statements by using some of the victim words from your journal, or you could use a word from Inside the Emotional Safety Zone list.

For example:

- Victim: I feel like _____ (name the circumstance) in my life is not fair.
- Guilt: When someone confronts me I feel like I have done something wrong.
- Anger: When I don't know how to handle a situation I feel out of control.

It is vitally important to understand the typical thoughts that lead to victim reactions and take your power away.

Our beliefs are another obstacle that can get in the way of effective change.

Using the Inside / Outside the Emotional Safety Zone list, take the feelings and attitudes you have just identified and add a typical belief that would fuel your emotions. It might even be helpful to include a brief description as to when you might feel this way.

For example:

- Victim: When I am a victim, my thoughts focus on feelings that "life is not fair." My typical fear-based belief around life is not fair is, "I am insignificant."
- Guilt: When someone is upset with me, my thoughts focus on my feelings of "I have done something wrong." My typical fear-based belief around I've done something wrong is, "I am not good enough."
- Anger: When I get angry, my thoughts focus on, "Getting angry helps me feel like I am in control." My typical fear-based belief around getting angry is, "I am a failure."

Defining your skewed perceptions and resulting behavior will give you even more conscious power to change.

An example of your resulting behavior would be:

- When I seek to control, I feel angry. My perception is, "I get angry when I feel I am being disrespected, and I find myself trying to control others with my angry behavior."
- "I find myself trying to control others when I feel disrespected." My behavior is: "I fight to gain respect by losing my temper."

This is an exercise that you may want to work on over time. When you become consciously aware of and take action to stop your reactive behaviors from controlling you, you gain the power to succeed.

The other side of living in The Victim Addiction is living an Accountable life. To live an Accountable life you connect to your personal power by acknowledging the life-changing choices you can make as you consciously choose to live outside your Emotional Safety Zone.

Begin by creating sentences that include motivating thoughts, attitudes and empowering beliefs. Be sure to connect to feelings that make you feel energized and excited about life; for instance:

- Accountable: I have the power to change my life for the better.
- Gratitude: I feel abundantly blessed with the lessons I have learned. They have helped me become the person I am today.
- Passion: I am experiencing the freedom to create happiness and success in every area of my life.

Now incorporate your beliefs.

For example:

- Accountable: When I live an accountable life, I believe that anything is possible. The belief that supports my new perspective is, "I have all the resources I need to live a happy and successful life!"
- Gratitude: When facing adversity, gratitude turns what I have into enough. The belief that supports my new perspective is, "I have all the resources I need to be happy."

- Passion: I have the energy I need to stand in the world and make a difference. The belief that supports my new perspective is, "I have the influence and ability to empower others for good."

When I choose to live in the qualities outside of my Emotional Safety Zone, I make a difference and have all the resources I need to succeed.

It's amazing what can open up when you see all you can become outside your Emotional Safety Zone. It is interesting how viewing life from a different perspective can give you gratitude for all the circumstances of your life.

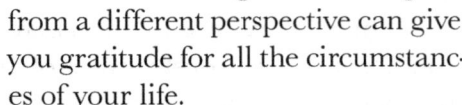

Gratitude is an amazing attitude that can literally change the way you perceive the world.

Gratitude is an amazing attitude that can literally change the way you perceive the world. Here is how an "Attitude of Gratitude" regarding some of the things I have struggled with has helped shift my perspective.

- I am grateful to my parents for giving me life.
- I am grateful for the struggles that have made me gentle, kind courageous and strong.
- I am grateful for "ex-man" the first, for giving me children to share my love and my life with.
- I am grateful for "ex-man" the second, for tenderly loving me in a way I had never known before.
- I am grateful for the peace that comes from knowing I am whole and complete and worthy of all the amazing things this world has to offer.
- I am especially grateful for my Savior who has lifted my burdens and restored the innocence and peace I was born to live.
- I am grateful for the foundation of my work, which is so eloquently declared in 2 Timothy 1:7; "For God hath not given us the spirit of fear; but of power, and of love, and of a sound mind."

What are you grateful for?

For one month, take the things in your life that have caused you the greatest amount of struggle and view them from an attitude of gratitude. Then, record your new perspectives in an "Attitude of Gratitude" journal. Have fun creating new discoveries.

Changing Your Attitude will Change Your Life

Attitudes are powerful motivators, and living with an attitude of gratitude can really make the world a brighter place in which to live.

Recently I watched my grandchildren perform the musical "Annie." Annie's positive attitude and happy disposition made even the darkest times seem bright. The attitudes we choose really do determine our success. For most, success doesn't come easy. In fact, some of the most inspirational success stories have come from people who had to overcome great odds over and over again before rising to the top.

Did you know that?

- Walt Disney was once fired from a newspaper for lack of ideas.
- Michael Jordan was disappointed in high school when his friend made the varsity basketball team and he did not.
- Elvis Presley auditioned to sing with a local band and was turned down and told he was going nowhere and should go back to driving a truck.
- Winston Churchill, former prime minister of England, failed the sixth grade.
- The record-setting home-run hitter Babe Ruth also holds the record for the most strikeouts.
- Helen Keller became blind before she was two.
- Thomas Edison's teachers told him he was too stupid to learn anything.
- Beethoven was told by a teacher he was hopeless as a composer.
- Albert Einstein didn't talk until he was four, didn't read until seven and was told that he was mentally slow.
- Isaac Newton did very poorly in grade school.

- Florence Nightingale was chastised for her desire to care for the sick and afflicted.

What is the formula that allows some people to move through the adversity they face and come out on top, when it would have been so much easier to give up? How do we endure in the quest when we are too tired, too discouraged and too challenged to persevere?

We must get out of our Emotional Safety Zone and challenge the thoughts, feelings, attitudes and beliefs that zap our motivation and keep us from our personal power.

Another important concept that has been reiterated in this book is the growth that can occur when we understand the differences between the rational and emotional mind. I like the analogy of a sports car given by marriage and family counselor Bob Stahn.

Analogy of a Sports Car

There are two important brain functions that become easier to understand when we compare them to a high performance sports car. In this analogy, the prefrontal cortex (rational brain) would be the steering and the brakes. The amygdala (emotional brain) would be the fuel and the accelerator.

If we used only the accelerator and fuel in the sports car, we would have the ability to move the car but would have no capability to choose in what direction the car would go. Conversely, if we used only the steering and brakes in the sports car, we would remain stuck turning the steering wheel back and forth and pressing the brake pedal, but going nowhere. In order to use the sports car effectively, we must use the accelerator and fuel, as well as the steering and brakes.

Imagine life in a community where people only used their emotional brain but none of their rational brain. What would that be like? Things might seem exciting, dramatic and spontaneous, but it would also be a frantic mess! People would be doing only what they wanted to do when they felt like doing it. Some would drive their cars as fast as the cars would take them down the residential streets, not caring what or who they ran into. Fights and arguments would be the norm. Murders over simple misunderstandings would be common.

People would be taking things just because they wanted to. There would be plenty of thrill and passion, but life would be dominated by complete disorder, even anarchy.

On the other hand, what would life be like if people used only the rational brain? Rules and laws would be strictly enforced and immediately obeyed. There would be complete structure in everything and everyone. People would do only what was logical and made perfect sense. However, there would be no passion or happiness in life.

People would be like robots, systematically moving through their pre-planned days without feeling. There would be no allowance for innovation, creativity or progression. Relationships would be more like business mergers than heart-to-heart connections. People would merely exist and would not be living. It would be safe and orderly, but without depth or meaning.

In order for our lives to be meaningful and effective, we must have a balance between the rational and the emotional parts of our brains. The rational brain provides structure in which the emotions can be freely expressed and utilized. Life within this balance is rich, deep, orderly and well managed.

As we engage the energy, momentum and creativity of the emotional mind, with the logic, reliability, and accountability of the rational mind, we can move forward in a powerful way.

When both minds are simultaneously connected, we have the ability to tap into our full potential and make significant contributions to life.

Engaging in life is valuing the power and energy stored in the unconscious mind. Viewing our triggers as a guide, pointing us in the direction of self-discovery, and using that power to access the wisdom and growth, is an essential element to enjoying our lives to the fullest.

In this next section, we will explore some different ways to enjoy living a rich fulfilling life.

Playing

Engaging in life is consciously changing our actions, and intentionally choosing to socialize, laugh and have fun.

As we engage in a new way of being in the world, we connect to some of the innocence and childlike wonder that we once enjoyed.

Do you know what makes you happy?

Do you take time to play?

Do you feel guilty taking time off work to do things just for the fun of it?

When was the last time you were spontaneous and went on a treasure hunt, had a water fight, built sandcastles on the beach, had a picnic at the park, or went down a slide?

Have you ever turned up the music just so you could dance in your office, bedroom, or even while washing your car? Do you sing in the shower? If not, I invite you to try it! I personally believe the world would be a much happier place with more shower singers!

Go ahead and enjoy your life! Kick up leaves or catch a snowflake on your tongue; dance in the rain! or go fly a kite! Wander through an art show, or sit in a hot tub reading a book while eating your favorite dessert.

Ya know? Fun! The stuff that happy lives are made of!

Some of us adults are so busy scheduling the "have to's" in our lives, we never take time to schedule in the "get to's." Did you know laughter and play actually create an amazing ripple effect? Laughter increases brain chemicals called endorphins that add to feelings of euphoria, decrease stress and pain, boost the immune system and can even suppress your appetite!

Each day is a new beginning, a day to engage in designing the life you have always imagined, a life that is full of love, gratitude, happiness and fun.

Engaging in life begins by understanding that most of our funnest memories occurred in the innocence of our childhood when life was wondrous and fantasy still existed.

Laughter

There is something magical about laughter. In fact, laughter is one of the quickest ways to wash away the blues.

Some of the funniest moments I have experienced have come from darling concepts my children have formed. For example, when my youngest daughter was small, she would sing "The Twelve Days of Christmas." She had her own wonderful rendition of the third day. She would sing, as loud as her little heart could, "On the third day of Christmas my true love gave to me—three French men!"

Laughter increases brain chemicals called endorphins that add to feelings of euphoria, decrease the sensation of pain, boost the immune system and even suppress appetite!

Life is full of all kinds of wonderfully laughable moments.

I had an experience when I was younger that didn't seem so funny at the time but now that I am older it makes me giggle every time I think of it. I liked this really nice boy, and, while talking to a friend, I learned that he was a lifeguard at the community pool in her neighborhood. She and I became regulars at the swimming pool.

Every time I would go, I would just sit in the pool and watch him do his job. I was far too shy to ever get up enough courage to actually talk to him.

One day, I quickly put on my swimming suit and rushed out of the dressing room so I could gaze at him, from a distance of course. I must have been there about 45 minutes when I noticed the young man I liked was walking in my direction! I can only imagine the incredibly stupid smile that must have been on my face as he approached. He leaned down and quietly said something to me. He spoke so softly, and my heart was pounding so hard, I couldn't really hear what he said. Seeing the confused look on my face, he spoke again. This time, just a little louder, but still not loud enough for others to hear and in the most polite way possible, he said, "Excuse me, miss, I know you cannot see it, but your bra is still wrapped around your waist."

I guess in my excitement to rush out to see him, I had flipped my bra around with the cups in the back to take it off, but I never unhooked it to actually remove it. I was always very modest and my swimsuit had a baby doll top, which was the style back then. It covered the front of me, but left the back open, so I had no idea what I had done.

I am sure you can imagine that, because I was so embarrassed, this boy lost all his appeal. I never returned to that pool again.

Looking back, I think I could write a book on laughable, dumb moments. For me, those moments are among the things that make laughing about life so much fun. I would love for you to share your silly, awkward moments with me on my website (www.TheVictimAddiction.com). We can call it our laughing place, a place we can go when times are tough and we just want to forget about life for a while.

There is a healing power in laughter that can be found in no other way.

When we consciously choose to have fun and appreciate our embarrassing moments, we have the energy needed to enjoy our lives to the fullest!

Friends

Friends can increase our laughter and make life so much more enjoyable, too! My friend Heather is a craft-making queen. One day, she called me and enthusiastically described her latest insights about heaven. She believes that when we die we will all receive a mansion in heaven. She described her mansion by stating, "My mansion will have thousands of rooms and every room will be filled with different crafts!" She laughed and said, "Tori, your mansion will be filled with boring books!" Her passion and creativity keeps my life filled with blingy fun!

Are you creating a life filled with wonderful friends with whom you are forming lasting memories? My son's darling wife, Kaci, keeps a kissing journal, and every memorable event she has is sealed with a kiss. Because her bright smile enlists others to take pictures, her tradition has inspired lots of smiles and an extra dose of kindness in the lives of others.

As a society, we need to get out and appreciate each other more! How much time do you spend to make and keep new friendships?

A rich and fulfilling life includes reaching out and sharing our lives with others.

Transforming our Defense Mechanisms

Another tool we can use to transform our emotional patterns and create the life we want will come as we transform our defense mechanisms into habits that will boost our energy and excel us to greater heights.

In your journal, you have recorded some of the automatic coping mechanisms that take over when you are in a state of reaction.

Understanding our coping mechanisms along with the ability to redirect our energy is one of the tools that can change our habits and enhance our happiness. Remember, it only takes 17 seconds of focusing on something that makes us feel good for the chemicals in our brain to start producing elevating chemicals that will change our mood and increase our happiness.

In order to transform your defense mechanisms make a list of things you enjoy that increases your energy and your mood. You know what I mean, the things that seem to bring an instant smile to your face. Once you list several things you like to do, put the list somewhere that you can connect to everyday, like a bathroom mirror or the dash of your car. Enjoy the things you have written by adding them to your daily routine. By consciously choosing to have uplifting habits as part of your daily routine, you will find it easier to shift your mood in emotional times.

Here are some examples of uplifting mechanisms:

- Listening to energizing music
- Meditation
- Exercise
- Dance
- Socializing with friends
- Cooking

- Writing letters
- Journaling
- Singing
- Playing the piano
- Drawing
- Viewing inspirational pictures
- Relaxing in a hot tub
- Getting a massage
- Visiting someone
- Going to the park
- Hiking

Connecting to something that inspires you is also a great way to elevate your energy. Connecting your values to the things that inspire you will give you further motivation to succeed.

Aligning our Values

Implementing uplifting mechanisms into your life will increase emotions of enthusiasm, peace and happiness. You can also take action by aligning your values, emotions and beliefs with the defined results you want to generate.

It can be fun to implement defined values into other areas of your life. To start, you may want to take one of the values from your island exercise. Add in emotionally charged motivations and empowering beliefs. Then, attach conscious behaviors to the process that will move you into action. It is also nice to involve others in your conscious action items. Make sure your action item is something you are really enthusiastic about.

Engage

Here is an example of what I am describing:

Item	Value	Emotional Motivation	Empowering Beliefs	Conscious Action
Library	Education	Confidence	I am Intelligent	Join a Book Club
Orphanage	Service	Empathy	I am Kind	Volunteer at a Crisis Center
Fitness Center	Health and Well-being	Balanced	I am Whole and Complete	Take a Zumba Class
Church	Spirituality	Peaceful	I Belong	Attend Regular Services
Mountains	Adventure	Excitement	I am Enjoying Life	Enroll in a Rock-climbing Class

Chapter 29

Accessing Your Inner Motivation to Succeed

*"I am not a product of my circumstances.
I am a product of my decisions."*

~ Stephen R. Covey

Creating a Happy Life

Before his untimely death, John Lennon shared that, when he was young, his mother often told him that happiness was the key to life. When he went to school, he was asked what he wanted to be when he grew up. He wrote down "happy." They told him that he didn't understand the assignment, and he told them that they didn't understand life. The ultimate goal in life is to live a good life and be happy.

Happiness is a choice, and, as we have learned throughout this book, happiness is something that is ours to create. In order to ignite the passion and motivation necessary to be happy, we must establish strong emotional connections that will engage happy thoughts, happy feelings, happy attitudes and empowering beliefs. We must see happiness, feel happiness and hear happiness in order to live in happiness.

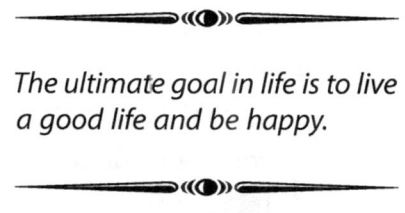

The ultimate goal in life is to live a good life and be happy.

In the chapter on neural pathways we addressed why motivational speakers encourage the use of mind maps, vision boards, and positive affirmations to promote change. In this chapter we will elaborate on motivating tools that we can immediately implement into our lives. Lao-Tzu said, "A journey of a thousand miles begins with one step." You must take the steps needed to design your life the way you want.

- Have you ever noticed how you spend your time?
- Do you use your energy to uplift and encourage others?
- Is your time occupied with mindless activities or are you building the kind of relationships that will last?
- Do the people you care about feel loved by you?
- What kinds of things are you doing to enjoy your life?
- What areas in your life would you like to enrich?

Knowing what you are passionate about will increase your ability to create strong neural connections and engage your inner motivation to succeed.

The first tool we will expand on, is how to create powerful affirmations.

THE PROCESS OF CREATING POWERFUL AFFIRMATIONS

The purpose of this process is to connect what we want to create to powerful affirmations that will promote feelings of energy and wellbeing.

On his website at http://jackcanfield.com/affirmations/ Jack Canfield gives five guidelines to follow when creating powerful affirmations

1. Start by entering the present tense. In other words, take the condition you desire and declare it as if it were already true.
2. Be positive. Place the emphasis on what you do want. For example: saying "I want to quit smoking," would keep the focus on smoking, versus "I want to live a life that is smoke free," which changes the focus from what is not wanted (smoking) to what is wanted (living a smoke free life).
3. Be concise. Shorter is better. Affirmations with fewer words are often easier to recall. Rhyming makes your affirmations even more memorable. For example, "I am feeling alive at 185."
4. Include action. Whenever possible, affirm yourself as a person who takes action. For example: "I am gratefully driving my

new Porsche along an open highway." Action engages the Law of Attraction, creating new results in our lives and opening us to further inspiration.

5. Include a feeling word. Powerful affirmations include content and emotion. Content describes the specific outcome that you desire. Emotion gets to the heart of how you feel about that outcome.

6. Create "I am" statements. I once heard Canfield say that creating "I am" statements that own your results is also very effective in creating powerful affirmations.

Writing positive affirmations will help us clarify the energy we want to connect to. Here are a few statements I use in my life:

- I am Honored at the Difference I am Making!
- I am Creating Balance and Feeling Peace in all areas of My Life!
- My Mind is Clear and Precise, My Body is Energetic and Healthy and I am Living a Life that I Love!

The second tool we will expand upon is mind mapping.

I love this image and received permission to use it by Paul Foreman at mindmapinspiration.com. It's a very creative illustration which combines empowering affirmations with mind mapping.

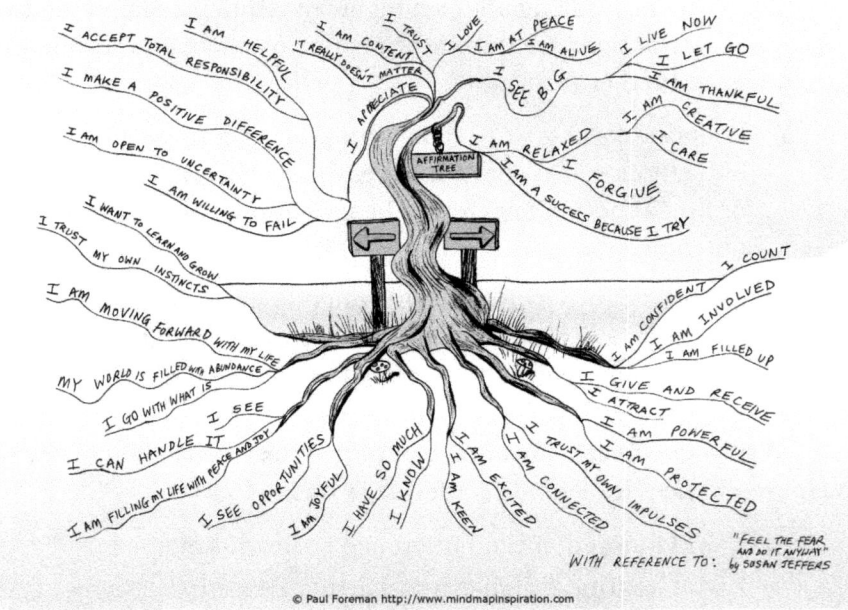

Mind mapping is a creative way not only to visualize what you want and how to get there, but it is also a good way to brainstorm areas in your life that you would like to expand. This process includes acknowledging current resources you can utilize and discovering exciting new ways to access and achieve your goals.

The ultimate goal of mind mapping is to strengthen neural pathways that will increase your drive and determination for success.

The ultimate goal of mind mapping is to strengthen neural pathways that will increase your drive and determination for success. To strengthen them, it is important that what you see, hear, think and feel are in alignment with what you want to create. Like this: My thoughts, "I love my trainings!" My feelings: "What I do for a living is very fulfilling. I get excited for each opportunity to share what I love." What I hear: "This training was amazing!"

Mind mapping will help you connect your vision and resources to your goals and objectives.

Five Stages of Mind Mapping

1. Analyze where you are at: Here are some suggestions of areas you might consider and questions you could ask to help you clarify your direction.

   Areas to consider are:
   - Health: Physical / Mental/ Emotional
   - Relationships: Family / Friendships / Romantic / Others
   - Communication: Where I feel understood / Areas I would like to improve
   - Growth: Personal / Spiritual / Educational
   - Social: Personal interaction / Social media interaction
   - Happiness: Recreation / Relaxation / Hobbies / Fun
   - Career / Business / Advances / Change
   - Finances / Money / Earning / Spending / Saving
   - Contribution: Areas I contribute / Areas I would like to expand
   - What do you enjoy about your _____? (Example: What do you enjoy about your physical health?)
   - What would you like to improve?
   - What would you like your outcome to be?

2. Chunk it Down

   In my training I use a version of the SMART Goal formula to identify goals.
   - Specific: Detail what you are trying to achieve.
   - Measurable: What benchmarks will measure your progress?
   - Action: What action can you take to accomplish your goal?
   - Realistic: Is your goal realistic for your current life?
   - Timely: When is the deadline to achieve this goal?

Take time to reward yourself when the goal has been accomplished. When you celebrate your successes, it increases your energy and excitement for other accomplishments.

3. Map Your Goals

Now that you have specific goals, you can map what needs to be done. This is also the stage where you will prioritize the action steps you will take and the timeline you will follow to accomplish your goals.

4. Take Action

In order to create the life you want, you must utilize the drive and determination you have just mapped out and apply it to daily action toward your objectives until you accomplish your goals. Don't be afraid to expand or update new ideas, just be careful that you don't complicate the process; stay focused on action items that will motivate completion.

Mapping should be done in a way that peaks your excitement every time you visualize your objectives.

The ultimate goal is to create the life you want. It will be much easier to do if you connect your success with the reward center of your brain by experiencing pleasure throughout the process and celebrating your accomplishments.

Here's a little secret that everybody should understand about setting goals: The drive and determination needed for success comes from the illogical nature of the emotional mind. So take the limits off! Get out of the familiar boundaries you have placed upon yourself and create goals that are outrageous and fun! If you can conceive it and you are willing to take daily steps towards it, you will achieve it! Remember, when you engage the emotional mind your potential becomes limitless!

Vision Board

The third tool will be creating a vision board.

A vision board is where you visually connect to the outcomes you desire. The fun thing about creating a vision board is that you put it together as if you were living your dream now. One of the dreams I am working on is a youth leadership camp. I know exactly what I want it to include, so when I was creating my vision board I found a lot of images of youth getting beyond the limits of their fears as they set their reservations aside to participate on a high energy ropes course. I also have pictures of youth working together overcoming obstacles in outdoor team building activities, along with pictures of youth participating in my training. I also have other things I love on my vision board, like family fun, hot tubing in the snow, lying on the beach, horseback riding, relaxing massages and fun with family and friends. There are also pictures of the vision I have for my business, which is finally starting to manifest in my life.

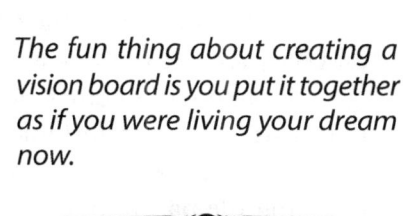

The fun thing about creating a vision board is you put it together as if you were living your dream now.

My vision board is a constant reminder that connects my vision with the excitement and inner motivation to succeed. It's exciting just realizing that every day I am one step closer to making my dreams come true.

Breaking Ineffective Habits

These are effective tools that connect what we want to strong neural pathways that create lasting change. Let me reiterate that the stronger our motivation is, the easier it becomes to break ineffective emotional habits. This occurs because every time we interrupt the connection to a neural pathway it weakens its ability to release electrochemical surges. It would be pretty easy to break a well-established habit if we were only dealing with one neural pathway connection, but our memories are connected to thousands of neural networks which can make it a lot harder.

Because restructuring old habits requires conscious rigor and may take some time, the emotional mind must be enrolled to successfully create desired results. In order to enroll the emotional mind, you must surround yourself with experiences that will increase evidence that your ineffective perceptions are no longer relevant to your current life and it's time for a change.

Once the emotional mind has a sense that your current perceptions are no longer relevant, there is an automatic shift that occurs. If you consciously direct that shift, change can be reasonably easy because the emotional mind will assist in breaking the ineffective connections and concentrate on something new.

Keep in mind that the emotional mind has no concept of reality and only focuses on how we feel.

Change will occur when we move away from something that makes us feel uncomfortable or move toward something that creates a sense of empowerment. You have the power to create that sense by releasing the past and focusing your energy on actively engaging in something new. Lasting change requires consciously interrupting any thoughts, feelings, attitudes or beliefs that involve ineffective emotional patterns. As we actively involve our emotional and physiological energy in a new perspective, we engage new neurons to branch out and create patterns for success. The more neural pathways we create, the stronger our ability to override existing pathways will become.

Keep in mind that forming new neural pathways may feel difficult at first because of the effort it takes for an electrochemical surge to forge through a pathway for the first time. However, this process gets easier each time we move in an intentional direction. Every time we take action to achieve our vision with what we see, hear, feel touch and taste, the brain sends electrochemical surges through the new neural pathways and strengthens them. The byproduct of strong neural pathways that support what you want to create is increased feelings of excitement and confidence, giving us the drive and determination needed to succeed. Each time we connect to empowering feelings, we gather new evidence that will further enroll the emotional mind. Consciously creating emotional results can take time, so be patient. It can take up to 45 days to establish a new habit or break an old one.

As we consciously restructure our ineffective emotional patterns, we can go on to create a life full of inner peace and lasting happiness.

This has been such a wonderful journey! Thank you for the opportunity to share what I have learned throughout my life with you. It is my hope that you don't just hope that your life will change, but that you will take the necessary actions, get curious about your emotional reactions and decide to make the changes necessary to create a life full of happiness and peace. You have all the power you need to live a rich and fulfilling life.

I would like to leave you with this wonderful story I was given permission to use by author Michael D. Hargrove and Bottom Line Underwriters, Inc.

Don't Hope ... Decide

While waiting to pick up a friend at the airport in Portland, Oregon, I had one of those life-changing experiences that you hear other people talk about, the kind that sneaks up on you unexpectedly. This one occurred a mere two feet away from me. Straining to locate my friend among the passengers deplaning through the jet way, I noticed a man coming toward me carrying small bags.

He stopped right next to me to greet his family. First, he motioned to his youngest son (who looked to be about six years old) as he put down his bags. They gave each other a long, loving hug. As they separated enough to look into each other's faces, I heard the father say, "It's so good to see you, son. I missed you so much!" His son smiled somewhat shyly, averted his eyes and replied softly, "Me, too, Dad!"

Then the man stood up, gazed in the eyes of his oldest son (who was probably nine or ten) and, while cupping his son's face in his hands, said, "You're already quite the young man. I love you very much, Zach!" They too exchanged a most loving, tender hug.

While this was happening, a baby girl (perhaps one or one-and-a-half) was squirming excitedly in her mother's arms, never once taking her little eyes off the wonderful sight of her returning father.

The man said, "Hi, baby girl!" as he gently took the child from her mother. He quickly kissed her face all over and then held her close to his chest while rocking her from side to side. The little girl instantly relaxed and simply laid her head on his shoulder, motionless, in pure contentment.

After several moments, he handed his daughter to his oldest son and declared, "I've saved the best for last!" and proceeded to give his wife the longest, most passionate kiss I ever remember seeing.

He gazed into her eyes for several seconds and then silently mouthed. "I love you so much!" They stared at each other's eyes, beaming big smiles at one another, while holding both hands. For an instant, they reminded me of newlyweds, but I knew by the age of their children that they couldn't possibly be.

I puzzled about it for a moment, then realized how totally engrossed I was in the wonderful display of unconditional love not more than an arm's length away from me.

I suddenly felt uncomfortable, as if I was invading something sacred, so I was amazed to hear my own voice nervously ask, "Wow! How long have you two been married?"

"Been together fourteen years total, married twelve of those," the man replied, without breaking his gaze from his lovely wife's face.

"Well then, how long have you been away?" I asked the man.

He finally turned and looked at me, still beaming his joyous smile. "Two whole days!" he said.

Two days? I was stunned. By the intensity of the greeting, I had assumed he'd been gone for at least several weeks, if not months. I know my expression betrayed me; I said, almost offhandedly, hoping to end my intrusion with some semblance of grace (and to get back to searching for my friend), "I hope my marriage is still that passionate after twelve years!"

The man suddenly stopped smiling. He looked me straight in the eye, and with forcefulness that burned right into my soul, he told me something that left me a different person. He told me, "Don't hope, friend ... decide!" Then he flashed me his wonderful smile again, shook my hand and said, "God bless!" With that, he and his family turned and strode away together.

I was still watching that exceptional man and his special family walk just out of sight when my friend came up to me and asked, "What'cha looking at?" Without hesitating, and with a curious sense of certainty, I replied, "My future!"

As you create your future, don't just hope for the changes you seek. Decide. Make a conscious effort to change the unconscious ways you have been giving your power away. Get beyond unconscious circumstances and live the life that you have always dreamed of!

Remember, "DON'T HOPE, FRIEND, DECIDE!"

www.ingramcontent.com/pod-product-compliance
Lightning Source LLC
Chambersburg PA
CBHW050547160426
43199CB00015B/2568